Theory of Action

International Library of Sociology

Founded by Karl Mannheim
Editor: John Rex, University of Aston in Birmingham

Arbor Scientiae
Arbor Vitae

Theory of Action
Towards a New Synthesis
Going Beyond Parsons

Richard Münch

Professor of Sociology,
University of Düsseldorf

Routledge & Kegan Paul
London and New York

First published in 1987 by
Routledge & Kegan Paul Ltd
11 New Fetter Lane, London EC4P 4EE

Published in the USA by
Routledge & Kegan Paul Inc.
in association with Methuen Inc.
29 West 35th Street, New York, NY 10001

Set in Times Roman 10 on 11 point
by Witwell Ltd
and printed in Great Britain
by T.J. Press Ltd.,
Padstow, Cornwall

Library of Congress Cataloging in Publication Data

Münch, Richard, 1945—
    Theory of action.

    (International library of sociology)
    Bibliography: p.
    Includes index.
    1. Action theory.   I. Title.   II. Series
HM24.M84   1987   302   87–4972

British Library CIP Data also available
ISBN 0–7102–1218–6

Contents

CONTENTS

Translation editor's note

This volume is a translation of the first part, plus concluding considerations (*Schlussbetrachtung*) of *Theorie des Handelns,* published by Suhrkamp, Frankfurt, in 1982. The remainder of the original book (Chapters 4–9) will appear shortly in translation, under the new title of *Understanding Modernity.*

Preface

Sociology, along with the other sciences of human action, cannot undergo further development solely by way of differentiation into specialized disciplines which are separated both in terms of subject matter and treatment, and in social terms. One needs only to recall the circumstances under which the discipline first emerged and grew to be aware that, if its further development is to be fruitful, more is needed than mere differentiation into coexisting directions, namely discussion, cooperation, and integration which retains any inherent tension. Neither a positivistic sociology, no longer aware of its own tradition and becoming absorbed in the blind collection of data or in empty theoretical formalism, nor an idealistic sociology rendered immobile by its backward-looking concern for its own classics, contenting itself with recounting everyday knowledge or flying high above the clouds in abstract developmental logic, represent in and of themselves approaches which can carry us farther forward. Any continuation of their mutul separation leads only to stagnation and the completion of ever more circles. Abstract positivistic or idealistic theory construction which neither takes account of the sociological tradition nor has empirical and/or historical relevance continually repeats the mistakes of the past. Positivistic empiricism and idealistic historicism make no progress beyond their own descriptions as repeatedly reapplied, and they draw no lessons from mistakes already made.

Modern science in general, and modern sociology in particular, owes its existence and the progress it has made not to the separation but to the integration of differing types of orientation. This book, together with its sequel, *Understanding Modernity*, is intended as a reminder of the conditions surrounding the creation and progress of sociology, and beyond it the sciences of human action – a reminder to serve as a basis for any further progress in the future. The tradition the book as a whole sets about renewing is that of the voluntaristic theory of action, the aim of which is to achieve a dialectical synthesis of the various directions of thought and methods of research. It will tap this tradition by rationally reconstructing the contributions of Talcott Parsons.

By rational reconstruction, I mean a reformulation and extension of the voluntaristic theory of action from the perspective of the present-day level of development. I have not therefore proceeded chronologically; instead, this book is devoted to an exposition of the voluntaristic theory of action as found in Talcott Parsons's work, which is then, in *Understanding Modernity*, used as the perspective from which to view a return to the contributions of Emile Durkheim and Max Weber.

The synthesis of differing orientations must not simply rest at the integration of different approaches, and of the theoretical and empirical aspects of sociology, but must reach beyond this individual discipline to seek links with the other sciences of human action. However, 'integration' should on no account be misunderstood as the suppression of tensions. Rather, there is a need for precisely this tension-free coexistence to be overcome, and superseded by a position where the different forms of orientation mutually penetrate one another, not eliminating tension, but instead making it productive by generating scientific progress. This means that discussions ranging beyond the boundaries of each individual approach should be institutionalized, that we should cooperate in joint projects and work on a common frame of reference which maintains the vitality of the tensions between different orientations within an integrated system.

In attempting to help integrate opposing orientations to action theory in this way, my intention is also, as far as possible, to present the voluntaristic theory of action in a readable and teachable form. That the voluntaristic theory's contribution to knowledge is insufficiently institutionalized is due in no small measure to the often esoteric fashion in which it is presented. This does not, of course, mean that it can be reduced to the undiscerning level of everyday knowledge and language. Rather, one strives for comprehensibility, readiness to communicate, and actual communication, though such endeavours are inevitably less effective than one would wish.

Two of the chapters in this volume on the theory of action are based upon essays which had already been published. Even so, this is not simply a collection of essays. The individual pieces have been reworked from their initial versions, and the second chapter has been extended far beyond its original scope. These have been supplemented by new contributions to provide as coherent and logical a reconstruction of the theory of action as possible.

The various chapters in the current volume were written over the space of five years during intermissions to more comprehensive undertakings on evolution, societal institutionalization, and the institutional specification of modern normative culture. These studies have now appeared in German in two books: *Die Struktur der Moderne* (The Structure of Modernity) and *Die Kultur der Moderne* (The Culture of Modernity). The empirical and historical outlines contained in the theoretical sections of this book are further elaborated in the above works. For the present, the foremost interest is in the theoretical perspective; empirical and historical interests are channelled into the later works. The development of the perspective in this theoretical contribution has been fundamentally influenced by practical work using the frame of reference of voluntaristic action theory. This is particularly true of the underlying Kantian perspective and of the theory of interpenetration, which crystallized in the course of an investigation into the birth of modern science. The effect was compounded because empirical/historical questions posed were continually tied back in to the discussion of problems on the theoretical level. It is essential to fruitful scientific work to proceed in such a way that theoretical and empirical/historical considerations can mutually penetrate each other and cross-fertilize.

While working on the material which has gone to make up this book I received a great many suggestions and critical comments, and a great deal of encouragement, for which I would particularly like to thank Jeffrey Alexander, Bernard Barber, Rainer Baum, Bernhard Giesen, Harry Johnson, Stephen Kalberg and Edward Tiryakian. I am also grateful to Werner Gephart, Bernhard Miebach and Karl-Heinz Saurwein for many stimulating discussions in the Social Sciences Institute at the University of Düsseldorf. That the book is now available in English, I owe to three different translators: first to Paul J. Gudel who prepared the original, unextended versions of chapters 1 and 2 for their initial appearance as periodical articles; next to Steven Minner, who would have completed the remainder but for his tragic and untimely death in a mountain accident. Steven translated chapter 3 of this volume; the rest was completed and partly edited by Neil Johnson, who also supervised the preparation of the manuscript. For this I am grateful to Monika Böttcher-Krause, Karin Knabe, Angelika Minner, Karin Rhau, Astrid Theus and Ulrike Wibbe. Thanks also to Jürgen Aretz, Heike Becker, Heinz-Weilhelm Droste and Jürgen Eiben for their bibliographical and proof-reading assistance.

Introduction:
The rational reconstruction of the theory of action

The theory of action represents the core of the sciences of human action. Its tradition within the discipline of sociology is such that all directions of thinking have made their own particular contributions to it. Anyone wishing to work on this tradition with the intent of developing it further with an eye to the future must set out from its present level of development and then go on to provide a new formulation of the work of the classics, maintaining their vitality and their relevance to the future. The performance of this task leads inexorably to the work of Talcott Parsons. Sociologists of the most different persuasions are at least unanimously agreed on the importance and the extent of Parsons's contribution to the theory of action. Equally, all are agreed on the immense scope of his work and hence its significance for all sciences of human action, well beyond the confines of sociology as such. Where, however, there is a great lack both of clarity and of unanimity is in the interpretation of his contribution.

Given the discrepancy between the general recognition of his work's significance and the limited clarity regarding its meaning and substance, any attempt to further develop the theory must first of all attain an understanding of Parsons's contribution to the theory of action which does justice to that work, before progressing to the continued development. This, indeed, will be the prime task of this book. The overall approach taken is not to give merely a history or partial history of the theory of action, but to achieve a gain in knowledge. The key question inherent in this perspective is: How far did Parsons succeed in developing a comprehensive theory of action capable of integrating the most varied theoretical approaches while assessing their limitations, of retaining their true content while eliminating their false content, and progressing beyond them? To answer this question we must turn to Parsons's stated aim that the *voluntaristic* theory of action should synthesize the opposing streams of thought of positivism and idealism, which in turn unify all other, more specific approaches. Thus the first matter to be cleared up is how Parsons's work contributed to this synthesis in each of it stages of development. Not until action theory's present state of development has been ascertained in this examination of its undisputedly most important exponent can we direct our attention back towards the classics. The task then – to be engaged in in the follow-up to this book – is to discover what contribution the classics themselves made to a synthesis of positivism and idealism to form a voluntaristic theory of action. The authors deserving special attention are sociology's two outstanding classics: Emile Durkheim and Max Weber. A history of sociology would proceed chronologically. The *rational reconstruction* of a theoretical development, on the other hand, must set out from the level of development reached up to the present day, which serves as a frame of reference for a new formulation of the classics' enduring contributions and for the elimination of errors they may have made. This is why Parsons is dealt with before Durkheim and Weber. Planning the material in this way, of course, also gives voice to the conviction that Parsons managed to reach beyond Durkheim and Weber.

Integrating the two opposing basic streams of Western thought – idealism and positivism – into a voluntaristic theory of human action constitutes the fundamental theme permeating Talcott Parsons's work. This theme can be formulated, on a metatheoretical level, in the question: 'How is a theory of action possible which combines theoretical abstraction with historical and empirical specification, and causal explanation with hermeneutic interpretation?' The corresponding question on the object-theoretical level is: 'How is human action possible which combines orderedness with individual autonomy?' The answer to the metatheoretical question is: Through the voluntaristic theory of action, which supersedes and integrates idealistic and positivistic theories of action. The object-theoretical question is answered thus: Through voluntaristic order, where purely ideal and purely factual, naturalistic orders are superseded and integrated. The above fundamental questions are also an expression of voluntaristic action theory's commitment to the basic values associated with modernity.

In his first major work, *The Structure of Social Action* (1937), Parsons made his classic formulation of the above theme: this first treatment involved an interpretation of the heterogeneous contributions of Alfred Marshall, Vilfredo Pareto, Emile Durkheim and Max Weber toward the theoretical integration in question. As he later developed his theme, Parsons also primarily included Sigmund

Freud's work on the theory of socialization and personality development within his group of classical sources. However, the classic contributions to voluntaristic action theory certainly need not be confined to these authors. Others such as Georg Simmel, George Herbert Mead or Jean Piaget could also easily be included in the group.

The turning point in integrating idealism and positivism in Western thought is provided by Immanuel Kant's critique of reason. The systematic significance of Kant's critiques for the voluntaristic theory of action in the work of Durkheim, Weber and Parsons is noticeable throughout. In his last major work, *Action Theory and the Human Condition* which appeared in 1978, Parsons himself emphatically underscored the significance of Kant in this respect. Only a Kantian perspective, then, can help us achieve an interpretation of voluntaristic action theory which does justice to the original work, is objectively tenable, and allows for its rational reconstruction and fruitful further development. This is the premise on which this particular attempt to take stock of and develop the voluntaristic theory of action is based. Its purpose is to make use of the Kantian perspective in working out the objectively most tenable structure for the voluntaristic theory of action in respect of the two metatheoretical and object-theoretical underlying questions formulated at the outset. I must stress again that this procedure is one of *rational reconstruction* in the light of these theoretical problems, and not a historical presentation of individual contributions and stages of development. The criterion applied throughout is: How should a particular item of theory or stage of development be interpreted if it is to go as far as possible towards answering the fundamental metatheoretical and object-theoretical questions? In this process a number of stages in the rational reconstruction of theoretical developments must be considered:

- During the first stage any errors occurring should be attributed to the interpreter of a theoretical text rather than to the text itself, until such time as he/she succeeds in eliminating the error by way of alternative interpretations.

- If this interpretational strategy no longer produces results, it is necessary to move on to the second stage where an author's subjective errors are corrected through constructive criticism in the light of an objectively tenable version of his/her contribution.

- If this strategy is also unsuccessful, a third stage is needed where the criticism is also directed at the theory's objective structure, which must be subjected to revision until such time as an objectively tenable structure is found which can prove itself in answering the fundamental metatheoretical and object-theoretical questions.

3

- Not until all these strategies have been tried without any further result should the fourth stage be embarked upon, where the construction of an entirely new alternative is undertaken. Such an alternative would have to be more comprehensive and better suited to solving our underlying theoretical problems than the voluntaristic theory of action. None of the alternatives currently on offer on the theory market can honestly claim to fulfil this requirement. None of them reaches beyond the scope of voluntaristic action theory; rather, they all fall back behind it. All of them, in one way or another, are either totally confined to the one-sided perspective of idealism or of positivism, or else the perspectives are combined in contradiction to one another, without any integration providing new progress.

In the rational reconstruction and extension of voluntaristic action theory undertaken here, the main emphasis will initially be placed on the first stage detailed above: seeking the objectively most tenable structure of the individual contributions and stages of development. In addition, however, the attempt will be made at a number of points to institute the second stage by correcting subjective errors the authors under discussion may have made, in the light of an objectively tenable structure of their contributions. Application of the third stage is limited to minor alterations in the theory structure. It would undoubtedly be premature at this time to engage in the fourth stage of replacing the voluntaristic theory of action by any existing alternative, for the immediate concern is to make clear the voluntaristic theory's structure and what it can achieve. Moreover, there is no similarly comprehensive alternative available on the theory market.

The rational reconstruction and extension of voluntaristic action theory begins by establishing the Kantian structure of Parsons's first majors, *The Structure of Social Action* (1937). This interpretational perspective is then used to reconstruct the individual steps in Parsons's theory development, right up to his final major work, *Action Theory and the Human Condition*. The attempt at reconstructing Parsons's work is concluded with a systematic presentation of the advance in knowledge voluntaristic action theory achieves over its positivistic and idealistic counterparts. The intention is that this advance, pointed out by Parsons right at the beginning of his career, should be demonstrated on the strength of the present stage of development attained by voluntaristic action theory.

The concluding consideration offers a résumé of the 'dialectic' preservation and replacement of positivism and idealism in the voluntaristic theory of action.

1 The structure of the Kantian core*

Introductory remarks

Over the last half-century, Talcott Parsons produced a body of work which was enormous in its scope, depth and continuity. No sociologist in the past has been able to escape the influence of this work, and not only sociologists but other social scientists too will inevitably meet and have to consider his work in future. On this point sociologists of all persuasions are agreed. The work began with Parsons's dissertation at Heidelberg on the concept of capitalism in the writings of Max Weber and Werner Sombart.[1] Several essays on Alfred Marshall and Vilfredo Pareto extended these early studies.[2] A first culmination point in this theoretical development was reached with *The Structure of Social Action*, a book which has become a classic in its own right through its constructive interpretation of the classic authors.[3] The remaining stages of Parsons's development are likewise marked by major publications, the last of which is the collection *Action Theory and the Human Condition*.[4] It has become an obligation for every sociologist, not only those working directly on theoretical questions but also all those engaged in the various fields of practical applications, to take into consideration Parsons's work – however complete or incomplete, correct or incorrect, it may turn out to be. Although firmly anchored in the sociological tradition, Parsons's work has an inherent scope which lends it a significance for modern thought far beyond the confines of sociology. It is especially relevant to all sciences of human action.

Although Parsons's sociology has become in this sense an institution, it is equally true that the conventional attitude toward his theory is one of critical aloofness. Sociologists do not like to be identified with his optimistic judgements on modern American Society, or with the label of 'conservatism' which Dahrendorf,

5

C. Wright Mills, Gouldner, and many other critics have affixed to his sociology.[5] In addition, the complicated model building in Parsons's sociology causes many sociologists to keep their distance from it.[6] To a critical and dialectical sociology, Parsons's theory appears blind to the omnipresence of conflict and change, incapable of explaining them and conservative in its final effect. To a phenomenologically based sociology, the theory is far too abstract and formalistic. As seen by the critique provided by empiricist positivism its concepts cannot be made operational and its structure has only conceptional schemata (taxonomies) to offer, and no empirically testable propositions and hypotheses. The style of presentation, regarded as difficult of access, is a unanimously disliked feature of Parsons's theory.[7] Certainly only a few sociologists have taken the trouble to follow Parsons's elaborate technical manipulations of his theory through his numerous works. Outside a narrow circle of disciples, the potential of his work has barely been tapped.[8] Frequently, the argument that his theoretical apparatus can only produce reifications and so blocks any access to reality has been used to avoid having to undertake the difficult task of testing systematically the adequacy of the theory's application to the world. One can use such systematic and thorough testing to exhibit the range and limits of a theory, but only if one is willing to go beyond wholesale criticisms.

The question how much explanatory power a theory as elaborated as that of Parsons possesses is not one which can be decided by general arguments or global judgements. After all, Parsons himself demonstrated more than sufficiently how rewarding such a testing of the explanatory power of his theory can be. Not the least part of this demonstration is the very range of his work, from general theory construction down to the analyses, frequently in occasional pieces, of concrete empirical-practical problems. What one comes to realize is that it is exactly this joining of opposites – of general theory development with empirical-practical analysis – which makes Parsons's sociology so fruitful. It makes possible that inter-penetration of theory and experience, of logic and practice, which is such a crucial prerequisite for the development of every modern science. In an autobiographical article published in 1970, Parsons points out this twofold character of his sociological work and emphasizes that his kind of theory building is neither logically deductive nor sheerly inductive, but rather resembles the continual process of the systematization of the law which one finds in Common Law jurisdictions:

'In this process [i.e. Parsons's theoretical development] ... I have indeed reacted to quite a number of externally presented stimuli of the sort that I have characterized, especially requests to write on topics suggested by others. In a sufficient proportion of such cases, I hope I have reacted somewhat in the manner of a competent common-law appellate judge: namely, that I have considered the submitted topics and problems in relation to a theoretical scheme, which – though its premises were not defined with complete precision and henceforth assumed as fully given in a logically complete sense – has had considerable clarity, consistency, and continuity. In a sufficient proportion of cases, it seems to me that this kind of procedure has yielded empirical insight and rounding out, extension, and revision and generalization of the theoretical scheme. At certain points this has meant intensive concern with formally defined theoretical problems, but at other points primary concern with much more empirical issues. In any case this is essentially what I have meant by the phrase 'building social system theory' as used in the title of this essay. ("On building social system theory: A personal history")[9]

We could describe this procedure as a specific form of the interpenetration of two subsystems of the production of knowledge which are themselves subject to their own laws: the subsystem of theoretical research and the subsystem of practical problem solving. In saying this we apply the central concept of Parsons's theory to his own sociological work. Only by developing such zones of interpenetration is it possible to synthesize the results of differentiated subsystems into a unified whole which would possess its own specific character and which would have more power to illuminate the world than either an undifferentiated unity or the sum of the particular subsystems themselves. Here it is theory without intuitions which remains empty, while intuitions without theory are blind.

The significance of this interpenetration of concept and intuition, of theory and experience, as a condition of modern science is nowhere made clearer than in Immanuel Kant's *Critique of Pure Reason*.[10] Among philosophers, it is Kant above all who articulates the specific epistemological structure of modern scientific knowledge, and Talcott Parsons's sociology is everywhere permeated with the structure of the philosophy of Kant. It is not only the aforementioned interpenetration of theory construction and empirical analysis in Parsons's concrete sociological work which leads us to this conclusion. His general theory of action and his theory of social systems are themselves thoroughly Kantian. If we look at Parsons's biography with this connection in mind, we notice that Parsons began to read Kant's philosophy intensively while studying at Heidelberg in 1925–6. In his autobiographical essay of 1970, Parsons describes his experience:

'In retrospect it seems to me that this experience was, even apart from the substantive importance of Kant for my problems, especially important training for my later work. It was reinforced by a seminar and oral exam on the same book under Karl Jaspers at Heidelberg in 1926. The importance lay in the fact that I undertook the detailed and repeated study of a great book, the product of a great mind, to a point of reaching a certain level of appreciation of the nature of its contribution, and not being satisfied with the myriad of current rather superficial comments about it. This experience stood me in good stead in working with the contributions of my own authors and coming to what I felt to be a high level of understanding of them in the face of many distorted interpretations current in the secondary literature, some of which were widely accepted.'[11]

Although even a superficial study of Parsons reveals the influence of Kant's epistemological conceptions, one can in fact go much farther and draw a precise parallel in structure and method between Parsons's general theory of action and theory of social systems, and Kant's own critical philosophy. This hypothesis gives us a way of reading Parsons which has up to now, been almost wholly neglected and this neglect constitutes a crucial deficiency in the reception accorded Parsons's work.[12] *Parsons's sociology cannot possibly be understood apart from a consideration of Kant's critical project.*[13] The philosophical perspective provided by Kant's critiques is introduced here so that it can provide a framework for the interpretation of Parsons's work as a whole. This will hopefully initiate a reconsideration of Parsons's theory of action and its various concretizations, a reconsideration capable of opening up perspectives on Parsons's work which will be free of the clichés that up to now have proved to be mostly obstacles to our understanding of it.

This thesis will first be established with regard to the structure of the theory of action as it is presented in *The Structure of Social Action* and in Parsons's constructive integration of his classical sources (Durkheim, Weber, and Freud), in order to isolate that core of the theory of action which is systematically expanded, without major changes, in all Parsons's further writings.

1.1 The interpretive perspective: Kant's critical philosophy

In his last theoretical publication, 'A Paradigm of the Human Condition', Parsons, fresh from a renewed, intensive study of Kant, enlarges on the significance of Kant's transcendental arguments for his own theory of action.[14] The indications contained in this, his last theoretical discourse, provide us with *a key to the proper understanding of his entire action theory and sociology*. Parsons shows special interest in Kant's dualistic construction of human knowledge, which can be viewed as a model for the general theory of action:

'Kant clearly thought in terms of dual levels: the categories of understanding and the sense data of empirical knowledge; the "categorical imperative" and the "problems" of practical ethics; the canons of judgement and esthetic "experience". There seems to be a striking parallel between his version of duality and the linguist's "deep structures" and "surface structures", the biologist's "genotypes" and "phenotypes", the cyberneticist's "high on information" and "high on energy", and indeed the sociologist's "values", or institutional patterns, and "interests". We therefore suggest that the first term in each of these pairs be used to designate a *meta*structure, which is not as such a property of the phenomena (also Kant's term) under consideration but is rather an *a priori* set of conditions without which the phenomena in question could not be conceived in an orderly manner.'[15]

Kant's *Critique of Pure Reason* is best understood as a reply to Hume's empiricism and to the scepticism which results from that empiricism.[16] Proceeding according to the tenets of a rigorous empiricism, Hume concluded that the knowledge expressed in the propositions of the natural sciences reduced ultimately to nothing more than collections of sense perceptions.[17] These sense perceptions, moreover, occur singly and, contrary to the claims of the causal laws of natural science, have no intrinsic connection with each other. There is no bridge from atomized singular perceptions to the general laws of science. According to Hume, habit alone leads us to believe in the necessity of the causal connection between two events which are always experienced as occurring in the same temporal order. Hume's point is precisely that this is mere belief, not knowledge.[18]

The attempt to construct a completely consistent empiricism had led Hume to doubt the possibility of scientific knowledge. Kant, on the other hand, began from a completely different conception of the nature of science. For him the validity of scientific knowledge was a given, a fact. His question was: How can we explain how such knowledge is possible?[19] His explanation took the form of a 'transcendental argument', by means of which he demonstrated that the possibility of scientific knowledge having universal validity for all men depends on the existence of certain preconditions. An important component of Kant's argument here is the distinction between the specific capacities of *a priori* categories and of empirical sense experience. It is impossible fully to understand the nature of scientific knowledge by reference either to the order embodied in its abstract principles or to its empirical content alone. For Kant, modern scientific knowledge is explicable neither as a habitual generalization from empirical experience, as in Hume's empiricism, nor as a series of deductions from the first principles of reason, as in the rationalism of someone like Descartes, but only as the mutual interaction of theory and experience. Experience that can become the touchstone of universal laws is itself only made possible by a table of categories and a set of general theoretical principles, which analytically order our sense perceptions. And it is only in so far as we constantly refer sense perceptions to these categories and principles that we are entitled to say of them that they express empirical and not merely logical regularities. Theoretical abstraction and empirical concretion are united in the statements of these laws.

This connection of opposites – the abstract and the empirical – is a specific historical occurrence whose product is modern Western science. The prototype of this interpenetration of theory and experience is the rational experiment, developed in a historical situation in which conditions were especially favourable to the interpenetration of spheres normally kept separate. These conditions were provided primarily by the scientific associations of the Italian Renaissance of the fifteenth and sixteenth centuries and the English scientistic movement of the seventeenth century. These associations united intellectuals with practical men of varying backgrounds – artists, engineers, artisans, merchants, politicians. Their collaboration produced what is by us today considered a matter of course: the interpenetration of theory and experience, of logic and practice, in modern science. Thus there were united for the first time functions performed previously by wholly separate social groups.[20]

Just as the *Critique of Pure Reason* is directed against empiricism in epistemology, Kant's *Critique of Judgement* is an attack on all attempts to construct a theory of aesthetic judgement by generalization from the collection of given individual judgements. A theory of judgement can claim universal validity only if it establishes a connection between *a priori* categories of judgement (such as the category of 'purposiveness as such') and the sensations of pleasure experienced by individuals as they contemplate works of art or the processes of nature.[21] And the same logic, the logic of the transcendental argument, structures Kant's *Critique of Practical Reason*. The latter work is particularly significant for us, because in it we can discern the main outlines of Parsons's theory of action.

In the *Critique of Practical Reason*, Kant argues against any attempt to found moral principles on the subjective considerations of utility of individual actors. That is, he rejects all utilitarian moral theories.[22] Just as we cannot account for the objective necessity of causal laws by reference solely to the content of sense perceptions, so we cannot derive the necessity of a moral law valid for all men at all times from the desires – or the calculations of utility – of individuals. Private calculations of utility may yield different results for different individuals, or for the same individual at different times. The criterion of a moral law, however, is that it is binding for all men at all times. We cannot explain the obligatory force of the moral law as the sum of all calculations of utility, because these calculations would yield extremely variable results, and we would have made no progress toward a concept of true obligation:

'The principle of happiness can indeed give maxims, but never maxims which are competent to be laws of the will, even if universal happiness were made the object. For, since the knowledge of this rests on mere data of experience, as each judgement concerning it depends very much on the very changeable opinion of each person, it can give general but never universal rules; that is, the rules it gives will on the average be most often the right ones for the purpose, but they will not be rules which must hold always and necessarily. Consequently, no practical laws can be based on this principle.'[23]

The characteristic of moral norms is that they lay claim to a validity which is independent of subjective utility considerations. Our obedience to them is not based on inclination, which is variable, but on duty, which is unchanging. As a philosopher, Kant makes no attempt to provide a sociological analysis of how this sense of duty arises, empirically, in men. His inquiry is directed toward the question: What are the conditions of possibility of a universally binding moral law? Once again, Kant demonstrates that the phenomenon in question is possible only through the linking of abstract categories and empirical ethical problems. Any particular rule of action can be adjudged valid to the extent that it enables us to attain a given end, but there is no direct path from this 'hypothetical' validity to a universal, unconditional validity, since our first particular rule might be called into question by other particular rules which function as means to other given ends. To bring order to the multitude of particular rules and to answer the question of their universal validity, we cannot begin from below, but must apply a scheme of categories from above. For Kant, order is produced by a 'categorical imperative': 'So act that the maxim of your will could always hold at the same time as a principle establishing universal law.'[24]

In so far as moral theory takes the categorical imperative as 'the supreme principle of morality', it can impose on the multiplicity of particular rules a unifying order which allows us to judge the universal validity of these rules. In this way, the development of a universal moral order is a consequence of the interpenetration of the two parameters along which human action can be judged: (1) the law of abstraction and of logical consistency and (2) the rules of mutual accommodation and of the satisfaction of needs and desires. A moral order must be based in some way on the association of the demands of abstraction and of logic and the needs of practical action. If these are kept separate, the former will generate only empty conceptual systems, while the latter will leave us with a multiplicity of particularized rules of action, each pertaining to a narrowly delimited sphere of human activity, containing no potential for a comprehensive morality.

We know from the comparative studies of Max Weber that it is not a foregone conclusion for any given culture that this interpenetration will occur. A systematic conception of natural law has been developed only in the West; in China, as well as in India, the conditions of interpenetration of abstract moral theory and practical regulation essential to such a development were lacking. In China, moral theory had become adapted to the practical interests of the bureaucratic elite of literati. In India theory and practice remained separated.[25]

Accordingly, Kant's philosophy articulates the presuppositions of modern Western society in both the theory of knowledge and the theory of morality. And it is precisely because it has this characteristic that Kant's philosophy provides us with a means for understanding Talcott Parsons's sociology, from its beginnings in Parsons's rereadings of Durkheim and Weber, through its incorporation of Freud, to the systematized fullness of the mature theory.

1.2 The crystallization of the theory of action as a theory of interpenetration: *The Structure of Social Action*

The significance of Kant's transcendental arguments as a key to the understanding of his own action theory, from its inception in *The Structure of Social Action* in 1937, was openly acknowledged by Parsons at the other end of his career, in 'A paradigm of the human condition' (1978). There Parsons regards Kant as providing the hinge for the turn from a 'positivistic' or 'idealistic' to a 'voluntaristic' theory of action. Kant is therefore a forerunner of Durkheim and Weber, who are read by Parsons in *The Structure of Social Action* as the founders, along with Pareto and Marshall, of a non-utilitarian, voluntaristic theory of action:

'This position of Kant's is clearly of central importance to the general theory of action. We hold that it is the locus of the most fundamental underlying premises or assumptions of *social* ordering at the human level. It should explicitly be defined not as the *data* of moral problems but as the *transcendental normative conditions of the ordering of such data*. This Kantian philosophical position clearly underlies both Durkheim's and Weber's treatment of the moral component of societies, especially modern societies.'[26]

In order fully to appreciate the thrust of Parsons's argument, we have to read *The Structure of Social Action* as the sociological equivalent of Kant's moral philosophy. Only in this way will we be able to understand how this first major work opens out into the theory of action in general and the theory of social systems in particular. Just as Kant developed his theory of moral philosophy as an alternative to philosophical utilitarianism, Parsons developed his theory of action as an alternative to sociological utilitarianism. This alternative Parsons terms 'voluntaristic action theory', the basic principles of which he finds adumbrated in the writings of Marshall, Pareto, Durkheim and Weber.

A central reference point here is Hobbes's formulation of the problem of social order.[27] A 'social order' can be said to exist to the extent that individual actors are connected by a system of shared behaviour patterns on the basis of which they can form rational expectations about each other's action. For example, if someone wants to make use of a pasture, he must be able to determine whether there are any other potential users of this pasture who might claim the same right to use it. If he cannot determine this, his use of the pasture is in principle not secure. At any time, a shortage of pasturage might cause others to dispute his right to use this pasture. He can successfully realize in action his aims and intentions only if he is able to defend himself against the attacks of others, and he can do the latter only if he has sufficient power. So it must be the goal of every actor to gain power over his fellows. The war of all against all is the inevitable consequence. But this state of war, in which every man must fear every other man, is an intolerable life for men. As Hobbes shows, in this situation – as in the so-called *prisoner's dilemma* – the most rational actions that men can perform on the basis of their individual subjective calculations of utility result in their being far worse off than if all had accepted some appropriate distribution of rights.[28]

As Parsons points out, Hobbes expresses in paradigmatic form the dilemma of utilitarian social theories.[29] If the aims of actions are completely arbitrary and if rationality is the only criterion for the selection of the means to those ends, then within a system in which resources are limited and actors are interdependent upon each other, subjective rationality in fact produces irrational consequences for every actor. Looking at this system from the outside, we can easily conclude that all the actors would obtain more satisfactory results if there were a distribution of rights and duties and if everyone could count on everyone else's observance of these rights and duties. In other words, there ought to be a normative order within the system. The utilitarian dilemma consists in the fact that within the system there is no motivation for the actors to try to alter their self-destructive situation. The most rational strategy is still the acquisition of superior power; the acceptance of a normative order requires the confidence that others too will stick to the norms. This in turn requires that everyone treat adherence to the norms not as one end among others, but as a higher end which is never submitted to the conditions of utility calculation. Thus we must give up the utilitarian premise that there are no necessarily permanent ends; the free calculation of utility requires precisely that the rank ordering of ends be allowed to change as the consequences we expect to follow from their realization change. (And this means that utilitarian calculation can choose among ends only by evaluating them as if they were means.) If the adherence to a norm is to function as a permanent high priority end, it must constitute the limit of the process of the calculation of utility: in other words, it must be ranked so high that it is never subjected to competition from other ends. So long as this condition is not satisfied, everyone is more likely to trust to his own resources of strength than he is to count on the adherence of others to the norms which define individual rights.

If we stay within the framework of a consistent utilitarianism, there is no way out of this dilemma. Hobbes's own solution postulates that the actors, taking the position of observers of their own situation, would realize that it is more useful for them to adhere to a common order. When the need of security becomes an end with a high enough priority, the actors will supposedly be ready to come to an agreement with one another and to transfer all of their power to a sovereign ruler.[30] But Hobbes's solution is inconsistent; it is not at all rational for the individual actor to make such an agreement:

'This solution really involves stretching, at a critical point, the conception of rationality beyond its scope in the rest of the theory, to a point where the actors come to realize the situation as a whole instead of pursuing their own ends in terms of their immediate situation, and then take the action necessary to eliminate force and fraud and, purchasing [sic] security at the sacrifice of the advantages to be gained by their future employment.'[31]

As long as the individual cannot rely completely on the fidelity of others to their mutual contract, it is not rational for him to enter into such a contract. And he can never trust in the fidelity of others unless such fidelity is no longer the object of utility calculations and hence becomes a higher-ranking determinant of action. This requires, however, a normative limitation of the principle of utility, binding for all actors; otherwise it will be safer to rely on 'force and fraud' as a means of protection against the predations of others. Such a normative limitation on the principle of utility would have to precede the agreement of the actors in the system to resign power resources; it could never be the result of such an agreement. Hobbes of course realized this, which is why he withholds from the citizens the right to cancel their contract so long as the sovereign can guarantee order.[32]

Thus it is not calculation of utility which motivates the citizens' adherence to the contract, since in regard to the contract we have the same distrust as everywhere else in the state of nature.[33] According to Hobbes, only the threat of external sanctions can assure the citizens' conformity to social norms. Order comes not from a contract spontaneously arrived at, but from a centralized authority.[34] Hobbes thus provides a solution to the utilitarian dilemma which has become the traditional utilitarian response to the fact that a free play of individual interests does not spontaneously yield social order. The solution turns on the idea of the centralization of decision-making power and the power to enforce sanctions. Essentially the same solution is offered in the model of 'collective resources' which James Coleman has advanced as a way of dealing with cases in which social exchange by itself proves unable to generate social order.[35] The same can be said for the work of Viktor Vanberg, who like Coleman is a modern utilitarian. The only alternative Vanberg is able to imagine to the formation of order out of a process of free exchange is the centralization of decision-making power.[36] Collective obedience to a norm is simply stipulated by a central authority and imposed through the threat of force. The tensions inherent within the utilitarian solution can be seen in the fact that we are no longer talking about 'norms', but only about centralized or decentralized 'decisions'. In fact, Vanberg tends to use the terms 'central decision', 'common decision', and 'social decision' as at least functional equivalents.[37]

What does motivate individuals to accept a centralization of decision-making power? In the various utilitarian models, the motivation can only be the fear of superior ability to impose sanctions, since the possibility of a spontaneous acceptance generated by a free play of interests has already been ruled out. This implies that a rational actor should want to obtain this superior power to impose sanctions himself. So we have landed back where we started, with Hobbes's war of all against all. A society can be expected to possess a stable order only if it contains a sufficiently pronounced hierarchy of power. But even this would be a very fragile order, endangered by every change in the availability of the resources of power. Thus the appeal to centralization of power is in the end no solution to the utilitarian dilemma, because it fails to touch the core of the problem: the need to limit the possible ends and means that individual actors may choose. 'A purely utilitarian society is chaotic and unstable, because in the absence of limitations on the use of means, particularly force and fraud, it must, in the nature of the case, resolve itself into an unlimited struggle for power.'[38] Simple centralization of power will be nothing more than an intermediate stage in the struggle for power unless it can found itself on some limitation on the usage of power other than the mere existence of a sufficiently hierarchized distribution of power within the society.

This is the argument on the basis of which Parsons maintains that within the system of utilitarian thought no solution to the Hobbesian problem of order is possible. If the human condition contained only those elements recognized by utilitarianism, there would be no social order. Like Kant in his criticism of scepticism, Parsons begins his own argument with the claim that social order *does* exist, even if in an always incompletely realized form, and that our task should be to try to explain how this is possible. Parsons's solution to the problem of social order is often called a 'normative solution'. The use of this phrase contains the assumption that Parsons explains the existence of order by reference to a common system of norms or values. Once Parsons has been oversimplified in this way, it is easy to take the next step and accuse him of not really explaining the existence of order at all, but only offering a definition. And thus the utilitarians feel justified in presenting again their old solutions – exchange or constraint or some combination thereof – while ignoring Parsons's demonstration that these solutions are inherently inadequate.[39]

If we do not want to miss the point of Parsons's solution to the problem, we have to read him from the perspective of Kant, and that means first of all recognizing that Parsons's solution can be neither normative nor utilitarian. Parsons presents a voluntaristic solution to the problem of social order. The term 'voluntaristic' indicates that social order need not be a completely causally determined factual order. As soon as a centralized force does not provide a factual order by causally determined compliance, social order is only possible as long as the actors voluntarily consent and bind themselves to a common normative frame of reference. A normative order of this kind, as opposed to a merely factual order, thus demands rational justification of particular norms by subsuming them to universally accepted values. In fact, Parsons's exposition of the voluntaristic theory of action requires that he fight on two fronts. We have seen that he defines his own position in opposition to the positivistic-utilitarian theory of action, which recognizes no criterion for the selection of human actions other than the rationality which weighs actions as means to ends. But he must also define his own position in opposition to idealistic theories of action – for example, that of German idealism, which understands all human action as an objectification of *Geist*. In opposition to both of these extremes, the voluntaristic theory of action maintains that human action must be understood as the result of an interpenetration of means-end rationality and a normative limitation on the free play of such rationality. Parsons refers to this relation as one of 'interdependence' of 'interaction': 'The voluntaristic system does not in the least deny an important role to conditional and other non-normative elements, but considers them as interdependent with the normative.'[40] Already at this stage in the development of his theory, Parsons has in mind that relation between analytically separate subsystems which he will later, in the 1950s, refer to as 'interpenetration'.[41]

What precisely is meant by interpenetration between the 'conditional' and the 'normative'? It does not mean that action is always, in every particular case, determined by both components. It means rather that social order is possible only if there is such an interpenetration between self-interested, rationalized action and a frame of reference which sets the limits of the process of the calculation of utility by ruling certain ends and means out of bounds altogether and by giving to others a stable priority independent of factual conditions and means-end considerations. Order can exist only if the actors are not free to shed their agreements with one another as easily as they might shed an uncomfortably starched shirt. The decisive question of transcendental logic is, then: Given that social order exists, what conditions constitute the framework within which social action necessarily takes place? Kant asks: If there is objective scientific knowledge and if sense experience by itself can provide us with only an unordered 'sensuous manifold', then whence the order and universal validity which are the defining characteristics of scientific knowledge? Kant's question and Parsons's question have the same form. And just as for Kant the answer to the question turned on the discovery of the *limits* set on the arbitrariness of sense experience, so for Parsons the answer to his question turns on the discovery of a limit on the arbitrariness of action determined solely by subjective considerations of utility. A social order cannot be established by utility considerations alone; there must be something else which provides the structure within which alone such considerations are possible.

The Kantian critical project is a comprehensive examination of the specific capacities of the human faculties of knowledge – sense perception, which supplies empirical data, and the understanding, which governs the formation of concepts and judgements. Kant's conclusion is that the orderedness of our experience, as it manifests itself in the fact that the canons of universal validity, the rules of logical consistency, and the laws of causality apply to it, is not something which is merely perceived, but occurs only through the *a priori* limitation of the possibilities of perception, the drawing of the 'bounds of sense', by the *rules* of concept formation and the modes of unity in judgement. In the same way, Parsons conducts an examination of the specific functions of the various elements of a system of action: (1) ends; (2) a situation consisting of (*a*) available means and (*b*) given conditions; and (3) a selective principle according to which means and conditions can be related to ends.[42] If the selective principle is a pure means-end rationality (Weber's *Zweckrationalität*) – for example, the calculation of utility – no social order can arise. A social order is possible only if there is a selective principle which exempts certain means and ends from utilitarian considerations and assigns to them a permanent priority. Within the limits thus established, action is motivated by considerations of utility and is as variable as empirical knowledge can be within the rules of understanding.

As Kant shows, there are only two kinds of selective principles: hypothetical and categorical. Only categorical principles can produce a constancy of choice of action through the variableness of situations of action.[43] We can make use of Kant's distinction in order to understand Parsons's argument that social order is possible only if action is guided, not solely by conditional selective principles, but also by normative selective principles which determine the scope of the validity of the conditional, hypothetical selective principles. These normative selective principles have the same functional significance for the theory of action that the pure intuitions of space and time and the categories of understanding have for classical mechanics in Kant's *Critique of Pure Reason*:

'A normative orientation is fundamental to the schema of action in the same sense that space is fundamental to that of the classical mechanics; in terms of the given conceptual scheme there is no such thing as action except as effort to conform with norms just as there is no such thing as motion except as change of location in space. In both cases the propositions are definitions or logical corollaries of definitions. But it is not necessary for present purposes even to raise the question whether human behaviour is "really" normatively oriented.'[44]

A normative selective principle is a categorical rule in Kant's sense.

Its validity is not dependent on the character of the individual situations in which it is applied. Concretely, this means that, if there is to be a social order, a rule such as, for example, that excluding the use of force and fraud must not have merely hypothetical validity contingent upon the actors' expectations of profiting from it. If the validity of the rule were merely hypothetical, it would often turn out to be more advantageous for actors to employ means which subvert the rule. This would prove the impossibility of mutual trust, and Hobbes's state of nature would be unavoidable. Further, the motivation to restrict oneself to peaceful means of exchange under a threat of sanctions imposed by an external authority would also be hypothetical, since the individual would accept this restriction only as long as he himself was not strong enough to seize the position of centralized authority and turn it against his fellows. In this case there would be no selective principle guaranteeing a constancy of motives for action and determining the use of peaceful means of exchange as the limit of social interaction.

The first thing we get out of Parsons's answer to the question of the possibility of social order is the realization that the selective principle setting the limits of self-interested action must be categorically valid for all actors. That means that the actors obey the rule because it is their obligation to do so, and not because they think it will be useful for them to do so. The paramount question for a sociological theory of social order must be: How is this categorical obligation possible? Only by understanding the function of the normative rules in Parsons's voluntaristic theory of action from this Kantian perspective can we grasp the full significance of Parsons's theory. From the standpoint of this Kantian perspective, it makes no sense to criticize Parsons for offering as an explanation of the existence of social order the very fact he is supposed to be explaining, that is, the existence of common norms. It is equally beside the point to counter Parsons by proposing again the solutions of traditional utilitarian thought – social exchange and, where this fails, a centralized authority with the ability to impose sanctions.[45] Parsons has shown these solutions to be fundamentally inadequate, and it was in uncovering the sources of their inadequacy that he first arrived at a formulation of the criterion a theory of social order must meet in regard to the function of normative rules in a system of social action. It is not enough simply to explain 'how norms come into existence'. One must explain precisely how a categorical obligation toward common norms comes about within a social system. Norms exist only when every actor in the social system can take general adherence to the norms to be a matter of course. This is possible only if adherence to the norms rests not upon merely hypothetical imperatives, but upon a categorical obligation which sets a limit to

19

the process of utilitarian calculation. Every explanation of 'the existence of norms' must simultaneously be an explanation of the source of the obligatory force of those norms. We will not be able to give this latter explanation if we continue to resort to free exchange or centralization of authority, or any other explanatory factor which remains wholly within the utilitarian framework.[46]

Parsons's analysis of the system of social action allows him to pose, in its correct form for the first time, the problem which the theory of social order must solve. It points out the direction in which a solution is impossible and the direction in which we must search if we are to find a solution. But Parsons does not simply replace the utilitarian theory of the genesis of norms with a normative theory which views social action solely as it is determined by categorical obligation. According to the voluntaristic theory of action, norms can be generated only through the interpenetration of action oriented toward a means-end rationality and a categorical normative obligation. Neither the one nor the other by itself yields a concrete social order. Where pure means-end rationality reigns, no social order is possible. But if there is nothing but the categorical obligation to obey norms, with no interpenetration with the various spheres of ordinary self-interested action, the result will be nothing but a 'sacred' order which will remain so remote from everyday behaviour that it will be incapable of imposing a concrete order. An order permeating all areas of social life can be expected only when the spheres of self-interested action and categorical obligation interpenetrate. This interpenetration is not something which can be taken for granted. The degree of such interpenetration in a given society depends on specific conditions which help or hinder it, conditions which it is the task of any theory of the development of norms to articulate.[47]

A theory of the development of norms must therefore be a theory of the interpenetration of opposed subsystems – in this case, the subsystem of action directed by means-end rationality and the subsystem of categorical duty. Nowhere else in the discipline of sociology has this basic idea, so essential for any theory of the development of norms and for every theory of social change, been elaborated as lucidly as in the writings of Talcott Parsons. It is all the more ironic, then, that among sociologists it has become almost a ritual to deplore Parsons's failure to provide an explanation of the development of norms and of social change; explaining social change means, after all, nothing other than explaining the institutionalization of a newly arisen order. The charge has been repeated so often that many now believe it purely on hearsay. One might conclude from this that sociologists in general are but little prepared to treat a truly complex theory adequately.

1.3 The sources of the theory of action: Whitehead, Durkheim, Weber, Freud

The most important influences on the development of the theory of action as a Kantian theory are Whitehead's epistemology and Durkheim's and Weber's sociology. These figures assumed in the course of Parsons's development greater significance than Marshall or Pareto, with whom they are bracketed in *The Structure of Social Action* as founders of voluntaristic action theory. Another very important figure in the development of the theory is Freud, whose work Parsons studied in depth only after the appearance of *The Structure of Social Action*. The question then is how these classics have to be read in the Kantian perspective.

Parsons's 'analytical realism',[48] as an epistemological concept, has its roots in the work of A. N. Whitehead.[49] Analytical realism claims that empirical phenomena acquire significance for a scientific discipline only when they are formulated in terms of the theoretical frame of reference specific to that discipline. This means that any discipline can consider only certain aspects of reality, never reality in its full concrete richness:

'Descriptive frames of reference in this sense are fundamental to all science. But by no means do they exhaust scientific conceptualization. Facts cannot be described except within such a schema. But their description within it has, in the first instance, the function of defining a "phenomenon" which is to be explained. That is, of the great mass of possible empirical observations we select those which are at the same time meaningful within such a schema and "belong together". They thus serve together to characterize the essential aspects of a concrete phenomenon, which then becomes the object of scientific interest.'[50]

We recognize this conception as a derivative of Kant's epistemology. The particular objects of a scientific discipline are themselves constituted through the interpenetration of empirical observation and a theoretical frame of reference. The first function of the theoretical frame of reference is to differentiate as sharply as possible the various aspects of reality, in order to enable examination of the causal relations that might subsist among these aspects. Its second function is to open up the possibility of abstraction, which makes possible the transference of knowledge from one field of phenomena to other fields of phenomena. These functions are best performed by a structure of categories which can be given increasingly greater specificity and analytical precision through the internal differentiation of a few basic concepts and which does not constantly have to keep introducing new concepts to handle its empirical input. Thus the theoretical frame of reference should make possible the abstraction from particulars, on the one hand, and the particularization of abstractions, on the other.

It is impossible to understand the mechanics of Parsons's theory apart from this background. The theory is designed to perform these two basic functions, and the later development of the four-function schema can be understood as the logical consequence of this fundamental commitment. It is supposed to make possible both abstraction and analytic differentiation, in order to provide the most precise assessment possible of the contributions of various aspects of reality in the causation of certain phenomena. This function of analytical schematization must be kept in mind when one tries to understand the development of the theory of action. Certainly this basic epistemological principle accounts for the emphasis, in all of Parsons's writings, on the process of concept formation as constitutive of the 'objects' of sociology. Yet, contrary to the frequent criticisms levelled against it, the theory of action consists of much more than mere 'taxonomies'. Those who find in Parsons's work nothing but a taxonomy have failed to read him carefully.

Whitehead had a mostly formal influence on Parsons; the influence of Durkheim, Weber and Freud was substantive. According to Parsons, Durkheim, Weber and Freud all share a *dualistic* conception of action. All three managed to avoid the pitfalls of reductionism which lay in both directions. Durkheim was not a sociological reductionist, Weber was not an idealistic reductionist, and Freud was not a biological reductionist – although these charges are frequent even today.

Criticizing the utilitarianism of Spencer in his study of the division of labour, Durkheim points out that social exchange always presupposes the existence of rules which are categorically binding.[51] These rules must be categorically binding if they are to serve as the 'frame' for the free association of individuals guided by considerations of utility. If these rules themselves were constantly open to considerations of utility, no one could have any confidence that those with whom he had entered into social agreements would abide by those agreements. There would be no peaceful exchange; and social exchange as such is peaceful exchange and is guided by rules which preclude the acquisition of goods by force and fraud; the only permitted means of acquiring goods is to offer equivalent goods or money in exchange. The adherence to these rules has to be categorical in character if there is to be sufficient mutual trust to serve as the basis for peaceful exchange. This categorical norm-adherence cannot emerge from the utility expected to result from exchange because this utility varies constantly. The adherence to rules cannot arise from exchange and free utility calculation, nor from the superior sanctioning power of the state – as utilitarian theory assumes. Durkheim holds, in Kantian fashion, that a stable limit on the free calculation of utility can only be the product of the moral-categorical authority of norms. Durkheim's overriding concern is with the conditions which allow the generation of such categorical obligations and the moral crises which are engendered in societies by the absence of such conditions.

Durkheim does more than stress the importance of obligation, however. The normative order must also be related to the needs and dispositions of individuals. Durkheim goes beyond Kant in his recognition that individuals must abide by norms not simply because they must, but because they desire to do so. Hence the crucial point of a theory of moral order must be the connection of social obligation with individual desire. This insight is fundamental to the theory of the interpenetration of the social system and the personality system.[52] It constitutes Durkheim's central contribution to voluntaristic action theory.

Durkheim's theoretical concerns begin with these basic questions and branch out in the direction of a theory of the institutionalization of norms in social systems and a theory of the internalization of norms within the individual personality.[53] Particularly important here is Durkheim's theorem that it is only in so far as the individual is part of a group on whose approval he is dependent that norms valid within the group can become categorically obligatory for the individual. For Durkheim, it is the lack of this bond between individual and group which explains the phenomenon of suicide – not only egoistic suicide but also anomic suicide.[54] But since such bonds exist only within groups which have both intensive and extensive contact among their members, the crucial question is: How can a society avoid particularization of these normatively governed bonds? Durkheim sought the solution to this problem in the strengthening of occupational groups as a basic element of social organization and in the institutionalization of common responsibilities in common assemblies which would enforce compromise decision-making.[55] In his sociology of religion, he came to the conclusion that individuals must be affectively tied to common values. These are in essence *sacred*, and must lend an outer form to the *profane* spheres of action. This relationship between sacred and profane represents the heart of Durkheim's Kantian perspective.

Durkheim also shows that the process of binding the individual to norms and the development of personality are not submitted in every case to zero-sum conditions. Division of labour has to be accompanied by the loosening of ties between an individual and a group; otherwise, the individual would be unable to participate in social life outside his primary reference group. The individual must be bound in succession to the normative demands of different groups; this is prerequisite not only for the development of a comprehensive normative order but for individualization as well.[56] The 'cult of the individual' is in this sense a form of social order in which institutionalization of a normative order and the individualization of the personality do not exclude each other, but reinforce each other. This discovery of Durkheim's is of decisive importance for Parsons's theory of institutionalization and internalization, because here Durkheim sets forth a theory of the interpenetration of social system and personality. Here lie the roots of Parsons's concept of institutionalized individualism.

We find such a theory of interpenetration in Weber's work, too, particularly in his comparative studies in the sociology of religion.[57] At the heart of Weber's account of the origin and development of Western society is a conception of the interpenetration of spheres which outside the West have remained separate or even opposed to one another. An especially important role is played here by the tension between religious ethics and the world, a tension which can be found, in the sense of a process of analytical differentiation, almost everywhere. This tension can be eased by any of four methods: *accommodation to the world, world flight, reconciliation*, or *mutual penetration*.[58]

Accommodation to the world is the solution of Confucianism.[59] This solution is found predominantly in societies in which religious ethics are articulated and expounded by a class which is involved in practical life and has its own status interests: for example, the Chinese literati. The consequence of this dominance of the sphere of means-end rationality over the sphere of religious ethics is the lack of an ethical order which could permeate the whole society. There can thus be only a limited ethical control of practical, utilitarian action.

The paradigmatic example of *reconciliation* is Hinduism.[60] The characteristic of this solution to the problem of the tension between religious ethics and the world is the separation of different spheres having their own internal order (the castes). These mini-societies are integrated on the theoretical level by the ideology of the causality of karma and reincarnation. There is no possibility here for a general religious ethics that would cover all of the different social spheres. There can only be particularized ethics for each sphere.

The paradigmatic example of *world flight* as a solution to our problem is Buddhism.[61] This solution tends to arise in situations in which religious ethics is primarily the concern of a class of intellectuals who are isolated from the concerns of practical life. The result is a sharp distinction between the ethics of the priests and the ethics of the laity and the absence of a general ethical code which could regulate the actions in the spheres of everyday life.

A *mutual penetration* of religious ethics and the world is found only in the West, and within the West its most complete realization is ascetic Protestantism.[62] Here alone have the practical spheres of economics and politics been ethically regulated, rather than consigned simply to the realms of utilitarian action and the manipulation of power. The typical Puritan business ethic is neither a mere appendage of economic acquisitiveness nor a pure emanation of religious ethics. It is instead the qualitatively new product of the interpenetration of two basically opposed spheres. Nothing comparable exists outside the West. This penetration of ethics into the domain of business is for Weber the specific mark of modern capitalism, in comparison with all non-Western and pre-modern forms of economic behaviour. It could have occurred only where two institutionally independent spheres came together while retaining their own essential character.

Although the institutional independence of the Christian religion resulted very early from the institutionalization of the custom of educating priests at universities, the penetration of the economic and political spheres by religion occurred only gradually and by steps. A giant step in this direction was the development of the medieval city, because in it, unlike the non-Western city, the religious community, the political community, and the market economy all were brought together.[63] But still there was a large gap between priestly ethics and lay ethics, and the bureaucratic organization of the institutionalized church tended to substitute control of external behaviour for the internalization of norms. Yet religion and the world were close enough to create even more extreme tensions between them as economic activity increased. These tensions were released by the Reformation, through a stronger ethical penetration of the world. The traditionalism of the German Reformation caused this process to be coupled there with a strengthening of absolutism. As a result, only in Calvinism and in the Puritan sects and denominations of England, the Netherlands and the United States was there a truly *reciprocal* penetration of religious ethics and the world. Important elements of this development were the radical elimination of any distinction between an ethics for the priests and an ethics for the laity and the importance given to internal control of behaviour, an importance conferred first by Calvin's doctrine of predestination.[64] Of paramount importance, however, was the tight binding of the individual to the group by its approval which was achieved within the free religious communities of Puritanism.[65]

We cannot understand the emergence of the modern normative order, which manages to be both universal and individualistic, and both rational and activistic, apart from this interpenetration of religious ethics and the world. The characteristic of this modern order is that it is able to maintain a common identity while encompassing a range of social activities that includes everything from philosophical theories of morality to practical problems of economic and political action. Only the West has developed the philosophical concept of natural law, and the reciprocal penetration of 'sacred' and 'profane' codes is peculiar to the West. Outside the West, these two realms have remained alien to one another, or one has dominated the other. In order to explain the genesis of the unique social order of the West, Weber has implicit recourse to a theory of interpenetration. Apart from this theoretical perspective, we will fail to understand Weber's explanation of the origin and development of Western society. It is the merit of Talcott Parsons to have distilled this theoretical perspective from Weber's sociological writings and to have made it the central idea of his own theory of action.

As the third source of the theory of action, Sigmund Freud is considered by Parsons to have made the same contribution to a theory of the interpenetration of social system and personality, from the perspective of the personality, as Durkheim made from the perspective of the social system.[66] For Parsons, this convergence is of fundamental significance for the future development of the social sciences: 'This convergence, from two quite distinct and independent starting points, deserves to be ranked as one of the truly fundamental landmarks of the development of modern social science.'[67]

Through his analytic differentiation of the personality into an id, an ego and a superego, Freud develops a perspective on personality which allows him to view it as a zone of interpenetration of the structure of drives, external reality, and cultural norms. In connection with this Freudian schema, Parsons emphasizes that already in the earliest (oral) phase in the psychic development of the child, the reality principle of the ego, as well as the affective motivation of the id, is shaped by interaction with social objects, primarily the mother, and so is the result of symbolic processes. This means that the ego and the id are no less cultural products than the superego, an assertion which Parsons claims that Freud found himself increasingly drawn to.

Freud's analyses of the forms of identification between mother and child, and of the differentiation of the object cathexes in the oedipal stage and in the later stages of latency and adolescence, are of great importance for the understanding of the process of socialization.[68] Identification is the result of the fact that the child in the oral phase is dependent on others for the satisfaction of its needs and desires: the basic mechanism of identification is the cathexis of the libidinal object. This object cathexis progresses from a more particularized dependence on pleasure to a more generalized and symbolically formed dependence on love. Identification is the basis for the internalization of cultural norms, which are represented by the object of identification. In the oedipal phase, however, there is a loss of early objects of identification, along with a differentiation of object cathexes and a corresponding growth of as many identifications as there are dyadic relations for the child within the different roles within the family and, subsequently, outside the family, in peer groups and classrooms. Simultaneously, a differentiation occurs between the child's identification with individual role-partners in the group and its identification with the group as a whole. In this process of differentiation of object cathexes and the loss of infantile identifications, the internalized cultural norms are generalized and detached from particular identifications. The superego which is the result of this process is thus not a replication of the institutionalized norms of a concrete group but rather a generalization from various systems of norms which enables the individual to take part in social life outside his original reference group and to attain a steadily increasing autonomy. What Parsons primarily takes from Freud is this conception of the simultaneous, mutually reinforcing expansions of the scope of the social system and the personal autonomy of the individual as part of one complex process, a process dependent upon a specific form of interpenetration.

Further prospects

So far, we have seen that Parsons lays the cornerstone of a theory of interpenetration in *The Structure of Social Action* and that we cannot adequately grasp this theory if we do not interpret it in the light of Kant's critiques. This Kantian perspective is also of the greatest importance for the understanding of Parsons's constructive integration of Durkheim, Weber and Freud into his theory of action. Through the integration of these classic authors, Parsons is able to exceed by far the theoretical range of the interpretations of them which are usually offered.[69] Moreover, without an understanding of this Kantian core, it is impossible to follow the further development of the theory of action. In fact, all of Parsons's further theoretical development is a series of refinements of this theoretical instrument for the analysis of relations to interpenetration. Before anything else, one needed an instrument with which one could analytically detach subsystems which possessed their own rule-governed order from the concrete manifold of reality. Once this was accomplished, one would be able to analyse these subsystems as pure 'ideal types' while also studying the nature and extent of their interpenetration. The fundamental theorem here is not the old doctrine of differentiation, according to which systems can increase their capacities through a process of functional differentiation, but the theorem of inter-penetration, according to which only a process which allows both the greatest unfolding of the internal laws of a subsystem and the greatest amount of interpenetration with other subsystems can produce a new level of development for the subsystems and the system as a whole. This new level of development is as much the result of the tension between the subsystems as it is the result of their unity. The interpenetration of subsystems unifies opposites *and raises the threshold level of tension* which the systems can accommodate while still retaining their identity and unity.[70]

Ethics and business, for example, are here not isolated spheres with rules and laws wholly unique to each. Yet they are relatively independent of one another. They are shaped by different social groups, by intellectuals or by business people, and pronounced tensions can thus be generated between them. Their mutual interpenetration, in which, for example, members of the same congregation become business partners, opens the possibility of the ethical regulation of business and forces ethics to be relevant to business life.

We can call a relationship formed thus between business and ethics a dialectical one, as long as we understand that we accept the biases of neither the idealistic nor the materialistic dialectics (in fact, these biases prevent the idealistic and materialistic 'dialectics' from being *true* dialectics at all).[71] In the zone of interpenetration between business and ethics there appears a new phenomenon: business ethics, which is neither pure business nor pure ethics, but something in between. It brings previously separate spheres together without incorporating one into the other, and it raises the level of each subsystem's tolerance for what had previously been incompatible with it, although this incompatibility can in principle never be totally eliminated. In such a system the possibilities of both economic action and ethical action are expanded. Interpenetration increases the scope and power of both spheres.

Ethics is not pure ethics with absolutely no practical or commercial relevance, but it is also more than pure business ethics with no link back to the main body of ethical thought. Similarly, business has transcended mere business acumen without any ethical quality, but it is also more than business ethics without business acumen. Each sphere, ethics and business, has expanded its area of influence to overlap with the other, and each is enhanced by the interpenetration. It is important that ethics has not increased its sphere of influence at the expense of commercial life, nor vice versa.[72]

Parsons's theoretical development after *The Structure of Social Action* moves clearly in the direction of refining his theoretical instrument for the analytical differentiation of subsystems and the analysis of the relations of interpenetration among them. The major landmarks in this development are: (1) the differentiation of cultural system, social system and personality, and the analysis of institutionalization and internalization in *The Social System* (1951)[73] and *Toward a General Theory of Action* (1951);[74] (2) the differentiation of levels of systems and the macroscopic-microscopic application of the four-function paradigm in *Working Papers in the Theory of Action* (1953);[75] (3) the introduction of the hierarchy of cybernetic control and of the media of interchange (*a*) on the level of the social system (money, political power, influence, value commitments) in *Economy and Society* (1956)[76] and after; (*b*) on the level of the system of action (intelligence, performance capacity, affect, definition of the situation), which dates from *The American University* (1973);[77] and (*c*) on the level of the human condition as a whole in 'A paradigm of the human condition' (1978).[78]

All these works are major steps in the development of the Kantian theory of interpenetration first formulated in *The Structure of Social Action* and can only be adequately understood in this perspective. Between *The Structure of Social Action* and *Action Theory and the Human Condition*, Talcott Parsons created a body of theoretical potential which, in its examination, exhaustion, and development, will keep not only sociologists, but researchers in all spheres of the sciences of human action, occupied for a long time to come.

2 The continuity of the development

Introductory remarks

In *The Structure of Social Action* (1937), Talcott Parsons articulated a theory of action the fundamental strategy of which corresponds to that of Kant's critical philosophy and the development of which up to *Action Theory and the Human Condition* (1978) must be understood as a systematic elaboration of this basic Kantian perspective. The hallmark of this perspective is the assumption that every action is to be understood as the product of a certain relation between analytically differentiable spheres or subsystems. These subsystems of human action are of two basic kinds: those with a *regulative* function and those with a *dynamizing* function. The paradigm of this distinction is found in the distinctions between the categories of the understanding and sense perception, between the categorical imperative and practical judgements, and between aesthetic categories and aesthetic sensation which we find in the critical philosophy of Kant.[1] It is only through the interpenetration of these spheres that cognitive, moral, or aesthetic experience can constitute itself. However, interpenetration is only one of many possible relations which may obtain between analytically differentiable subsystems of action. Between these subsystems there exist fundamental tensions. Max Weber's typology of the relations between religious ethics and the world provides us with a ready set of categories for thinking about the various ways in which these can be eased: the accommodation of the potentially regulative subsystem to the dynamic subsystem, their mutual isolation, their interpenetration, the one-sided constriction of the potentially dynamizing subsystem by the regulative subsystem.[2] Interpenetration, however, is that form of relation through which opposed spheres or subsystems can both expand without thereby creating mutual interference. Interpenetration is the mechanism by which the potential of every system is converted into actuality; it is the mechanism of self-realization and evolution.

Closely connected with this theoretical core of Parsons's action theory is his *voluntaristic* solution to the problem of order, particularly as this problem manifests itself in social order. As soon as we recognize that human action is intentional action, we can no longer understand it as completely causally determined by *dynamic* factors. On this plane of intentional action, order is possible only if the actors share common values, which in principle they acknowledge *of their own free will*. This recognition of common values is itself possible only if the *individuals* are not acting within a framework of purely instrumental rationality (or 'means-end rationality'), but are able to take an increasingly universal standpoint of *collective solidarity* which transcends the solidarity of particular groups. Shared values must be anchored in this collective solidarity. Furthermore, the recognition of more specialized norms pertaining to human action is dependent on their being rationally *justifiable* through their subsumption under the common values. Finally, this normative framework is necessary in order to give form to the dynamic spheres. On the other hand, when we grant to these dynamic spheres an autonomous efficacy or power, we can no longer understand the order of action as depending solely on a one-sided constriction of the dynamic spheres through the imposition of a pre-existent normative framework. We must understand it as dependent on the interpenetration of the normative framework and the dynamic spheres, which relate to one another as form and substance. A one-sided restraining relationship would not allow us to account for the autonomy of individual action. Such a relationship would correspond to Durkheim's conception of mechanical solidarity, within which the concept of the individual has no place. The combination of the autonomy of the actions of individuals with social order is possible only as the interpenetration of a normative frame of reference and the dynamic spheres of action, which include the wants and needs of individuals.[3] 'Interpenetration' is in this sense a generalization from the normative idea of the coexistence of the actions of autonomous individuals and social order which is, in the framework of action theory, the central idea of modernity. The values on which the theory of action as constitutive of a field of fundamental inquiry is based are therefore rooted in the normative idea of modernity.

The core of the theory of action is a set of premises which have the character of *postulates* and not simply (as is so often asserted) a taxonomy.[4] In comparison to the positivistic and idealistic theories of action, the voluntaristic theory achieves progress in knowledge according to Karl Popper's model.[5] What is true in positivistic and idealistic theories is preserved in voluntaristic action theory, while their errors are eliminated and new areas for explanatory applications of the theory are opened up.

If we look at Parsons's integration of Durkheim, Weber and Freud into the theory of action from this perspective, we see how much material of potentially constructive value for systematic sociology Parsons has made accessible in the work of these classic authors.[6] And it is only against this background that we can understand the latent structure of Parsons's development of his own theory. This development should be understood as a progressive amplification of the Kantian core which is first set out in *The Structure of Social Action*. This is true of the analysis of institutionalization and internalization as interpenetrations of cultural system, social system and personality, and of the introduction of the pattern variables in *The Social System, Toward a General Theory of Action* (both 1951), and *Family, Socialization, and Interaction Process* (1955); it is true of the differentiation of the subsystems of action and the analyses using multiple 'system references' with the help of the microscopic-macroscopic applications of the four-function paradigm in *Working Paper in the Theory of Action* (1953); it is true of the introduction of the cybernetic hierarchy of controls; and it is true, finally, of the theory of the generalized media of interchange, which Parsons first developed for the social system in *Economy and Society* (1956) and then extended to the system of action generally in *The American University* (1973) and to the system of the human condition in *Action Theory and the Human Condition* (1978). This unitary development represents a systematic expansion of the scope of the theory, from the social system to the general system of action to the system of the human condition. Characteristic of this development is its continuity in relation to the core which is present in *The Structure of Social Action*, that is, the Kantian theory of interpenetration. It is this continuity which will be demonstrated here in detail.[7]

The thesis of the 'Kantian core' and the 'continuity of the development' relates to the latent structure (the deep structure) of the theory of action and is independent of both Parsons's own conscious attempts to describe the latent structure and the inconsistencies and discrepancies of the theory's surface structure. If we accept for the moment Karl Popper's distinction among a 'first world' of material objects, a 'second world' of subjective consciousness, and a 'third world' of objective symbol structures, we can say that the theory put forth here concerns the third world of objective symbol structures rather than the second world of subjective awareness.[8] My purpose here has been to reconstruct the core of the theory in such a way as to permit the greatest possible integration of the various stages of Parsons's theory into a *coherent* system, so that Parsons might seem to manifest progress instead of simply change. Even this task has been in the service of a broader goal, which is to make the strongest case possible for Parsons's theory in the face of its critics and to show as clearly as possible the great variety of the theory's possible applications.

2.1 The interpenetration of cultural system, social system and personality: *The Social System, Toward a General Theory of Action* – I

In *The Structure of Social Action*, Parsons differentiated the system of action into only two spheres: the sphere of instrumental ('means-end rational') action, in which there exist only hypothetical imperatives, and the sphere of categorical-normative obligation. In *The Social System*, this two-term system of action was replaced by a three-term schema which begins with the differentiation of the cultural system, the social system and the personality system. The constitutive elements of these systems are as follows: those of the cultural system are *symbols*; those of the social system are social interactions on one level and, on the next higher level, *social roles*; finally, those of the personality system are *need dispositions*.

In Parsons and Shils's 'Values, motives, and systems of action' this differentiation of subsystems is incorporated in a new frame of reference for action theory which extends the frame of reference of *ends*, *situation (given conditions, means)* and *norms* formulated in 1937.[9] The new schema assumes an actor orients himself to a *situation* in which he acts. The actor can be an *individual* or a *collective*, that is a corporate actor, acting intentionally in each case. The essential elements of the action frame of reference are the situation, in the sense of external given conditions, and the actor's orientation to that situation. The situation comprises *physical*, *social*, *cultural* and also *organic objects*, which fit into this classification provided they represent some aspect of the external given conditions to which the actor is oriented. Any of the actor's own physical, social, cultural or organic characteristics can belong to the situation if they represent a given or an environmental element to which his orientation is directed. These were the conditioning factors for action in the 1937 model. The later model provides an analytical extension in the sense that normative and cultural objects can also function as conditioning factors by virtue of their location in the action frame of reference. The actor's *orientation* to the situation encompasses ends, means and norms from the 1937 model. This orientation is broken down according to the differentiation of the personal, cultural and social action systems, and is hence described respectively as motivational, symbolic-cultural or social. In the light of later development of the theory of action, the adaptive orientation must also be added here. However, the immediate concern as these orientations were further differentiated was with the motivational and symbolic-cultural, value-related orientations. These in turn can be divided into three models and their respective parallel components, namely a cognitive, a cathectic (affective) and an evaluative-motivational orientation, matched by value-orientations (symbolic orientations) classified respectively as cognitive, appreciative and moral. Again, later developments would require us to add the category of a constitutive, meaning-seeking (religious) motivation. Also, the social and adaptive orientations for action would need to be broken down in a similar way.

If we compare the 1951 action frame of reference outlined above with that of 1937, the orientation of action on the general level to ends would be attributed to the personality system, while orientation to norms would appear within both the cultural and the social systems. The latter demonstrates the clearer differentiation emerging between the obligating and limiting function of *social* norms and the generalizing function of *cultural* norms. At this stage the behavioural system, under which the use of means must be categorized, was still missing from the model. On the more specific level of modes of orientation, means are classed under the cognitive, ends under the cathectic and appreciative, and norms under the evaluative and moral orientations of action. The missing element on this level is the generalizing function of a symbolic frame of reference, which is provided by the constitutive, meaning-seeking orientation.

As we can see, the 1937 frame of reference was not superseded but enhanced by the 1951 model, though it should be noted that a number of the classifications did not appear until later. The main structure of the theory as it stood in 1951 consisted in the analytical distinction between the personal, social and cultural systems. At this stage the idea of interpenetration between these three subsystems emphatically takes a central role in the analysis. Each concrete unit of action – the action of a collective or individual in a situation – is interpreted as the result of a certain type of interrelationship and a certain degree of interpenetration between the three subsystems, each of which when looked at individually functions according to its own laws. The stage has thus been reached where, as well as the concept of interdependence, Parsons also begins systematically and regularly to use the term interpenetration when he wishes to describe a particular type of relationship between these subsystems:

'Thus conceived, a social system is only one of three aspects of the structuring of a completely concrete system of social action. The other two are the personality systems of the individual actors and the cultural system which is built into their action. Each of the three must be considered to be an independent focus of the organization of the elements of the action system in the sense that no one of them is theoretically reducible to terms of one or a combination of the other two. Each is indispensable to the other two in the sense that without personalities and culture there would be no social system and so on around the roster of logical possibilities. But this interdependence and interpenetration is a very different matter from reducibility, which would mean that the important properties and processes of one class of system could be theoretically *derived* from our theoretical knowledge of one or both of the other two.'[10]

And in Parsons and Shils's contemporaneous 'Values, motives, and systems of action', their contribution to *Toward a General Theory of Action*, interpenetration is explained as a specific kind of relationship between analytically differentiated subsystems:

'A third basis of their intimate relation to each other is the fact that they *interpenetrate* in the sense that no personality system can exist without *participation* in a social system, by which we mean the integration of *part* of the actor's system of action as *part* of the social system. Conversely, there is no social system which is not from one point of view a mode of the integration of parts of the systems of action which constitute the personalities of the members. When we use the term *homology* to refer to certain formal identities between personalities and social systems which are to be understood in terms of the above considerations, it should be clear that we in no way intend to convey the impression that a personality is a microcosm of a social system, or that a social system is a kind of macrocosmic personality.'[11]

The interpenetrating subsystems possess different qualities, but they are 'homologues' of one another. This means that elements of one system can become elements of the other. In the zone of interpenetration thus created, a new quality appears, which forms a bridge between the previously separate subsystems of action. Each individual action is now seen as a product of the interpenetration of these subsystems. The reciprocal penetration of instrumental action and normatively obligated action requires the *institutionalization* of normative culture in the social system and the *internalization* of normative culture in the personality system.[12]

A normative culture as a general system of values – for example, the fusion of individualism, universalism, rationalism and activism which characterizes modern society – can be understood as a symbolic code, which undergoes continuous modification through the course of its history by means of its interpenetration with the social and personality systems. Its function is to provide for the possibility of variation while preserving the specific cluster of values which characterizes the action system (pattern consistency). This cluster or pattern of values must therefore be sufficiently generalized to permit a given type of action system to adjust to new conditions without having to alter its fundamental structure. The scope for variation which this code grants to action is therefore too broad to guarantee the orderedness of social interaction in any given situation. As a result, social order cannot be conceived of as simply the consequence of the existence of a normative culture. The culture must be institutionalized in a social system, and this means that it must be specified as a set of binding obligations.

In a social system, normative culture is fleshed out, given a concrete content of meanings. Correspondingly, other possible contents are excluded. The hallmark of a social system is the obligation imposed on the members of the society to accept a certain variant of the basic cultural pattern. This variant, and the obligation to accept it, must attain to a certain degree of self-evidentness, even though there may be other possible variants of the cultural pattern. This self-evidentness can come about only through an isolation of the members of the social system from the outside and an intensification of their solidarity with one another, so that deviations from the cultural pattern become violations of the obligations of group solidarity. The interpenetration between social systems and an overarching cultural system makes possible an increase of social solidarity within each individual social system and an increase in the solidarity between the systems. These two increases do not exclude one another in this case, but instead depend on one another. Whenever the specific normative ideals of a social system are projected into and embedded in the cultural system, they must be sufficiently generalized so that they do not come into conflict with the normative demands of other social systems. Conversely, through this interpenetration cultural values are sufficiently specified in the form of practical rules so as to make possible the identification of the members of diverse social groups with the same cultural pattern. In this way, the cultural pattern is interpreted so that it meets not only the rarefied 'contemplative' needs of an intellectual elite but also the practical, more mundane needs of various other social groups for ethical regulation. The result is necessarily a greater overlap, on the level of the social organization of this interpenetration, of the subsystem of practical problem-solving with the subsystem in which the interpretation of the cluster of cultural values is paramount, such as the systems of higher education and scholarship, religious congregations, and other cultural institutions.

Social order, however, requires not only the capacity of the cultural pattern to maintain its basic nature through variation and the institutionalization of a concretization of the cultural pattern through obligations imposed on the actors by their mutual solidarity. Order must also be compatible with the capacity of the actors for autonomous action. Here, too, 'interpenetration' is Parsons's answer. Its specific form is the internalization of normative culture in the personality through the process of socialization. After reading Freud, Parsons approached this range of problems from the standpoint of Freudian psychoanalytic theory, but he simultaneously preserved the contributions of Durkheim and Weber to the theory of socialization:

'In my reading of Freud, I gradually realized the importance of what I and others came to call the phenomenon of "internalization" (Freud's own term was "introjection") – both of sociocultural norms and of the personalities of the others with whom an individual has been interacting, above all a "socializing agent" (the latter case some-times being called "identification").

This idea first emerged clearly in Freud's thought in the conception of the superego, though one may say it was present from an early stage, especially in the conception of transference (for example, the treatment of the analyst as if he were the analysand's father). Freud came to consider moral standards, particularly as implemented by the father, integral parts of the child's personality, through some phases of the learning process. Gradually the scope of this aspect of Freud's theory of "object relations" widened in the course of his later work to include not only the superego but also the ego and even the id. At about the same time, it became clear to me that a very similar conception, developed from a quite different point of view, was essential to Durkheim, especially in his conception of social control through moral authority. The idea was also at least implicit in Weber's treatment of the role of religious values in determining behavior, and appeared with great clarity in the work of a group of American social psychologists, notably G. H. Mead and W. I. Thomas. The conception of the internalization, in successive series, of sets of cultural norms and concrete social objects has become a major axis of the whole theory of socialization, figuring in new forms even in the most recent treatments of the problems of higher education.'[13]

This way of looking at the process of socialization made its first appearance in the analysis of the interpenetration of the cultural system, the social system and the personality system in *The Social System*. It was further expanded in *Family, Socialization, and Interaction Process* (along with the inclusion of the behavioural system [behavioural organism] as a fourth system of action), where it is explicitly connected with Freud.[14]

The internalization of normative culture is a process in which institutionalization occurs in reverse. As socialization runs its course, the individual is bound first of all to a given specification of the normative culture – and, of course, also to the members of a concrete family. A child is bound to his family by very strong ties of love and respect, and it is through these ties that he is bound – through increasingly specific reattachments of regard or disregard for desirable or undesirable ways of acting – to an acceptable variant of the normative culture. In the extreme case, in which a child's total capacity for love and regard was occupied by the parents and in which the family was isolated from the larger community, we might see a complete identification of the actor with his family role. The individual would in that case be incapable of concretizing the normative culture independently, in situations outside the family. The less the internalization of the normative culture transcends the limits of the family and kinship relations, the less will it generally be possible for the actor to generalize the normative culture sufficiently to permit him to respecify it in different social systems. The process of socialization therefore must lead its recipient beyond the family to continually more comprehensive specifications of the normative culture, and it must continually move him beyond each set of solidarity relations that he establishes. The interpenetration of the various solidarity relations and the specifications of the normative culture which are connected with them is the most important factor in the establishment of a common basis for the identification of different normative systems with one and the same fundamental pattern. The individual becomes emancipated from one-sided group pressure in this way.

One mechanism of the interpenetration of normative systems and solidarity relations is the integration of emotional and instrumental guidance in the family. Sometimes these functions are divided between the mother and the father. In such cases the division of labour must be accompanied by social solidarity between the parents. The child's capacity for identification with the normative orientation of the parents is created only through his emotional ties to them, while it is through their demand that the child behave in accordance with norms which are external to the family that the child is able to transfer this identification to the normative system beyond the family.[15] This same two-sidedness, of an emotional attachment of the individual to a group which then subjects that individual to normative demands which originate outside the group, must be exhibited in the actor's relation to all the groups which succeed the family as participants in the process of socialization: peer groups, school classes, professional groups, occupational groups, religious congregations, neighbourhood associations, etc.[16] In the course of this socialization the individual continually has new worlds opened up for him within the world of a normative culture, and his attachment to the normative culture is generalized and freed from the tyranny of concrete specifications.[17] The whole process of socialization, therefore, is a process in which the individual, *through* the internalization of the normative culture, attains to increasing autonomy of action, but it is also a process in which the bond between the individual and the normative culture is strengthened, because this bond comes to depend less and less on any particular relations of the individual.[18] The interpenetration of different socializing entities in this way makes possible a form of interpenetration of cultural system, social system and personality which permits an increase in the inherent qualities of each. The normative culture is made more consistent through the process of generalization, while its institutionalization in various social systems simultaneously becomes more specific; the bonds between the individual and these specifications become tighter, while the autonomy of the personality simultaneously is increased. Conversely, the less pronounced the interpenetration is, the less consistent the normative culture appears, the less is social interaction governed by connections between individuals and the normative culture beyond those which were formed in the context of very particular social groups, and the fewer possibilities there are for personal individuality:

'Personalities and social systems are, according to the implications of this view, not directly homologous; they are differently organized about different foci of integration and have different relations to the sources of motivational energy. But they are more than merely "analogous", they are literally "made of the same stuff"; as we have so often put it, they are not merely interdependent, they *interpenetrate*. Above all, it is important that the *focus of organization* of both types of system lies in certain apsects of the relevant culture patterns, namely the value-systems which have been institutionalized in the social system, internalized in the personality system. Moreover, these are not merely "the same kind" of cultural values, they are literally *the same* values, looked at and analyzed in terms of different system-references. Neither of these system-references is the "right" or the "real" system reference, both are equally real and stand on the same ontological level.[19]

In *The Social System*, then and in 'Values, motives, and systems of action', coauthored with Shils, Parsons achieved a definite extension and refinement of this theoretical instrument, with the help of which complex relations of interpenetration could be understood in all their significant detail. The notion of interpenetration itself, which in *The Structure of Social Action* Parsons had had to handle by means of the interrelationship between the instrumental and categorical-normative orientations of action, was made more precise and detailed to apply to the world. Therefore it is completely inaccurate to say, as has often been said, that at this stage of his career Parsons turned away from the theory of action toward the theory of systems and was from this point on misled into substituting the system for the individual. The object of inquiry in *The Structure of Social Action* is not isolated actors or actions but the systems formed by social action; here Parsons is already primarily concerned with the problem of how the existence of social order within such a system can be explained. The voluntaristic theory of action is from its first formulation a theory of the social system, while a general theory of action is not attained until the later works mentioned above:

'The conception of a theoretical system as my major focus of interest first crystallized in the series of studies leading up to *The Structure of Social Action*. At this stage, it was confined to the social system case; only in the course of the work in 1949–1950 which eventuated in *Toward a General Theory of Action* did the idea of a *general* theory embracing not only social systems, but also psychological and cultural systems fully crystallize.'[20]

While in *The Social System* Parsons placed the interpenetration of the cultural system, the social system and the personality system in the foreground, he at the same time laid the foundations for a new type of analysis, which could work with a multiplicity of system references simultaneously and which would open an entirely new way of thinking about the old problem of the relation of individual and society. *The Social System* represents a clear theoretical advance over *The Structure of Social Action* in that the theoretical apparatus of the former permits the integrated analysis of cultural, social and personality systems while transcending the limited perspective of a simple systems functionalism.[21]

Parsons went on to apply this technique of analysis to the problems of institutionalization and internalization which we have sketched here in a series of works which meet the high standard set by *The Social System*. Perhaps the most significant of these works is *Family, Socialization, and Interaction Process*, coauthored with Bales. Parsons wrote his contributions to this volume in the wake of his reading of Freud. He makes use of Freudian theory to analyse internalization as the result of the interpenetration of ego-ideal, superego, ego and id, and to mark out the phases of the socialization process. A further refinement resulted in the theory of the generalized media of interchange on the level of the general system of action. Institutionalization and internalization are regarded here as the products of the interpenetration of the cultural system, the social system, the personality system and the behavioural system. This interpenetration is produced by the generalized media of interchange – *definition of the situation, affect, performance capacity, intelligence* – each of which is anchored in a particular subsystem but also extends into each of the other subsystems. At this stage of the development of the theory, the decisive step is the inclusion of a multiplicity of levels and a multiplicity of interpenetrating systems on the level of the general theory of action. The main theoretical effort is directed toward the discovery of the conditions necessary for the development of a higher degree of freedom of action within the frame of reference of an increasingly generalized set of values. The attainment of higher levels of socialization signifies for Parsons, in this context, not commitment to the normative beliefs of any given group or social class, or even society as a whole, but a commitment to a universal framework of values which transcends particularities:

'This view casts serious doubt on the allegation that functional analysis of social systems implies an imperative of conformity. We must keep in mind that we are here speaking of the general action level, and that the term 'moral' refers to any culturally grounded justifications of selection among alternatives for action, whether they be for sustaining a given social system, or for its revolutionary overturn, or for any of the wide variety of withdrawing or otherwise deviant modes of association.'[22]

2.2 The pattern variables: *The Social System, Toward a General Theory of Action* – II

The introduction of the pattern variables represents the next stage in the development of the theory's ability to differentiate subsystems of action and analyse their interpenetration. The pattern variables comprise the following five pairs of opposites:[23]

Self-orientation	Collectivity-orientation
Diffuseness	Specificity
Affectivity	Affective neutrality
Particularism	Universalism
Ascription (quality)	Achievement (performance)

41

The first of these pairs lost its systematic application when the four-function paradigm was introduced. As a group, the above terms all represent patterns which guide action in differing situations. This is best understood in terms of the human individual, under conditions of freedom, having the choice between the above alternatives or, more precisely, in terms of human action varying between them in the symbolic normative sphere rather than in the material, conditional sphere. The extent to which action tends one way or the other depends on the relative weight of the pattern variables at the level of each of the action systems: on the social level we are concerned with *role patterns*, on the personality level with *disposition patterns*, and on the cultural level with *cultural patterns*. The greater the degree of autonomy in human action, the greater the degree of interpenetration that is required on the levels of the various action systems.

In each pair of variables the left-hand variable restricts the scope for ordered action. All these variables characterize relatively primitive stages of action, whilst those in the right-hand columns allow considerably more scope for ordered action. The latter group represents levels of action which are phylogenetically and ontogenetically highly developed. Nevertheless the more developed type of action would be impossible but for the fact that its more elaborate patterns are founded in the 'primitive patterns' of the first column. Again, their interpenetration is vital. We can examine the pattern variables in the light of concrete interactions taking place between two imaginary actors, 'ego' and 'alter', which cover all action system levels. They can then be interpreted as follows:

- *Self-orientation* is an orientation in which the frame of reference for action is determined by the satisfaction of individual wants. *Collectivity orientation* implies that the individual acts in the wider and ultimately universal frame of reference of collective solidarity, transcending his own egoism.

- *Diffuseness* in social orientation signifies the involvement of the concrete individual on both sides of the interaction between ego and alter, and the continuation of constant relationships such as trust no matter what the situation or the service being performed. *Specificity* in social orientation indicates a restriction of mutual expectations to certain aspects, and to the particular positions individuals occupy in the context of action. Hence role expectations can be regarded as specific, because they concern not the individual himself, but just one of his positions in a social network.

- *Affectivity* in social orientation implies that the mutual expectations and actions of ego and alter are guided by their positive or negative feelings for each other. *Neutrality*, on the other hand, requires that mutual expectations and actions should not be determined by these positive or negative feelings.

- *Particularism* in social orientation means that the frame of reference for an individual's action provided by solidarity and norms is narrower than the context of the action itself, and the interdependence with the action of others. The individual only feels obligated to those closest to him, and to the norms which apply to this relationship; he does not feel obligated to those who are more remote or to the norms which would apply in that instance. This is accompanied by a sharp distinction between in-group and out-group morality. *Universalism* on the other hand requires the individual to have a constant solidarity with all those to whom he is interdependently related, whether directly or indirectly. The norms applied to these relationships have a general validity, that is for all actors in all contexts.
- *Ascription (quality)* refers to a social orientation in which the mutual expectations and actions of ego and alter are determined by in-born indicators such as belonging to a particular class, race, caste or sex. *Achievement (performance)* implies a social orientation where the mutual expectations and actions are regulated by voluntarily acquired attributes and voluntarily realized achievements, examples of which might be educational diplomas, particular achievements at work, or the spending of money.

The pattern variables can be used to indicate with precision the specific relations between opposed modes of orientations of action which have been joined together by the interpenetration of different subsystems of action. One can examine the interpenetration of cultural system, social system and personality system as a specific combination of these orientations of action. They are not, however, mutually exclusive orientations. The terms of each pair can interpenetrate as well, thus increasing the scope of both terms together.

The constant generalizing of solidarity relations beyond the limits of the groups in which those relations are originally formed, a process which constitutes the socialization of an individual, is the generalization of that individual's *collectivity orientation*, but it also and simultaneously provides more scope for *self-oriented* action. The originally diffuse loyalty to the group is extended by its mediation through loyalties outside the group – for example, through the instrumental role of the father, or through peer groups or school classes. These provide a basis for the transformation of *diffuse* attachment into specific attachments embodied in *specific* roles. In similar fashion, the progressive extension of *affectively* forged relations between the object of socialization (the socializand) and agents of socialization through *neutral* relations makes it possible for the 'primordial trust' which is acquired in affective relations to be carried over to neutral relations. It is not necessary, then, that a new affective basis for each of these latter relations be fashioned, as would otherwise be the case. These successive interpenetrations of social systems produce both *particularized* connections to the norms of various groups and a similar connection to a *universal* norm, which exists independently of any relation to concrete groups. Finally, the gradual transition from the recognition of individuals solely on the basis of their *membership* in one group (the family) to a system of allocating approval and disapproval on the basis of the performance of desirable or undesirable *actions* provides the basis for an ability to control behaviour by a differential allocation of approval and disapproval without the danger that the individuals who are censured will react by withdrawing altogether from the network of social relations. In each of these cases, we see in the first term of each pair a mechanism which limits the possibilities of action. The gradual transition to the second term expands the scope of action. In this way, dispositions toward action which originally can be realized only in limited spheres become available to many systems.

The pattern variables are designed as a means of characterizing specific dimensions of interpenetration in subsystems of action and social subsystems. Parsons's need for something like the pattern variables arose out of his desire to investigate the role of interpenetration in specific problem areas. The pattern variables primarily appear in his work on the socialization process, particularly in the writings on socialization in the family, in adolescent peer groups and in schools. A related group of writings comprises the studies of the modern professions, particularly those of the relation between doctor and patient. The first of these studies was the essay 'The professions and social structure' (1939); numerous works on the professional complex followed.[24] The core of these works is the idea that the professional–client relationship is a zone of interpenetration of the intellectual disciplines, the social systems which determine the criteria governing the fulfilment of the various roles of the client, the personality and behavioural systems of expert and client. Here again, the crucial problems are to locate a form of interpenetration which makes possible an increase in the demands of all these subsystems and to locate a specific combination of action orientations which limit the sphere of action and action orientations which expand it. The relationship between professional and client requires clear external delimitation combined with an inner solidarity which can provide the foundation for mutual trust. The need for trusting cooperation in the relationship makes it natural that the client emphasize the diffuse, affective, particularistic and qualitative aspects of the relationship. On the other hand, the professional's ties to the canons of his discipline and to the social systems which are dependent on the client's role performance force him constantly to lead the client toward the specific, neutral, universalistic and performance orientations, all of which are effective only on the basis of the 'limited' orientations.

2.3 The four-function paradigm: *Working Papers in the Theory of Action*

The next refinement of Parsons's theory was the introduction of the four-function paradigm (or A–G–I–L schema) in *Working Papers in the Theory of Action*, which Parsons wrote in collaboration with Robert Bales and Edward Shils. The four-function paradigm was the result of combining Bales's categorization of the problems which systems face, which he developed during his work on task accomplishment in small groups, with Parsons's pattern variables. The first use of the paradigm was as a model for the types of deviance from norms, and thus also as a model for the related types of social control, but even in the *Working Papers* it was already being generalized beyond the boundaries of this specific problem and being given multiple applications. The paradigm defines the problems which all systems face and relates each problem to a certain combination of action orientations which provides a solution to the problem. The action orientations themselves are divided into object categorizations and attitudes. Object categorizations express the actor's cognitive perception of the objects which constitute his environment, in relation to each other and in relation to his goals. He can perceive them as universal or particular, performative or qualitative. Attitudes signify a cathectic relation to objects, which can be specific or diffuse, neutral or affective. The *Working Papers* go on to make the following specific connections between systems problems and the orientations of action:[25]

A. *Adaptation* as a systems problem requires the mobilizing of resources as a basis for the realization of goals. The solution of the problem of adaptation requires a combination of universalistic and performative object categorizations, along with specific and neutral attitudes.

G. *Goal attainment* (and goal selection) requires a mechanism which allows ends or goals to be arranged hierarchically in all specific situations in which choices of goals must be made. The proper combination of action orientations here is that of performative and particularistic object categorizations and specific and affective attitudes toward the objects.

I. *Integration* requires the cohesion of the units in the various systems (social action in the social system, the connection between stimulus and response in the behavioural system, need dispositions in the personality system, symbols in the cultural system) with one another, their solidarity. The appropriate action orientations here are particularistic and qualitative object categorizations, together with diffuse and affective attitudes.

L. *Latent pattern maintenance* requires the ability to preserve the basic structure of the system, together with the ability to adjust to changing conditions within the framework that the basic structure provides. The solution to these problems presupposes a combination of qualitative and universalistic object categorizations, together with neutral and diffuse attitudes.

These connections between systems problems and action orientations were then further differentiated into subdimensions by Parsons; this process reached its climax in his essay 'Pattern variables revisited: A response to Robert Dublin'.

As a basis of classification in differentiating the four functions, Parsons introduced at this stage two axes for the orientation of action: the axis between external and internal orientation, and the axis between instrumental and consummatory orientation. Externally oriented action is determined by outside conditions, as opposed to the internal, normative orientation. The consummatory orientation means that a goal would be sought for its own sake, while the instrumental orientation implies that the action is engaged in as the means toward a further set of ends. If these axes are cross-tabulated with reference to the A–G–I–L schema the following functions emerge:

A. Adaptation brings together the external and the instrumental orientations of action.
G. Goal-attainment and goal-selection combine the external and consummatory orientations.
I. Integration encompasses internal and consummatory orientations.
L. In the field of latent pattern maintenance, the internal and instrumental action orientations coincide.

These two axes for the orientation of action can be viewed as a parallel to the basic categories in the action frame of reference set out in *The Structure of Social Action*. The external-internal axis is equivalent to the opposition of given conditions to norms, and the instrumental-consummatory axis to the distinction between means and ends.[26]

Compared to the frame of reference set out in 'Values, motives, and systems of action', the new schema achieved a further generalization and also plugged some of the remaining analytical gaps. The functions defined above can be attributed to the subsystems and action orientations in the 1951 schema as follows: goal attainment and selection belong with the personality system and with the motivational and cathectic, appreciative orientations; adaptation belongs with the behavioural system, not introduced until later, and with the adaptive orientation (which requires further expansion) and the cognitive orientation (which was already in existence); integration is linked with the social system, the social orientation (again, expansion needed) and the evaluative, moral orientation (in contrast to the moral orientation's earlier, cultural definition); finally latent pattern maintenance is linked with the cultural system, the evaluative, symbolic orientation and the meaningful, constitutive orientation (which must be added as a new item). Each function determines the orientation of the action system in relation to the environment which surrounds it.

In attributing the pattern variables to the four basic functions of action systems and to the appropriate aspects and subsystems of action, it is possible to bring more precision to the scheme just introduced. Each of the four basic functions has expressions of particular *aspects* of action attributed to it as follows: the *primary* attribution is of one particular manifestation of the appropriate aspect of action in relation to one of the pairs of opposites outlined earlier; the *secondary* attribution is of particular manifestations of the same aspect of action in relation to the other three pairs of opposites. Thus, for the *fulfilment of a function* to be *maximized*, an extreme manifestation of the relevant aspect of action in relation to one side of the pair of opposites in the primary attribution is needed, supported on a secondary level by its manifestation in relation to the other three pairs of opposites (see Figures 1 and 2).[27]

G. *Goal orientation*, as the aspect of action associated with the realization of goals, has a *primary* axis of variation from the greatest diffuseness to the greatest *specificity*. A maximal realization of goals requires a high specificity in goal orientation. The greater the tendency for an individual's or a collective's goals to be variable, indeterminate and less clearly defined, the more diffuse is the goal orientation. Specificity is at its height when only one goal is being sought which is fully determined and clearly defined.

On the *secondary* level, the actors must have an *affective* bond with their goals. Pursuit of these goals should not be a matter of indifference or superficiality, but should awake a positive feeling in them. The frame of reference for the goals should not be too wide, as this would make it impossible to determine them clearly. What is needed is a *particularistic* frame of reference. A scientist who is simply searching for 'the truth' (that is, with a universal goal orientation) is far less likely to achieve concrete results than if he were to seek out the truth regarding clearly defined subject matter using precisely specified procedures. The final requirement for goal realization is a performative orientation toward achievement. That is, the means deployed to realize the goal(s) may not be subject to prior determination by qualitative ascription. This is necessary, for instance, when it comes to allotting tasks to individuals and determining the methods and technology to be used. In this sense a

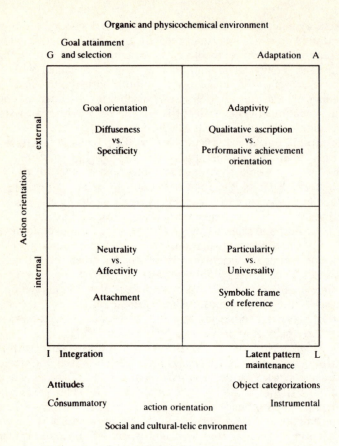

Figure 1 Pattern variables and functions of action subsystems – I

performative achievement orientation means that the sole criterion for establishing the division of tasks and techniques applied should be their suitability for the purposes of goal realization.

A. *Mobilization of means,* as the aspect of action fulfilling the function of adaptation, can vary on the primary level from the greatest qualitative ascription to the greatest *performative achievement orientation.* It is the latter which is essential to maximal adaptation. Qualitative ascription in the field of mobilizing means implies a restriction of the choice of means by habit and tradition. Particular means are employed, or particular individuals carry out particular functions, because that is the way it has always been. This naturally limits the ability to adapt to new situations. On the other hand, the performative achievement orientation implies when related

48

Organic and physicochemical environment

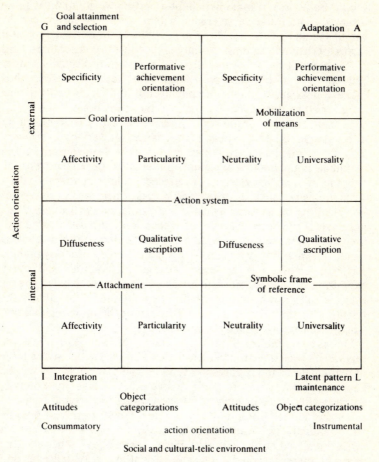

Figure 2 Pattern variables and functions of action subsystems – II

to the choice of means that only those means will be chosen which are most successful in a given situation.

On the *secondary* level, the means being weighed against one another should be unmistakably *specified* to enable any judgement at all to be made on their suitability for the task. The more the different means are clearly delimited one from another, the more specific they are. An indeterminate, diffuse application of means allows no advancement in learning. The actors should not remain affectively tied to 'popular' means: they must maintain a *neutral* relationship to them. Emotionally conditioned limitations on the variation of means, including the division of functions between individuals, should not exist if a maximal adaptation to new situations is to be achieved. The frame of reference within which the means can be varied should be as far-reaching as possible. Moreover, instrumental forms of behaviour must as far as possible be generalized and independent of the situation, allowing any form of behaviour, once learned, to be mobilized at will. A *universal* frame of reference thus makes it possible to adapt more intelligently and far-sightedly to new situations than does a particularistic frame of reference.

L. The *symbolic frame of reference*, as the aspect of action directed toward latent pattern-maintenance, can vary on its *primary* axis from maximal particularity to maximal universality. The maximal maintenance of latent patterns is dependent on the existence of a *universal* frame of reference. A latent pattern, or deep structure, is a system of values and norms which lies at the root of every-day action, and can produce many different types of act. Thus grammar is the deep structure of speech, on the basis of which all kinds of utterance can be produced. 'Particularity' in this context would mean action was guided by limited rules which would be rendered inapplicable by every change in situation and every expansion of interaction. 'Universality', on the other hand, means that the rules can be applied in different situations; this allows the retention of the rules as a latent structure to be more widespread, whether materially, socially or temporally.

On the *secondary* level, the frame of reference must be *qualitatively ascribed* to the action, that is it must be the stable basis of permanence amid changes in situation, and may not in any way be changed by the criteria of performative achievement. For example, truth and the rules of logic must serve as an unalterable frame of reference: science would not be possible if they themselves could be freely altered. The frame of reference must also show a certain *diffuseness*, and not be specified like a concrete goal; otherwise, the frame of reference would not be able to continue in existence beyond the achievement or alteration of a single goal. It must be possible to derive a number of different goals from it by interpretation. Because of its necessary breadth, the frame of reference cannot attract a great deal of affectivity. A close affective bond would be much more likely to lead to a particularization of the frame of reference. Emotionally, the individual is tied to that with which he is immediately familiar, to the action frame of reference shared with those closest to him. For a frame of reference to have validity when it stretches beyond those areas dear to his heart, there must be a greater *neutrality* toward its increased scope. The individual must be prepared to tolerate many varied interpretations as legitimate. There is more neutrality, the greater the range of interpretations which are viewed as legitimate.

I. The *mutual attachment* of elements in an action system, such as actors in the social system, is an aspect of action which is keyed to the integration of the action system. As such, its *primary* axis of variation is between maximal neutrality and maximal affectivity. Integration, to be maximized, is dependent on a high, positive and *affective* interrelationship of the elements of action, that is of the actors. Neutrality in this context would mean elements being joined together, as in the case of an act taking place between two actors, with no heed of the person or matter involved, with indifference. Affectivity means that the elements are joined according to the feeling a person, or the matter in hand, generates. In social action it is essential for solidarity to be based on this affectual bond, independent of the situation and of utility expectations. One person does something for another, or observes common rules, out of a love for the other person or for the rules, and not because he seeks personal gain, or is forced to act this way by outside circumstances.

On the *secondary* level, the affectual bond must be *diffuse* in character, and not remain confined to features of the actors which are too specific. Diffuseness in this sense means one person is tied to the entire, concrete personality of another, whatever he or she may do, rather than influenced by particular characteristics. In any other situation, the durability of the bond would always be placed in jeopardy. The status of each member of a collective must be *qualitatively ascribed*. One's acceptance as a member with concomitant rights and duties should not be dependent on particular achievements. A performative orientation to achievement only undermines solidarity. The frame of reference for those joined by an affectual bond must tend toward *particularity*, as they can then immediately and unambiguously identify with it and recognize themselves as the carriers of common values and norms. Thus, they represent a closed community.

The individual combinations of primary and secondary pattern variables should only ever be related to the maximal fulfilment of a function, and to the relevant aspect of action. The simultaneous fulfilment of the functions demand firstly, that the combinations be limited to their respective aspects of action, and secondly that the pattern variables be graduated in the zones of interpenetration between subsystems.

A more detailed break-down of the links between pattern variables and action subsystems was Parsons's purpose when he replied to Robert Dubin's critique in 'Pattern variables revisited'. In this case he joins the attitude to objects as the orientation set, with the function of latent pattern maintenance, and the categorization of objects (modality set) with the function of goal attainment. The orientation set is identifiable by the combinations of diffuseness and specificity, and affectivity and neutrality, while the modality set is associated with the combinations of particularity/universality and of qualitative ascription/performative achievement orientation. In the other two subsystems, the integrative and adaptive, a different approach is taken and all four combinations of conflicting variables are included in a diagonal relationship to each other. The resulting combinations are as follows (see Figure 3):

L.   *The orientation set*
L.   Needs for commitment combine diffuseness and neutrality.
G.   Consummatory needs combine specificity and affectivity.
I.   Needs for affiliation combine diffuseness and affectivity.
A.   Interests in instrumental utilization combine specificity and neutrality.

G.   *The modality set*
L.   Objects of 'generalized respect' combine qualitative ascription and universality.
G.   Objects of affective cathexis combine performative achievement orientation and particularity.
I.   Objects of identification combine qualitative ascription and particularity.
A.   Objects of utility combine performative achievement orientation and universality.

I.   *The integrative set*
L.   Pattern maintenance combines qualitative ascription and neutrality.
G.   Goal attainment combines performative achievement orientation and affectivity.
I.   Integration combines diffuseness and particularity.
A.   Adaptation combines specificity and universality.

A.   *The adaptive set*
L.   Existential interpretation combines universality and diffuseness.
G.   Expressive symbolization combines particularity and specificity.
I.   Moral-evaluative categorization combines qualitative ascription and affectivity.
A.   Cognitive symbolization combines performative achievement orientation and neutrality.

The development of the four-function paradigm was progressively freed from its connection with the pattern variables, and the paradigm was progressively generalized beyond its originally limited area of application, so that it could be continually respecified and applied to new ranges of objects. In this way, the paradigm assumed more and more the character of a general theoretical instrument for the analytical differentiation of reality. From the point of view of the development of the theory as a whole, the most significant events of this period are the use of the four-function paradigm in the analytic differentiation of subsystems of action, the repeated application of

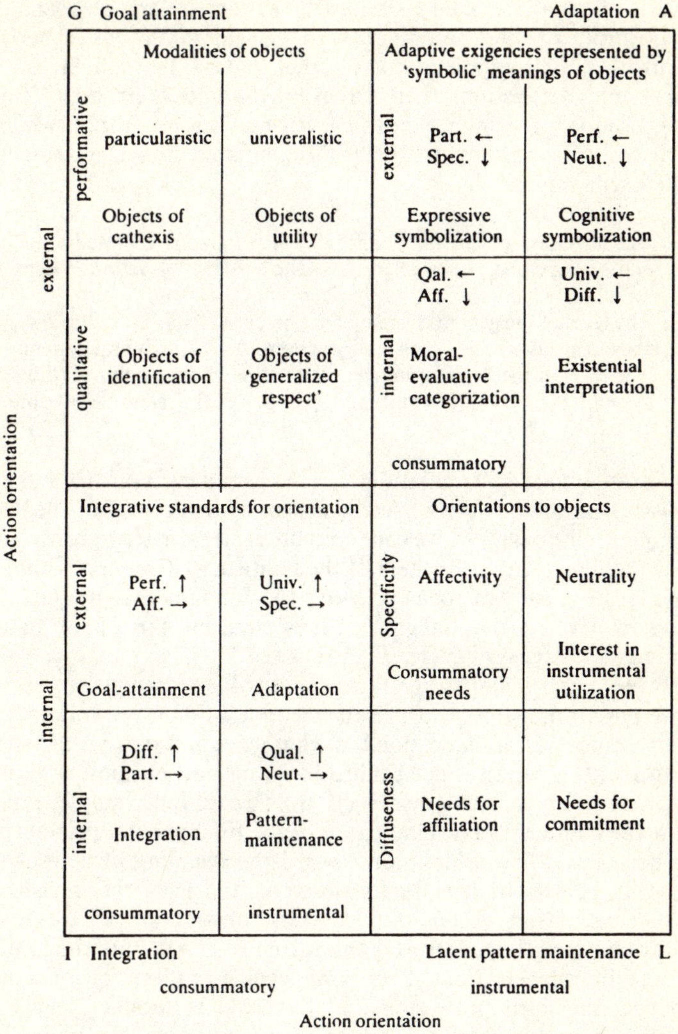

G   Goal attainment   Adaptation   A

Action orientation

	Modalities of objects		Adaptive exigencies represented by 'symbolic' meanings of objects	
performative (external)	particularistic	univeralistic	(external) Part. ← Spec. ↓	Perf. ← Neut. ↓
	Objects of cathexis	Objects of utility	Expressive symbolization	Cognitive symbolization
qualitative			Qal. ← Aff. ↓	Univ. ← Diff. ↓
	Objects of identification	Objects of 'generalized respect'	(internal) Moral-evaluative categorization	Existential interpretation
			consummatory	
	Integrative standards for orientation		Orientations to objects	
external	Perf. ↑ Aff. →	Univ. ↑ Spec. →	(Specificity) Affectivity	Neutrality
	Goal-attainment	Adaptation	Consummatory needs	Interest in instrumental utilization
internal	Diff. ↑ Part. →	Qual. ↑ Neut. →	(Diffuseness) Needs for affiliation	Needs for commitment
	Integration	Pattern-maintenance		
	consummatory	instrumental		

I   Integration   Latent pattern maintenance   L

consummatory   instrumental

Action orientation

Figure 3 Pattern variables and functions of action subsystems – III (based on T. Parsons, 'Pattern variables revisited: A response to Robert Dubin', in *Sociological Theory and Modern Society*, New York: Free Press, 1967, Figure 1, p. 198)

53

the paradigm to the problem of the internal differentiation of various individual subsystems and to the problem of the differentiation of levels of analysis having different system references, and the connection of the paradigm with the hierarchy of cybernetic controls.[28] The application of the A–G–I–L schema to the subsystems of action, their environment and their microscopic-macroscopic ordering yield basic levels of analysis, each of which in turn could be further internally differentiated into a microscopic-macroscopic hierarchy:[29]

1. The level of the 'human condition', which Parsons explored at the very end of his career, consists of: L – telic system, I – action system, G – human organic system, A – physicochemical system.
2. The level of the general system of action consists of: L – cultural system, I – social system, G – personality system, A – behavioural system.
3. The level of the social system consists of: L – social-cultural (fiduciary) system, I – societal community, G – political system, A – economic system.

These analytical differentiations can be carried even further and used to focus on and isolate a specific aspect of reality out of the entire complex. For example, we can focus on the legal system, considering it as the integrative subsystem of the political system, and within the legal system we can focus on, say, the fundamental principles of modern law as the integrative subsystem of the latent pattern maintenance subsystem (see Figures 4 and 5).[30]

What is particularly significant about this technique of analytic differentiation is that, through the location of an aspect of reality in the schema, we can understand in what ways and to what extent the nature of this aspect is determined by its interpenetration with other subsystems on various other levels. So we can, for example, explore how the character and significance of the fundamental principles of modern law – the orientation toward the meaning of actions (L), equality before the law (I), freedom (A) and legal rationalism (G) (which is itself differentiable, into abstraction[L], excluded contradiction [I], analysis [G] and formalism [A]) – are the product of the interpenetration of cultural legal discourse, rational legal science, the legal profession and the legal community. This last relation already provides a link to the next higher level of analysis. Ultimately, however, the decisive significance will belong to the subsystem we want to investigate and *its* function. On the next higher level of analysis, we can understand legal culture as a product of the interpenetration of the legal community, judicial decisions, the legal process and the constitution, which here provides the connection to yet the next level of analysis. One level higher, the law finds itself in

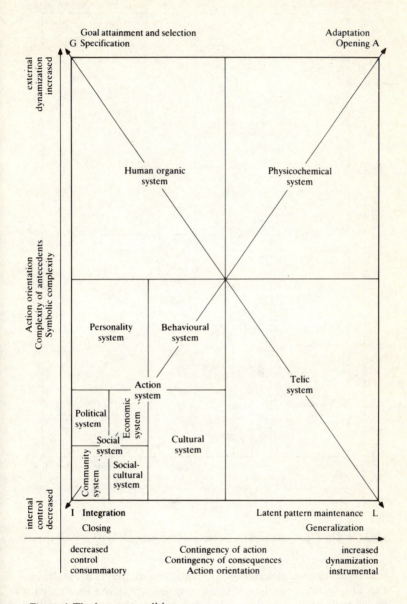

Figure 4 The human condition

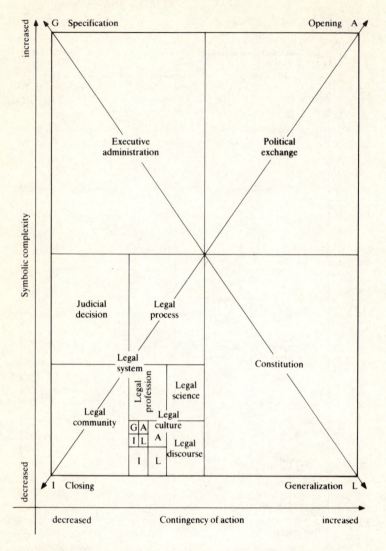

Figure 5 The legal system in the context of the political system

the zone of interpenetration of constitution, political exchange, executive power and the societal community, which is the mediator to the next level of analysis. One level higher again, we would find the political system in the zone of interpenetration of fiduciary system, societal community, economy and personality system, which is the link to the level of the general theory of action.

What we have been presenting here is an *analytical* reconstruction of the legal system. This is fundamentally different from talking about the structure of a *concrete* legal system. In a concrete legal system, certain aspects of the analytical model may be missing completely, and others may be disproportionately dominant. A concrete legal system may produce judicial decisions totally lacking any basis in the cultural and social spheres and inaccessible to the opening procedures of the legal process. Such decisions would be determined solely by the political component, by the application of political power. Assertions of this sort are *empirical* applications of the theoretical model, which itself encompasses all of the analytical dimensions.[31]

This distinction between *analytical* reconstruction and *concrete* reality, between *theoretical* model and *empirical* application, applies equally to all the models which will be presented in the course of this book.

Fundamentally, the model of action subsystems can be applied in two different ways, which in turn can be combined with one another. It can be used to explain the action of an individual or a corporate actor. Concrete action is understood in this case as the resultant effect when the various forces (that is, subsystems) have their bearing on the action in the action space. The more the action subsystems are empirically differentiated from each other, the more the effect of these forces on the concrete action is in turn dependent on the relationship of the subsystems both to each other and to their environment. In the latter case certain characteristics of an action subsystem can be explained on the strength of its own structure and of its particular interdependence with other subsystems in its environment. These two explanatory routes do not use totally different theoretical models, but rather different interpretations and applications of one and the same model. The first approach involves looking at an individual or group's action in the action space and the second an observation of the relationship between the subsystems in that action space, which indirectly determine the ultimate concrete action.

2.4 The cybernetic hierarchy of conditions and controls: 'An approach to psychological theory in terms of the theory of action'

The introduction of the cybernetic hierarchy of conditions and controls allows us to determine more precisely the kind of interpenetration which occurs between individual subsystems.[32] From the A-system through the G-system and the I-system up to the L-system, the level of information increases, that is, the ability of the system to guide action by means of symbolic articulations (for example, rational argument) increases. The subsystems with a higher level of information have the ability to guide or control action in the subsystems which are less rich in information. They do so by defining the limits of action in the subordinate subsystems. For example, a system of generalized values defines the limits of solidarity formation, goal selection and resource mobilization. Conversely, from the L-system up through the I-system and the G-system to the A-system, the level of motivational energy available for action increases. In this hierarchy, the higher subsystem has a dynamizing effect on the lower ones, that is, it expands their sphere of action. This would endanger the degree of order in the lower subsystems, if this dynamization were not delimited through its penetration by a more highly ordered system. The expansion of the market has a dynamizing effect on the ethics of a community (I-system) because it loosens the ethical constraints on action. This could lead to the dissolution of the entire societal community and the disappearance of ethical regulation altogether if the penetration of pure market activity by the societal community did not produce an ethical tempering of this activity and thus keep the dynamizing effect of the expansion of the market within its proper limits. The precipitate of this interpenetration would be business ethics, which mediates two subsystems which would otherwise operate solely according to their own inner laws.

One way of understanding these inverted hierarchies of control and dynamization more precisely is to newly construct the fourfold classificatory scheme which is formed by the distinctions of internal–external and instrumental–consummatory orientations of action, which Parsons introduced after his first formulation of the A–G–I–L schema as the foundation for the analytical differentiation of subsystems.[33] A starting point for this new construction is the distinction between symbols and individual acts as basic elements of every action system. The nature of the relation between symbols, in the form of systems of meaning, normative systems, expressive symbol systems and cognitive systems considered as expectations of actors' symbolic articulations, on the one hand, and actions themselves, on the other hand, is of decisive significance both for the orderedness and control of systems and for their openness and capacity for dynamization. The relations between symbols and actions are already specifications of the more general relations between antecedents and consequents which obtain between all events. Symbols may vary between the poles of highest complexity and highest orderedness; actions vary between the poles of highest contingency and highest predictability.[34]

Symbolic complexity forms the vertical axis (ordinate) and contingency of action the horizontal axis (abscissa) when the 'force field' of an action space is illustrated by a system of coordinates. The action space is delimited by four extreme points as follows: minimum symbolic complexity and minimum contingency of action (I – closing), maximum symbolic complexity and maximum contingency of action (A – opening), minimum symbolic complexity and maximum contingency of action (L – generalization), and maximum symbolic complexity with minimum contingency of action (G – specification). Action moves within the action space as defined by these extreme points, and takes place in fields of action which are always nearest to a particular extreme point, and hence subject to its force field.

Both aspects of action systems (symbolic complexity and contingency of action) can be combined with one another in different ways. A method providing the greatest possible variation in setting out the relations between symbolic complexity and contingency of action is the drawing up of a hierarchically ranked fourfold table. Repeated application of this table yields continually finer-grained determinations of the relations between symbols and actions and a microscopically–macroscopically ordered differentiation of system levels. One can move upward, embedding the system of action in the system of the human condition, or downward, using the schema to make further differentiations of the action system and the social system (see Figures 4 and 5).[35]

With this system of classification, we can formulate precisely the relation of each function of a subsystem to our two basic elements – symbols and actions – and our two basic properties – complexity and contingency. Four and only four basic relationships obtain between complexity of symbols and contingency of action: generalization, specification, closedness and openness. The construction of this sort of relation between symbol and action is a way of characterizing the function of every structure and process of action. Thus, discourse yields a generalization of symbols combined with actions of high contingency as their implementation. Authority is that structure of social action which makes possible obligatory commitments to specific actions in the face of alternatives which are presented with a high degree of symbolic complexity. Community closes the universes of symbolic presentations and actions through its insistence on the self-evidentness of the obligations of its members. Exchange opens the spectrum of symbolic articulations and actions: this is the social structure embodying the least amount of restraint on possible actions and expectations. On the level of the general system of action, a symbolic code as the structure of the cultural system is the most highly generalized and as such allows a high contingency of action. The specification of concrete goals out of a multiplicity of symbolically presented alternatives necessitates the forging of a personal identity. The self-evidentness of duty requires the bonds which a social system provides. The opening up of expectations and actions necessary for adjustment to changing conditions requires the learning, through a system of rewards and punishments, of ways to manipulate the physical-biological world.

It is necessary to distinguish these controlling and dynamizing relations between subsystems, which exist on the theoretical level, from the actual relations which obtain between corresponding empirical subsystems. The relations between empirical subsystems can range from the *accommodation* of the potentially controlling subsystem to the dynamizing subsystem, through their *reconciliation,* their *mutual isolation* and their *interpenetration*, to the one-sided *domination* of the potentially dynamizing subsystem by the controlling one.[36]

By defining the functions of systems through the classification of the relations between the elements of a system and their most abstract properties, one can justify the choice of these functions: at this level of abstraction the classification is exhaustive. The abstractness of the functions is what allows them to be specified for various subsystems, sub-subsystems, etc., without the danger of committing that error, so feared by Parsons, which Whitehead calls 'the fallacy of misplaced concreteness'. The microscopic–macroscopic, 'sliding scale' nature of the classificatory scheme allows for the drawing of ever finer distinctions and for the continual identification of intermediary types which lie in the zones of interpenetration of the basic types. The repeated application of the classificatory scheme performs here the function that in mathematics is performed by systems of numbers, of which the simplest is the binary system. By means of the repeated application of the same set of numbers, the binary system does everything the decimal system does. The four-function paradigm is this type of system, one which through the repeated application of a small group of basic categories is able to capture all aspects of reality.[37] The four-function paradigm is itself a duplication of a simpler two-term schema (absence of orderedness vs. maximum of orderedness) through the application of this simpler schema to the two basic elements (symbols and actions).

As an example of the way in which repeated application of the fundamental schema can yield ever finer determinations of functions as intermediary stages between, and zones of interpenetration of, the basic schema, let us look at exchange as a form of social interaction. Exchange, as the structure of the economic system, performs in the social system the function of opening the framework of action. It has a dynamizing effect. As a subsystem of the social system, it can have this effect only within the framework of a social order which already limits the possibilities of action and establishes *peaceful* exchange as the only legitimate form of the private acquisition of goods. Within the social system, this limitation cannot arise out of the activity of the acquisition of goods itself. It can arise only out of the penetration of the activity of acquisition by normative rules governing exchange and founded on commitments to a societal community which proscribes violations of the rules. The 'market community' is that form of community which is located in the zone of interpenetration of exchange and the societal community. The market community carries the guidance of the community into acquisitive activity and, on the other hand, transmits the dynamizing effect of exchange to the community.[38] This makes possible both the expansion of exchange activity and the expansion of the moral order, which now finds for itself a sphere of application to which it had heretofore been a stranger. Through this interpenetration of exchange and societal community, a society can become both economic *and* moral and can decrease the incompatibilities between these two spheres. These incompatibilities would be especially marked in societies in which the development of the acquisitive life was not accompanied by an expansion of the bonds of community but instead the formation of communities extending beyond kinship relations remained impossible, as has more or less been the case outside the West. In these societies, money truly does become what Marx took it always to be, 'the debasement of the moral and economic order of things'.[39] Here is that unbridgeable chasm between the sphere of economic rationality and the sphere of the ethic of brotherliness which Weber diagnosed as a consequence of the failure of religious ethics and the world mutually to penetrate.[40] The compatibility or incompatibility of social spheres is a consequence of the organization of their relations with one another; the mechanism by which essentially incompatible spheres can be made compatible is not simply differentiation, but the independent social anchoring of their cores in such a way that they must interpenetrate, so that in the zone of interpenetration a new quality will be formed as a bridge between them.

Another form of dynamizing and controlling interpenetration exists between exchange and authority and between exchange and cultural discourse. The expansion of commercial exchange has a dynamizing effect above all on cultural discourse and on the system of authority. On the one hand, it strains the consistency of cultural patterns and, on the other hand, it strains the ability of the system of authority to make and enforce decisions. This dynamizing effect can once again be held within limits only if the value system can be injected into exchange through value generalization, thus determining what will count as legitimate activity in the area of exchange. But in addition the system of authority must be able to enforce the limitations on market activity beyond the self-evident rules of the market community.

The classification of controlling and dynamizing effects according to the relations of symbolic complexity and contingency of action shows that the I–system possesses the highest level of orderedness. In the social system this means that it is through the societal community that the realm of symbols and the realm of action become closed *as* realms possessing self-evidentness. Therefore, it is from the societal community (not from the L–system, the social-cultural or fiduciary system) that the strongest limiting effect proceeds down through the system as a whole. On the other hand, the generalization of the value system which takes place in the social-cultural system exercises a dynamizing effect with regard to the self-evident elements of a community, in that it extends the realm of action which is legitimized by general values. If we change Parsons's cybernetic hierarchy in this way, putting the I–system at the highest level of control, we can grasp more precisely the dynamizing effects of the cultural system on the level of the general system of action, of the social-cultural system on that of the social system, and in general of any L–system on any level of analysis. Precisely taken, the subsystems can no longer be classified in a hierarchy. The model of the action space expresses much more precisely their mutual relations and the character of their effects on action.

Discourse, as the structure of the social-cultural system, acts to mark out the space of acceptable interpretations of a society's value pattern. Accordingly, it has a generalizing effect with regard to the concretizations of the value pattern which hold for specific social spheres. It promotes cohesion among the different normative orientations which are valid for specific social spheres by anchoring them in a consistent value pattern. This insures unity in diversity and continuity in change and facilitates the formation of consensus between adversary positions. On the other hand, the marking out of a space for the interpretation of the value pattern through discourse can also beget conflict. Discourse can hold itself aloof from the concretizations of values contained in social institutions and place on those institutions new demands that they justify themselves. When the claims of cultural discourse begin to make constant, exorbitant demands on social institutions, the value pattern is supplying not the kernel of the society's sense of identity, but the kernel of its ultimate fragmentation. A third possible relation between the cultural system and the other spheres of a society would be the tight binding of the former to a determinate social group which is dominant in the societal community, as, for example, Confucianism formed the ideology of the ruling class of literati in China.[41] The tight connection between the value pattern of American society and the white Anglo-Saxon Protestant community, the WASPs, produced a similar effect. In extreme cases of this type, the social value pattern comes to take the form of the value orientation of a ruling social group and it loses its power of generalization as well as its ability to facilitate the *inclusion* of different social groups in *one* societal community.[42]

Which of these three relations between the cultural system and the system of the societal community actually obtains depends on the degree of interpenetration of these two systems. The formation of consensus between different social groups and continuity in the face of change are dependent on the mutual penetration of both systems. If the cultural system possesses sufficient institutional independence from the societal community and yet reaches out into it, and if the societal community can reach out into the cultural system without losing its own institutional base, then the cultural system can exercise a generalizing effect on the concrete value orientations of individual groups, which on the basis of this assimilation of their value orientations are given a common identity. The extension of the societal community into the cultural system gives the value system an adequate grounding in the societal community and a relationship to the value orientations and practical requirements of social groups. The dynamizing effect produced by intellectual interpretation of the value pattern, which because of the intellectual orientation toward rational construction inclines toward a more stringent consistency of ethical convictions, is limited through its connection to a societal community. If, on the other hand, culture is the affair of intellectuals only, its inherent dynamizing tendency will be greatly accentuated, and the cultural system will begin to have a divisive effect on the society. Conversely, where the cultural system is merely the appendage of one dominant social class, it cannot provide a *foundation for a common identity* for the different communities within the society. In both cases, the interpenetration of culture and societal community is lacking.

The educational system, especially the university, has a particularly important role in the formation of this complex relation of differentiation and interpenetration between culture and societal community: 'It seems reasonable to suggest that the system of higher education is particularly important in the development of mobile "markets" for the factors of solidarity.'[43] Not all educational systems fulfil this function in the same way, as one can easily see from a glance at different systems. While the American system of education, for example, relies more on interpenetration, the European system, traditionally, tends to segregate and isolate intellectual culture from the other spheres of the society, which presents a considerable potential for conflict within these societies.

In this connection, one can give more precision to the frequently cited distinction, drawn by David Lockwood, between social integration and system integration.[44] By 'social integration' is meant, as Lockwood holds, the emergence of collective solidarity as a function of the societal community. 'System integration' would denote, more precisely than in Lockwood's distinction, the interpenetration of analytically differentiated subsystems as *one* among many different possible relations between subsystems. The theorem of the cybernetic relations of control and dynamization belongs to the Parsonian theory of action as a way of making more precise the theorem of interpenetration, as a way of analysing relations between subsystems. This theorem too should not be misunderstood as an assertion concerning *concrete* systems. It does not entail a 'cultural determinism' or a functional primacy of the cultural system in a concrete sense.[45] The theorem of the high position of the cultural system as an *analytical* system in the cybernetic hierarchy applied to *social institutions* postulates that institutions can lay claim to a truly normative validity, as opposed to a mere empirical validity dependent on power and interest, only if they can establish themselves as specifications of a more general system of common values. I have given a still higher place in the hierarchy to the societal community because these culturally justifying institutions can possess normatively *binding* validity only if the value system is anchored in at least a possibly universal community of solidarity which, through the self-evidentness of the obligations it imposes, sets a limit to the potentially endless rational questioning and examining of the value system. This hypothesis is traceable to the theorem, already present in *The Structure of Social Action*, that the social order as *normative*, that is, as an order which includes the freedom of the individual rather than as a causally determined, empirical order, cannot be reduced to the interplay of power and interest.[46] The Parsonian theory of action never denies the empirical effectiveness of power and interest, or of conflict, as is so often asserted.[47] Conflict is a dynamic factor which tends toward the dissolution or reorganization of existing institutions. The reorganization of old institutions and the establishment of wholly new ones, however, are subject to the same conditions as every other attempt to establish social order. And here, if it is a question of *normatively valid* institutions, constellations of power and interest in themselves are as much insufficient conditions as cultural legitimation and a communal foundation are indispensable conditions. Moreover, power and interest cannot even be the only moving factors in change. The cultural legitimation of insitutitions through rational argument, and the expansive movement of the socialization process, through which the individual is continually growing into more extensive social circles, exercise a pressure on concrete institutions to change in the direction of a more general justification of norms by values.

2.5 A digression: Interpenetration and differentiation

What is meant by 'interpenetration'? Having credited this concept with such a central significance in the frame of reference of voluntaristic action theory, it is important that we should now embark on a number of more thorough clarifications of the concept and on examinations of the conditions for interpenetration and the relationship between interpenetration and differentiation.

Let us imagine a societal collective which will be our corporate actor. This collective, just like an association or a business, has the use of organizational procedures for arriving at decisions which are eventually made and carried out 'in the name' of the collective as a whole. When an association's committee draws up a budgetary plan which is then accepted by majority vote at the association's meeting, then both the decision and its eventual execution can be attributed to the association as the corporate – or collective – actor. If it is a government which draws up the budget and it is accepted by a majority of the country's parliamentary assembly, again the decision and the action in implementing the budget can be attributed to society as a corporate actor. From this we can see that the decisions of a *corporate* actor and their implementation rest upon a *political* structure, that is, on the mobilization of legitimate power within the framework of an authority structure. This does not, however, mean that 'society' is definable only in political terms. The political aspect is so clearly in evidence only because the political structure is in closest contact with immediate collective decision and action. Before they can in fact be realized as concrete action, such decisions always need to fulfil a number of further preconditions. Material resources, cultural legitimation, collective solidarity and individual motivation are all factors which must be mobilized if a decision is to become collectively binding and then be carried out in reality. Only to the extent that these resources are actually brought together does collective action really take place and only then is it even possible to speak of the existence of a collective. Society is the name given to a collective which fulfils this requirement for collective action and also, amongst all comparable collectives, possesses the greatest scope for collective action. An actor acts in a situation. This is also true for society as a collective actor. But we can also see society as a system of interdependent actions taking place in an environment.

A characteristic of a so-called simple or primitive society is that particular institutional provisions for mobilizing the necessary resources for collective action are available only to a limited extent. (This 'limited extent' must be emphasized, as a totally un-differentiated society does not exist in practice.) The primitive society in our example might have a council of elders which distributes work, settles disputes, gives meaning to the life of the society and makes collectively binding decisions. These various problems can be given some systematic order if this society is seen within the action space of the 'human condition' defined by four extreme points. The four extremes comprise four analytically distinguishable dimensions in the actor's environment, namely: the environment of physicochemical processes or 'material given conditions' (A), the goals set by other (collective and individual) actors (G), the conflicts between collectives or individuals within a society (I) and the transcendental conditions for the constitution of meaning in human action (L).

These four environments confront society with various problems, in the spheres of obtaining material resources, reaching and implementing collective decisions, maintaining collective solidarity and constituting a meaning to life within society. The four environments can confront society with difficulties of various degrees in coming to terms with these problems. Material given conditions demand lesser or greater efforts in obtaining resources. The many and varied goals set by collectives and individuals with power of their own hinder to a greater or lesser extent the making and implementation of collective decisions. Conflicts between collectives and/or individuals vary in prevalence and, accordingly, the maintenance of societal solidarity is inhibited to a greater or lesser extent. Human experiences can have various degrees of irrationality, making the constitution of meaning either more or less difficult to form.

Should the environments pose only minor problems, then particular efforts and actions by society to overcome them are not required. In paradise, where there is always material abundance, and never any contradiction between goals, any conflict, or any irrationality, there is no need to develop economic and other technical instruments or any particular provisions toward solving political, communal and spiritual problems. However, this does not mean as a corollary that a society will necessarily produce these particular provisions if the environments pose major problems. What is more likely to be the case is that a large society is unable to overcome such problems and breaks down into smaller units on a more primitive level.

If major problems are to be overcome there has to be an increased interaction between society and environment, which we can term *interpenetration*. This signifies that the environment, through the problems it poses, influences the society, and society for its own part influences the environment by developing certain regular, in-stitutionalized actions, which shape the environment without depriving it of its independent existence. The various regular actions form subsystems which mediate between society and the particular dimensions of the environment as zones of interpenetration.

Let us take the cultivation of cereals as a simple example. This represents a subsystem in the zone of interpenetration between society and the material environment. The material environment requires of society that it perform certain regular activities and hence is an influence upon it. Conversely society influences the environment by shaping the landscape according to its utility. Society thus incorporates part of its material environment. The cultivation of cereals, by virtue of its physicochemical and organic basis, is part of the material environment. In its social organization, it is part of society. Cereal cultivation unites within it the social organization and the physicochemical and organic basis, and hence represents a system in itself which is conditioned neither solely materially nor solely socially. It is in terms of the interpenetration of society and material environment that this system can be explained.

'Interpenetration', as illustrated by this example, denotes a process in which a system has such an influence on the environment, and the environment such an influence on the system, that the two transform each other at the margin, without mutually changing their central cores. The more pronounced the marginal zones are, the more they tend to form definable subsystems which mediate between the system and the environment. The more closely they themselves are linked to each other, the more they together form a subsystem which combines within it aspects of the system and aspects of the environment[48] (see Figure 6).

The generation of marginal zones has a number of particular preconditions in the system's relationship to the respective dimensions of the environment. If we take society as the system, then in terms of the relationship to the material environment, it is *trial-and-error learning processes* which promote the development of the *instrumental, economic subsystem*. Quite different preconditions are required when it comes to the relationship between the society and the goal-setting and power of other individual and collective actors. The more heterogeneous the goals, and the greater the tendency for the various individuals and collectives to have power at their disposal, the more the making and implementation of decisions by society requires a *monopolization of legitimate power* by the societal collective and the transfer of decision-making authority to particular councils and decision-making bodies. In this way a *political subsystem* develops, as an intermediary between the societal collective and the goal-setting of individuals and collectives. Yet another set of preconditions is called for by the interpenetration of the societal collective with the multiplicity of particularized collectives and individuals, so that society maintains its solidarity. In this case

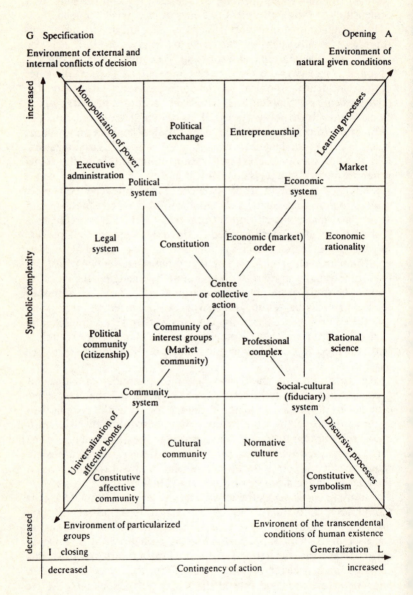

Figure 6 Differentiation of society by interpenetration

it is the *universalization of affective bonds*, as supported by rites and symbols, which encourages the development of a societal *community system*, bringing together the particular groups in an all-encompassing community. Finally, the societal collective's inter-penetration with the transcendental conditions for meaningful human existence poses its own special requirements: in this case *discursive processes* are the appropriate preconditions which help bring the *social-cultural (fiduciary)* subsystem into being, mediating between society and the transcendental conditions for the constitution of meaning. Societal action is thus rooted in a further frame of reference concerned with the meaning of life.

Once the above-named systems have interposed themselves as shown, as societal subsystems between society itself and the environment in its four distinct dimensions, then the process of interpenetration is ready to begin again on the next higher level. The more these subsystems have taken on an independent identity in overcoming their specific problems, the more they themselves come to represent environments to each other and the more pressing the problem of mediating between them becomes. The societal subsystems have their own values, norms, roles and carrier collectives. Their interpenetration, then, is a question of interaction between their role carriers and carrier collectives.

In modern societies the instrumental-economic subsystem is 'carried' by the values of economic rationality, the norms of market order, the roles of producers, consumers, employers, employees, sellers, buyers, etc., and by the collectives of employers' and employees' associations. The political subsystem is represented by the values of democracy, the norms of the democratic parliamentary decision-making process, the roles of members of the government and of parliament, voters and lobbyists, and by the collectives of political parties and interest groups. The community system comprises the values of human and civil rights, the norms of compromise-seeking and settlement of disputes through the legal system, the role of the citizen, and the collectives of classes, social strata and religious, professional, ethnic, linguistic, regional and other groups. The social-cultural system is based on the values of intellectual rationality, the norms of discourse, the roles of intellectuals, experts, clients, laymen, etc., and on the collectives of intellectual and professional associations. The interpenetration of these societal subsystems requires the interaction of the above role carriers. The more regularly the interactions take place – in joint councils, for example – the more they too tend to form subsystems between the societal subsystems. Hence new subsystems have interposed themselves between the first subsystems. Once the process is completed society has been broken down from four basic systems into sixteen more finely *differentiated* subsystems.

Thus one can see that differentiation as described here occurs as a result of interpenetration. The process begins with the interpenetration of society and environment, leading to the differentiation into four basic systems, the interpenetration of which leads once again to the formation of sixteen subsystems. It should be understood that this differentiation is a differentiation beside which integration remains preserved. Society and environment thus have their mutual ties extended by further, finer chains. Even in the outward direction, the differentiation becomes more detailed through new interpenetrations. Between the centres of the economic, political, community and social-cultural systems and their respective environments, new subsystems interpose themselves which then become the new extreme points of the societal system:

The market is the mediating zone of interpenetration between economic action and the environmental shortage of economic resources.

Executive administration is the mediating zone of interpenetration between political action and the environment of external and internal conflicts of decision.

The constitutive affective community is the mediating zone of interpenetration between community action and the environment of particularized groups.

The constitutive symbolism of religion is the intermediary between discursive communication in the social-cultural sphere and the transcendental conditions of meaningful human existence.

Between the social system's extreme points listed above, further subsystems are generated by internal interpenetration as follows:

- The penetration of economic action by the political orientation results in economic entrepreneurship.
- The penetration of economic action by the community orientation results in economic (market) order.
- The penetration of economic action by the social-cultural discursive orientation results in economic rationality in the form of rational calculation and rational technology.
- The penetration of political action by the economic orientation results in political exchange between interested parties and representatives.
- The penetration of political action by the social-cultural discursive orientation results in the political constitution, representing a discursive frame of reference for political action.
- The penetration of political action by the community orientation results in the legal system, which forms a communal basis for political action.

- The penetration of community action by the political orientation results in the political community of citizens.
- The penetration of community action by the economic orientation results in the interest-based market community.
- The penetration of community action by the social-cultural discursive orientation results in the cultural community.
- The penetration of social-cultural discursive action by an adaptive, economic orientation results in rational science.
- The penetration of social-cultural discursive action by the political orientation results in the professional complex, which combines discursive procedures with systems of authority based on differences in professional competence.
- The penetration of social-cultural discursive action by community orientation results in normative culture. Cultural orientations obtain their normative binding force by being anchored in the community.

However the differentiation of the social system into sixteen elements is by no means the end of the line for the process of societal differentiation through interpenetration. Apart from further internal differentiation, the process can notably also produce further differentiations between the social system and society's physico-chemical, human-organic and transcendental environments. At this point we have reached the level of the general action system[49] (see Figure 7).

- The social system is a combination of interdependent social interactions. Values, norms, social roles and collectives all represent structural components of the social system.
- In the zone of interpenetration between social action and the goal-orientation of the human organism, the human personality is formed. The personality system is a combination of constant dispositions evident in all the actions of a particular actor.
- In the zone of interpenetration between social action and physico-chemical processes, the human behavioural system develops with its learning capacity. The basic elements of the behavioural system comprise stimulus-response relationships and, on a higher level, cognitive schemata.
- In the zone of interpenetration between social action and the transcendental conditions of meaningful human existence, the cultural system is formed. Symbols should be seen as the constitutive elements in the cultural system.

Once again, a further differentiation of these subsystems in the action system emerges from external and internal interpenetration. The following subsystems come to light as a result of external interpenetration in the direction of the physicochemical, human organic and transcendental environments of the social system.

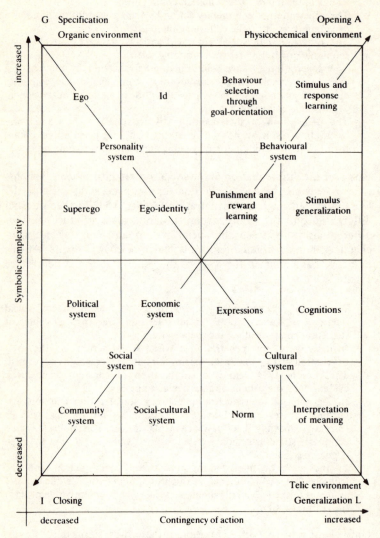

Figure 7 Differentiation of the action system

- Stimulus-response learning mediates as a zone of interpenetration between adaptive behaviour and the physicochemical given conditions of the environment.
- The ego as the individual's centre of decision-making mediates as the zone of interpenetration between personal dispositions and man's organic needs and impulses.
- The interpretation of meaning mediates as the zone of interpenetration between symbolic orientations and the transcendental conditions of meaningful human existence.

Internal interpenetration of the subsystems of action generates, over and above the differentiation of the social system already dealt with, the following new subsystems:

- Selection of behaviour through goal-orientation results from the penetration of adaptive behaviour by personal dispositions.
- Punishment and reward learning results from the penetration of adaptive behaviour by social interaction.
- Stimulus generalization results from the penetration of adaptive behaviour by cultural symbolism.
- The id, as the hedonistic aspect of personality, results from the penetration of personal dispositions by adaptive learning.
- Ego-identity (the ego-ideal), as the generalized aspect of personality, results from the penetration of personal dispositions by cultural symbolism.
- The superego, as the order-generating aspect of personality, results from the penetration of personal dispositions by social obligations.
- Cognitions, as the opening aspect of the cultural system, result from the penetration of cultural symbolism by adaptive learning.
- Expressions, as the specifying aspect of the cultural system, result from the penetration of cultural symbolism by personal dispositions. Works of art are an expression of personality in this sense with a general symbolic and cultural validity.
- Norms, as the closing aspect of the cultural system, results from the penetration of cultural symbolism by social interaction and communal association.

A still higher degree of differentiation is achieved on the next level up in the analysis, by interpenetration of the action system with the other subsystems of the human condition. Outside the action system on which we have so far concentrated, the differentiation of the other subsystems is sketched out below. In this instance the mutual penetration of the subsystems has to be conceived of anthropocentrically, that is, from the point of view of the constitution of the human condition as seen by the human individual himself[50] (see Figure 8).

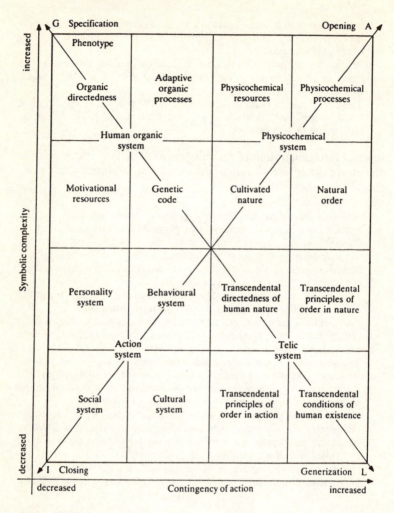

Figure 8 Differentiation of the human condition

- Physicochemical resources should be interpreted as the result of the penetration of physicochemical processes by human organic processes.
- The cultivation of nature should be understood as the result of the penetration of physicochemical processes by human action.
- The natural order should be thought of as the result of the penetration of physicochemical processes by the transcendental conditions for order.
- Adaptive organic processes should be viewed as the result of the penetration of the human organism by physicochemical processes.

- The genetic code of the human organism should be seen as the result of the penetration of the human organism by the transcendental conditions of organic existence.
- The motivational resources of action represent the result of the penetration of the human organism by meaningful action.
- The transcendental principles underlying the order of nature can be interpreted as the result of the penetration of transcendental conditions by physicochemical processes.
- The transcendental principles of directedness in human organic life should be viewed as the result of the penetration of transcendental conditions by the human organic structure.
- The transcendental principles of ordered action can be understood as the result of the penetration of transcendental conditions by symbolic, cultural human action.

The differentiation and integration achieved by interpenetration between society and environment, or between the societal, action and human condition subsystems, is still only one type of relationship among a number of other possibilities. These relationships vary according to how clearly formed and how strong society, environment and the subsystems are, and according to the degree of development attained by the mediating systems. If we take society as the point of reference in our analysis, we will encounter the following variations:

1 Society, environment and mediating systems are all only slightly developed: society will be underdeveloped and poorly integrated with the environment.
2 Society and environment are only slightly developed, but the mediating systems more strongly: society will be underdeveloped but integrated with the environment.
3 Society and environment are strongly developed, but the mediating systems only slightly: conflict between society and environment will result.
4 Society is strongly developed, but the environment and mediating systems only slightly: society will dominate the environment.
5 Society and the mediating systems are slightly developed, but the environment strongly: in this case the environment will dominate society.
6 Society and the mediating systems are strongly developed and the environment weakly: here there is a less pronounced dominance on the part of society, namely the over-steering of the environment by society.
7 Society is slightly developed, but the environment and mediating systems strongly: society will be over-steered by the environment.
8 Society, environment and mediating systems are all strongly developed: society and environment will be differentiated and integrated.

In as far as mediating systems have actually developed, the way in which they mediate depends on their structure; this can tend in a particular direction within the action space, or can combine a number of such directions. Viewed on the level of the social system, four distinct structures are possible. The mediating systems could feature a *discursive* structure, and in this case the mediation tends to be one of *reconciliation*. The structures can take on the form of authority. In this case the mediation will be based on political *enforcement*. The structures can be those involving exchange. The mediation would then entail *openness and instability*. Finally, the structures can be of a communal nature, in which case the mediation would be characterized by *closedness and immobility*. It is only if all these structures are combined in the mediating systems that the highest degree of *interpenetration* between society and environment becomes possible.

The above-listed types of relationship between society and environment can similarly be applied to the internal relationships between the societal subsystems. As far as the relation between interpenetration and differentiation is concerned, we can establish the following: Interpenetration brings about a differentiation of subsystems, and the integration of these subsystems depends in turn on a new interpenetration in the form of the generation of more subsystems which act as mediating systems. In the process, it is possible for subsystems to be generated by interpenetration and differentiation which are not subsequently integrated by further interpenetration. The process of interpenetration thus reaches a certain level of differentiation where, through limited integration, it progresses no further. In principle, the process of interpenetration is infinite. Measured against this standard, all societies achieve an insufficient degree of integration of the subsystems created by differentiation.

2.6 The theory of the generalized media of interchange

2.6.1 The interpenetration of the social subsystems: *Economy and Society*

Parsons reached a new stage in the analysis of analytically differentiated subsystems with the introduction of the theory of the generalized media of interchange, which he formulated successively for the subsystems of the *social system* (money, political power, influence, value-commitments),[51] the *action system* (definition of the situation, affect, performance capacity, intelligence),[52] and finally the system of the *human condition* (transcendental ordering, meaning, health, empirical ordering).[53] The starting point for this theoretical development was a renewed encounter with economic theory, occasioned by an invitation from the Department of Economics at Cambridge University to deliver a guest lecture in honour of the memory of Alfred Marshall. This invitation led to an intensive period of work with Neil J. Smelser, out of which emerged the coauthored *Economy and Society* in 1956. In this book, Parsons and Smelser developed a theory of the economic system and a theory of money within the framework of the general theory of action. The theories differed from pure economic theory in that they viewed economic action as mediated through the interpenetration of analytically differentiated social subsystems – the economic system, the political system, the integrative system and the cultural system.[54] In the foreground of the analysis stood the relations between the economic system and the other three subsystems. These relations appeared here, for the first time, as relations of interchange, in which money as a generalized medium of interchange played a central role. And next to money, the medium of interchange anchored in the economic system, there began to emerge indications of the concepts of political power, influence and value–commitments as media anchored in the political system, the integrative system, and the cultural system, respectively.

All of the media of interchange possess certain common characteristics which make them particularly suitable for the establishment of a certain type of relationship between systems, one which combines differentiation and interpenetration. Each medium possesses the following qualities:[55]

1   Media of the social system and the action system are *symbolic* in character, that is, they are signs of other objects which one can recall through the medium under certain circumstances. Money symbolizes a certain quantity of goods or services which can be obtained with it.
2   Media are generalized, that is, one can with their help re-present a variety of objects, independent of concrete circumstances.
3   Every medium is founded on the institutionalization of a '*medium code*', that is, on binding normative rules which set the conditions of acquisition and use. Through the institutionalization of a code, a medium becomes a valid means of interchange, but only within a clearly defined context in which it can be used for achieving determinate goals. Money becomes a medium of peaceful exchange through the existence of the institution of property. Political power is the legitimate medium of the collectively binding implementation of decisions only through the existence of a valid order of authority. Influence is the medium for the motivation of action only through the

existence of an order of prestige. Value-commitment is a medium which engenders loyalty to social institutions only because of the existence of an order of common values under which institutions can be subsumed.

4   Through its institutionalized code, each medium is given a *specific* significance, on the basis of which each can be distinguished from the others and which gives each medium a delimited area of valid application.

5   Media *circulate*, in two respects: first, they can be passed around among actors; second, each medium is able to pass over the boundaries of the system in which it originates and thus make possible a specific form of interpenetration of subsystems.

6   A particularly significant characteristic of media is that they are not subject to zero-sum conditions. This means that when one actor increases the amount of a medium that he has at his disposal, he does not necessarily reduce the availability of the medium to other actors. For this to be so, material production of the societal object to which any medium relates must be increased, so that the total quantity of the medium may also be increased without depreciation. Only then, for example, can the 'printing of money' bring about a real increase in the stock of monetary value in a system. Similarly, the increased production of compulsorily binding decisions is a precondition for the real increase of power, the raising of the level of social solidarity is a precondition for the increase in influence and the increased production of knowledge is a precondition for the real increase of intelligence. The same transcendence of zero-sum conditions holds for the relation of the media to each other: an increase in one does not require a decrease elsewhere.

7   Parsons describes the media of social action in terms of two intersecting dichotomies. In the process of motivating social action, media can on the one hand originate in the surrounding situation and exert their influence on the external action (conditional factors), or on the other can originate internally and influence the intentions of the action (normative factors). Furthermore, they can bring about either the negative consequence of avoiding particular actions, or the positive one of carrying out particular actions:[56]

–   A positive effect bearing externally upon the action from the situation is generated by money. A less generalized form of this means of motivating social action is represented by concrete incentives or rewards. These act as a type of basis of security for money.

–   A negative effect bearing externally upon the action from the situation is generated by political power. In less generalized form, this means of motivating social action is seen in concrete negative sanctions, particularly the threat and use of force, as a type of basis of security for political power.

- A positive effect bearing from within the actor upon the intentions of action is produced by influence. In less generalized form, this is seen in concrete applications of influence by convincing an actor, which are a type of basis of security for influence in the general sense.

- A negative effect bearing from within the actor upon the intentions of action is produced by value commitments. The infringement of values gives rise to internal feelings of guilt. In less generalized form this means of motivating social action is seen in the activation of commitments to *more concrete* norms as a type of basis of security for general value commitments.

- (In this context we can conceive of commitments as a purer medium for community action, similar to Parsons's value commitments; however, we would attribute them not to the social-cultural system but to the community system. They too work from within and bear upon the intentions of action, with the infringement of norms causing guilt feelings in the community. Less generalized forms of this means of motivating social action are concrete affective ties to communal norms as the basis of security for more general commitments.)

- (*Rational arguments* as media of social-cultural action have a positive effect on the intentions of action. Less generalized forms of these means of motivation are empirical confirmations of individual pronouncements, acting as a basis of security for more general arguments.)

8   The media of social interaction can be related to value principles toward the fulfilment of which they actually contribute. The extent to which the value principles are fulfilled is measured by standards of coordination:[57]

- *Money* is oriented to the value principle of *utility*. The relevant standard of coordination is the *solvency* of a company or an entire society.

- *Political power* is oriented toward *effectiveness*, as expressed in decision-making ability. In this case the standard of coordination is *compliance* with political decisions.

- *Influence* (commitment) is oriented to *solidarity*. In this case *social consensus* should be seen as the standard of coordination.

- *Value commitments* (arguments) are oriented to the *integrity* of latent cultural patterns. The standard of coordination is the *consistency* of the latent cultural pattern.

At the level of the social system, the following zones of interpenetration are created through the reciprocal guidance of action by the appropriate generalized media (see Figure 9):

L ⟷ A   Value commitments (arguments) define the cultural framework of economic action. The use of money extends the scope for cultural

79

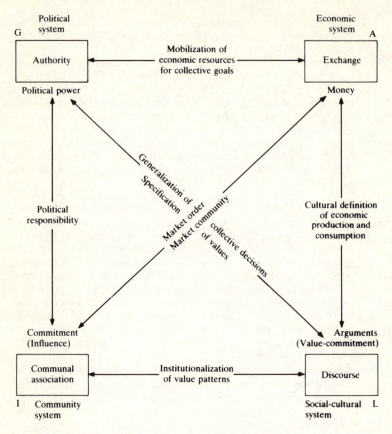

Figure 9 The social system's zones of interpenetration

action because it liberates the orientation to cultural standards from ascriptive ties. The result is the *cultural definition of economic production and consumption*.

L ⟷ G   Through value-commitments (arguments), collective decisions are embedded in a *general* framework. Conversely, general values are *specified* in the process of collective decision-making through the application of *legitimate* political power.

L ⟷ I   Through the use of value-commitments (arguments), the normative orientation is placed within a general framework of communal activity. The binding of social-cultural discussion to the gaining of influence in the community (to the commitment to a community) sets the normative limit to this discussion. Out of these two processes arises the *institutionalization of value patterns*.

G ⟷ A   The use of money facilitates the mobilization of economic resources for the achieving of collective and individual goals; the long-standing security of economic resources necessitates a collective responsibility which goes beyond the interests of individuals, is independent of particular power groups, and is supported by legitimate and generalized political power. The result is the *mobilization of economic resources for collective goals.*

G ⟷ I   The binding validity of collective decisions requires the anchoring of articulations of interest demands in a comprehensive community through the acquisition of influence in this community (the commitment to it). The conversion of these legitimately defined interests into collective decisions in the process of decision-making must be supported by the exercise of legitimate political power. It is in this context that *political responsibility* develops.

I ⟷ A   The submission of economic action to the economic order – the order of the market – arises out of the acquisition of influence in a community (the commitment to it). The use of money broadens the scope for action within the limits of the community. In this situation, a *market order* and *market community* are formed.

We cannot go into all of these relations of interpenetration in detail here. As an example, we shall look at the relation between the *social-cultural (fiduciary) system* and the *economic system* with the help of the theory of media (see Figure 10).

The characteristics of the media which are of decisive significance for the theory of interpenetration are the institutional anchoring of the media and their ability to circulate beyond the bounds of the subsystem of their origin. Both qualities help meet the conditions of interpenetration: the differentiation of subsystems and their simultaneous mutual opening to one another. Parsons and Smelser make this characteristic of the media quite clear in their discussion of the relations of interchange between the economic system and the other three systems, and in this way they distinguish their analysis of the medium of money from all purely economic theories of money.[58] Money is the mediating term which makes possible the interpenetration of the economic system and the cultural, integrative and political systems, because it can circulate among these systems and thus not only convey the demands of the process of the rational acquisition of goods into these other subsystems but also bring back from these subsystems their claims on the economic subsystem. Parsons and Smelser demonstrate this dual function of money primarily in their analysis of the interchange between the business firm, the basic unit of the economic system, and the household, the basic unit of the social-cultural (fiduciary) system:[59]

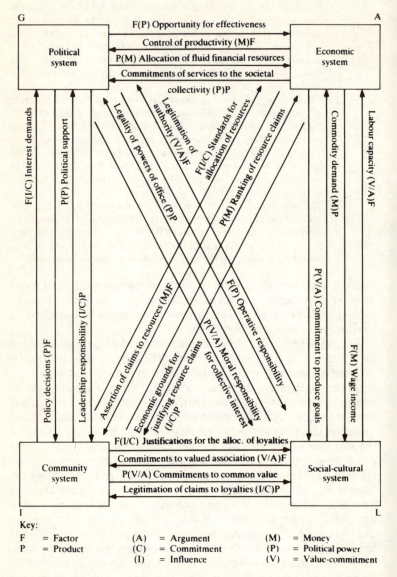

Figure 10 The input–output paradigm of the social system (based on T. Parsons and G.M. Platt, *The American University*, Cambridge,-.: Harvard University Press, 1973, Figure A.3, p.432)

'Household members what to "live" according to a given pattern; the firm's goal is to "produce", secure rewards, and accumulate facilities to continue producing. Some mechanism must mediate between these two distinct orientations.

On the one hand, money represents the *generalization* of purchasing power to *control decisions* to exchange goods; on the other hand it symbolizes attitudes. The former is the "wealth" aspect of consumers' income, the latter the "prestige" aspect. If it cannot command goods and services money is not acceptable as wages; if it cannot symbolize prestige and mediate between detailed symbols and a broader symbolization it is not acceptable on other grounds. Only with this dual significance can money perform its *social* functions.'[60]

In particular, between the business firm and the household there is both an interchange of factors (*labour capacity* and *wage income*) and an interchange of products (*commodity demand* and *commitment to production of goods*). The firm is anchored primarily in the economic system and the household primarily in the social-cultural (fiduciary) system. That does not mean that the economic system comes to a stop at the door of the concrete household. It means that the household is an empirical unit in which analytically differentiated subsystems with their own internal orders can affect one another and mutually penetrate. The household is on the one hand an economic unit which participates in economic activity as a source for labour capacity, as a producer or a consumer, and thereby is subject to the economic order. On the other hand, the household is a significant place for socialization and as such is a bearer of the cultural order:

'The relationship between the economy and the latent pattern-maintenance and tension-management subsystem is essentially analytical, i.e., it illustrates the crucial point of interaction between two differentiated functional subsystems. But the economy does not 'end' at the market for consumer goods. Indeed a good deal of the working capital of the economy is, even in our society, located concretely in households in the form of consumer durables in the process of depreciation.'[61]

One can consider the labour market and the consumer market as zones of interpenetration of the economic system and the social-cultural system, in which firm and household constitute the units of mediation between the interpenetrating systems.[62] In the interchange of factors, labour capacity and wage income, the interpenetration of these two systems means that the qualifications of the workers – for example, their value orientations, their cognitive-technical abilities, their sense of discipline – are determined by their socialization in the family and other loci of socialization that bear primarily cultural responsibility. This process of socialization does not necessarily proceed in a sense which is contrary to economic life; this becomes more true the more the process of socialization is expanded. The qualifications of workers derive chiefly from cultural standards, which the firm cannot evade in the process of defining its own qualification requirements. In the firm, the qualifications of the workers confront the demands of economic rationality,[63] which expresses itself through the differential distribution of wage income, on the basis of economic criteria of scarcity. Wage income is thus determined primarily by criteria of economic rationality and only secondarily by culturally imparted qualifications, while labour capacity is determined primarily by cultural standards and only secondarily by economic standards. Wage income is a primary, economically determined input factor in the household, where it forms the basis for the formation of a specific life-style, which in turn yields a certain orientation to cultural standards. Here wage income sets an economic limit to the realization of cultural standards and provides a way for the economic system to penetrate the social-cultural (fiduciary) system. Concrete consumer demand, however, is a product of orientation toward cultural standards and to that extent provides a way for the social-cultural system to penetrate the economic system. The corresponding commitment of the business to produce goods is not, however, simply derivable from cultural standards of consumption. Instead, those standards will be broken down by the business's orientation toward economic rationality, to which it is forced by market competition. The commitment to produce goods is therefore determined primarily by the economic system and secondarily by cultural standards, while commodity demand is determined primarily culturally and secondarily economically.

In accordance with this conception, Parsons included 'value-commitment' as the medium specific to the social-cultural (fiduciary) system. In the interchange of factors, value-commitments oblige the individual to orient himself toward standards of discipline and cognitive rationality – for example, in the shape of the Puritan ethic – relating to his capacity as a worker, while the use of money as the payment for performance pushes both the business which pays it and the worker who receives it toward economic rationality, thereby setting a limit to the reach of cultural standards. In the interchange of products, the use of money pushes both the producer and the consumer toward economic rationality as a limit to the orientation toward cultural standards, while the value-commitment of the producer to the production of goods demands, on the introduction of cultural standards of business ethics and quality, that a limit to self-interest be defined.[64]

The significance of money and value-commitment lies in the fact that through their characteristics of being institutionally anchored and possessing specific qualities they become the conservators of the institutional cores of their respective subsystems, while through their characteristics of circulability, symbolization and generalization they make possible the interpenetration of their systems of origin with other systems while protecting their own system's integrity. The institutional binding of money to the order of property and of value-commitments to the value pattern is the basis of the differentiation of the two systems. The fact that these media circulate permits the entrance of economic demands into the cultural system and of cultural demands into the economic system. Their symbolic and generalized character is what allows them to make connections with the concrete demands of systems other than their system of origin. It is only the generalized character of money that permits the distinctive linking of differentiated subsystems which we refer to as interpenetration. As a generalized medium of interchange, money can be used however one likes, in accordance with concrete cultural standards, in the service of the goal of consumption. From its anchoring in the economic system develops the external space of its application to the goals of consumption. Culturally formed desires for consumption provide the material which is given *form* through submission to the laws of the economically rational employment of money. If there were no generalized medium, there would be no basis for rational economic calculation and economic activity would be overwhelmed by concrete standards of consumption that would be inaccessible to rational calculation. We can see this in all primordial forms of economy which lack that coherence which can be provided only by the use of money.[65]

As a generalized medium, value-commitments can control action in all situations of labour and production. The anchoring of this medium in the cultural value pattern gives to value-commitments that constant, invariable meaning through which action in these situations does not occur according to mere whim, but remains always tied to the cultural value pattern. The development of generalized value-commitments allows the shaping of economic activity by the cultural value pattern. If the commitments to values are too concrete, it will be impossible to transfer them to any other areas of life. In the other areas, purely internal laws, such as the rules of self-interest, would then be free to hold sway. The generalization of value-commitments, though, permits them to be specified in concrete situations in such a way as to be harmonizable with economic demands. Economic demands provide in this case the material of action which through generalized value-commitments is given ethical form but is not stifled by its demands.

The control exercised on the relation between the economic and social-cultural (fiduciary) systems by money and value-commitments as media of interchange allows for an expansion of the range of both systems, without their interfering with one another or one overwhelming the other. By the creation of credit (through banks in the economic system and through educational institutions in the cultural system), zero-sum conditions are overcome.[66] Within both systems, an increase leads to increased capacity for production. Money can be invested and applied to a wider range of interests. Value-commitments can be invested, and the sphere in which they can be validly implemented can be expanded, for example, if the socialization performed by educational institutions can be opened up to wider areas of the specification of value-commitments.

Analysing relations of interchange between subsystems by means of the theory of media permits us to grasp such dynamic processes as deflation or inflation of media.[67] Deflation and inflation are crises which indicate a decrease in the ability of the system in question to fulfil its function. Deflation is a decrease in the demand for goods, as this is expressed in money, which ultimately leads to a corresponding decrease in the capacity for production. In like manner, a deflation of value-commitments is a decrease in the potential breadth of implementation of general values; it impairs the ability of the general value pattern to shape action in widely disparate areas of life. Monetary inflation is caused by a rise in demand which is not followed by an increase in production. In the same way, inflation of value-commitments occurs when the claims of value-commitments on various areas of life are not accompanied by a corresponding ability of these value-commitments ethically to shape action in these spheres.

The development of generalized value-commitments naturally has specific presuppositions in the organization of the socialization process. Only when successive stages of socialization into interpenetrating subsystems trigger that interpenetration between the cultural, social and personality systems of which Parsons had already had intimations in *The Social System* (1951) can value-commitments be sufficiently generalized. The formation of value-commitments as a general medium of interchange already presupposes, therefore, an interpenetration, which must occur before the medium can raise the level of combined differentiation and interpenetration of the social subsystems.

The swallowing up of economic theory by the general theory of action opened up for Parsons a new way to refine his theory, a way which indicated to him the future development of the theory. In the wake of *Economy and Society,* Parsons added to the theory, as further media of interchange, political power for the political system (1963), influence for the societal community (1963), and value-commitments for the cultural system (1968). Through all of this, he remained firm in the idea that these media of interchange were to be viewed as mechanisms which secured the interpenetration of subsystems and their simultaneous differentiation.

Let us now examine the reciprocal relationships between the other social subsystems.[68] In the context of the relationship between the *social-cultural* and *political* systems we find the specification of cultural value patterns and the generalization and legitimation of collective goals. Here the *operative responsibility* of political representatives for the implementation of cultural values in political decisions represents a factor input from the political to the social-cultural system, controlled by political power. The exercise of political responsibility is dependent on the transfer of political power. Nevertheless the integration of political decisions into the cultural frame of reference, or their exclusion from it, is a matter for social-cultural discursive procedures. In the opposite direction the *legitimation of authority* is a factor input from the social-cultural to the political system, controlled by value-commitments (arguments). Authority is not able to legitimize itself. It is only ever legitimized in as far as social-cultural discursive procedures allow it to be justified through rational argument based on general values. Turning now to the level of products, the *moral responsibility* of political representatives *for collective interest* should be seen as a product output from the political and into the social-cultural system. Cultural political decisions determine a frame of reference within which social-cultural action in schools, universities, theatres, concert halls and the like, takes place. The way in which these products are 'consumed' is determined, in the context of social-cultural action, by value-commitments (arguments). In the opposite direction the *legality of powers of office* should be viewed as a product output from the social-cultural to the political system. The legality of decision-making authority is dependent on the ability to justify it rationally and discursively in the context of the cultural pattern of values. In political action this legality of decision-making authority is consumed in every-day decisions, for when they are carried out this implies the application of political power.

The reciprocal relationship between the *social-cultural system* and the *communal system* is extremely significant for the institutionalization of value patterns. In this context *justifications for the allocation of loyalties* controlled by influence (commitment) represent a factor input from the communal and into the social-cultural system. This is a matter of distributing loyalties toward interpretations of meaning, norms, expressions and cognitions which are themselves not rationally based, but are supported by the commitment to a community. A factor input from the social-cultural to the communal system consists of *commitments to valued association,* controlled by value-commitments (arguments). Membership of particular communal associations rests not on compulsion, but on free will and on a consensually held appreciation of these associations (clubs, political parties and the like) maintained through rational argument. In terms of products, *commitments to common value* are a product output from the communal to the social-cultural system. This gives expression to the fact that allegiance to common values ultimately cannot rest upon rational argument, but can only emerge from the affective attachment to those values of the members in a community. Within social-cultural action these values are nevertheless brought to bear on action through value-commitments (arguments). A product output in the opposite direction, from the social-cultural to the communal system, is the *legitimation of claims to loyalties.* That is to say, loyalty requirements need to be rationally and discursively justified by reference to common values, and do not simply come about as a result of affectual attachment. Within this social-cultural frame of reference the fulfilment of claims to loyalty is nevertheless based, in communal action, on influence (commitments).

Let us next examine the reciprocal relationship between the *political* and *economic* systems, within which the mobilization of resources and collective goal determination have to be integrated. In this instance the *control of productivity* through economic activity is a factor input from the economic to the political system, controlled by money. Political programmes cannot be put into practice in the absence of this economic basis. In the political system, economic resources are deployed in the pursuit of collective goals. In the opposite direction the *opportunity for effectiveness* is a factor input controlled by political power, from the political and into the economic system. The legislature determines the framework for effective economic action. A prerequisite for economic action is a predictable order which it cannot create of itself, hence it is dependent on the political implementation of such an order. On the product level, *commitments of services to the societal collectivity* can be seen as a product output from the economic to the political system. Services performed by public employees, or by private undertakings on public contracts, are economically motivated and provided according to economic criteria, yet their application within the political system is controlled by political power. In the opposite direction, the *allocation of fluid financial resources* is a product of the political system determined by the monetary policy of the politically accountable central banks, of governments and of parliaments. Nevertheless the deployment of capital resources in the economic system is controlled by money and by economic criteria.

A particularly characteristic example of the theory of generalized media is provided by the analysis of the political support system as the zone of interpenetration between the *political system* and the *community system*. This zone of interpenetration forms in the relation between citizens and political representatives. There is an interchange of factors in *interest demands* and *policy decisions*, and an interchange of products in *political support* and *leadership responsibility*, which are mediated by political power and influence (commitment). As long as the articulation of political interests relies on the wielding of influence, which was created and generalized to serve the societal community (is bound to the commitment to a community), the articulation of political interests is not simply a question of naked power, but is connected to the legitimation of the community. The articulation of interests provides the matter which is given form by the reliance of political decision-making on political power – for example, by the reliance on majority rule. The more political support is conferred according to the criterion of the performance of the political representatives on behalf of the societal community, the more is the acquisition of political power determined by the order of the community. Conversely, leadership responsibility is not an affair of pure power politics either, at least to the extent that it must rely on influence (commitment) in order to be effective for more than a short time. The political power which can be thus acquired on the political market, as it were, is here the matter which is given *form* through being connected to the criteria of the acquisition of influence. Political support must be understood as a product output from the communal to the political system. This support is 'consumed' within the political system when decisions are carried out through the use of political power. Conversely the responsibility of political leadership represents a product output from the political to the community system. It is in communal action that this responsibility, closely tied to influence (commitment) is 'consumed'.

Finally, the reciprocal relationship between the *economic system* and the *community system* is concerned with the allocation of resources according to communal standards. *The assertion of claims to resources* is in this case the factor input from the economic to the community system, determined by money. Claims made on resources are economically motivated and articulated in terms of money. Conversely *standards for allocation of resources* represent a factor input controlled by influence (commitment), from the community system to the economic system. These normative standards need to be rooted in commitments to a community. On the product level, *economic grounds for justifying resource claims* are a product output from the economic to the community system. The economic criterion of scarcity serves as the frame of reference on which the justification of claims in communal action is based. Within this frame of reference, the justification of claims is supported by influence in the community (by the commitment to the community). In the opposite direction, the *ranking of resource claims* in budgetary procedures represents a product output from the community system to the economic system. The criteria which allow such a ranking to be constructed need to be both normatively and communally rooted. Within economic action, consumption of resources provided through a budget is economically motivated, and guided by money.

As we have now seen, through the introduction of the generalized media of interchange, Parsons achieved a further refinement of the differentiation and interpenetration of social subsystems. The theory of the generalized media of interchange is thus a logical step in the development of the theory of action, which is based on the dualistic conception of the system of action as a zone of interpenetration of conditional and categorical action orientations. Of particular significance in the development we are considering here is the discovery that money as the medium of the economic system functions both as the bearer of the institutional core of that system and as the means by which the economic rationality institutionalized in the economic system penetrates into other social subsystems. If money assumes a special role in the establishment of relations of differentiation and interpenetration, then the other subsystems must develop media with a similar capability if they are to maintain an equal status with regard to the processes of differentiation and penetration. That the development of generalized value-commitments permits the differentiation of the social-cultural system and the penetration of other areas of life by the cultural value pattern is one proof of the correctness of this statement of the function of the generalized media of interchange. It was not, therefore, from the purely economic properties of money that Parsons extrapolated when he formulated the theory of the generalized media of interchange – it was instead the logic of the analysis of the relation of interpenetration, which always undergirded the theory of action. It was the classification of the theory of money within this theoretical framework which opened the way to the general theory of the media of interchange. Without the help of this framework, there would have been no bridge from money to the other media of interchange.[69] The theory of media represents a new level of theoretical explanatory ability if it allows us to use the institutionalization of generalized and symbolic media which guide action to explain higher levels of the integration of individual freedom and social order than we were able to account for previously. The questions which the theory of media allows us to formulate are bound to the same fundamental normative idea of modernity which was present in the theory of action from the beginning:

'This is the theme that the media constitute mechanisms whereby an action system is able to achieve a new level of "value-added" combination. This implies, on the one hand, a freedom of action for its individual component member-units, but on the other hand, new mechanisms of control which make the functioning of such freedoms feasible at increasingly generalized levels.'[70]

2.6.2. The interpenetration of the action subsystems: The American University

The elaboration of the theory of the generalized media of interchange in terms of the social system came to a close in 1968 with the publication of Parsons's essay on value-commitments. The development of the theory from here took place on the level of the system of action as a whole. Parsons worked out this part of the theory in the course of the comprehensive examination of the educational system, especially the university, as the core of the cognitive and professional complexes, an examination he made between 1968 and 1974. Here the generalized media of interchange became 'definition of the situation' for the cultural system, 'affect' for the social system, 'performance capacity' for the personality system and 'intelligence' for the behavioural system.[71]

The generalized media of action can be related to meaning patterns, as each is oriented to the fulfilment of such a meaning pattern. This fulfilment is in turn measured against standards of value. The basis for the foregoing is that meaningfulness is the distinctive hallmark of human action:[72]

- *Definitions of the situation* are oriented toward the *constitutive grounds of meaning* of the human condition. The appropriate standard of value is the *value rationality (Wertrationalität)* of action, grounded in moral authority. This definition of the standard, reaching as it does into the domain of social action, could be more generally constructed, and more closely linked to the cultural dimension, if replaced by the expression 'meaningfulness of action in a cultural framework'.
- *Affect* (affective attachment) is oriented toward the *institutionalization of meaning* relevant to society. In this case the value standard is the *unity in meaning* (harmonization) of identities based on social imperatives. This signifies the integration of the individuality and sociality of man.

- *Personal performance capacity* is oriented toward the *internalization of relevant meaning* for the personality. *Means-end rationality (Zweck-rationalität)* serves as the standard of value, based on practicality, that is, the possibility to carry out actions.
- *Intelligence* is oriented toward *grounds for cognitive validity and significance*. In this case the value standard is the *cognitive rationality* of action, grounded in cognitive standards.

What this theoretical accomplishment means for the analysis of relations of interpenetration is shown most clearly by the theoretical consideration of the cognitive complex in *The American University* (1973), a monograph coauthored by Parsons and G. M. Platt. On the level of the system of action, the university appears as the core of the cognitive complex,[73] which forms a zone of interpenetration of all four action subsystems, with priority given to cognitive rationality, and which includes all four media of the action system in relations of interchange.[74]

Cognitive learning and the acquisition of competence are the primary achievements of the personality, and these in turn require the application of *performance capacity* as a generalized medium, which determines the ends of action in this learning process. The acquisition of cognitive competence presupposes further capacities, which do not lie within the sphere of the personality system. There must also be present an obligation to standards of rationality, which can come about only through their institutionalization in a social system and through 'the attachment of the individual to the group' as Durkheim put it. The penetration of the social system into the other subsystems requires that it be generalized through a medium of interchange that we can call *affect*. The affective grounding of cognitive rationality, the generalization of affective ties as the medium of solidarity relations, and the role these processes play in the development of a pluralistic society – these are the real subjects of Parsons and Platt's study of student socialization. Every learning process presupposes, to the extent that it is intended to be generalizable and communicable, the penetration of that process by a common framework. In the case of cognitive learning, this is the function of knowledge which is anchored in the cultural system and therefore lies outside the personality system. The penetration of cultural knowledge into different personality systems requires a 'relay mechanism' which permits abstraction from concrete knowledge and which also preserves the identity of this knowledge, not allowing it to be completely 'personalized'. This is possible only through a generalization of knowledge beyond concrete situations; *definition of the situation* as a generalized medium of interchange has to develop as a response to this need. It guarantees a common overarching perspective on all concrete situations in which knowledge is instantiated. Knowledge can then be specified and applied to various problems without losing its identity. It can take on a multiplicity of specifications while its essential core stays consistent. Here again, zero-sum conditions are overcome through the control of the relations of interchange by generalized media. Beyond these specific capacities of the personality system, the social system and the cultural system, cognitive learning also requires certain other capacities – the ability to perceive, to symbolize, to remember – which originate in the behavioural system. Progress in cognitive learning can be made only when these abilities are united with the capacities anchored in the other subsystems. That means that these capacities must also be generalized to be able to enter into multifaceted relations with the concrete products of the other subsystems – concrete knowledge, concrete obligations to rationality, concrete personal goals – and use them as matter on which they impose a form. This generalizing capacity we can call *intelligence*; it raises the level of penetration of the cultural, social and personality systems by the behavioural system.[75] Clearly, achievements in the area of knowledge are based only partially on pure intelligence. It is not the case, as is still widely believed, that given complete equality of opportunity, the intelligence of individuals would become the sole factor in the distribution of income, position, power and prestige (see Figure 11).

The development of generalized media of interchange as a mechanism for connecting differentiated subsystems is here also a condition of the interpenetration of subsystems. The media allow the subsystems to develop simultaneously without mutual interference and thus provide a crucial prerequisite for the development of the cognitive complex in general and cognitive competence in particular. On the level of the general system of action, the theory of media is a significant theoretical tool for the exploration of relations of interpenetration.

Moving now to an examination of the reciprocal relationships between the individual action subsystems, we can distinguish the following zones of interpenetration:

L ⟷ A   From the interpenetration of knowledge, controlled by definition of the situation, and learning capacities, controlled by intelligence, we observe the *enhancement and implementation of knowledge*.

L ⟷ G   From the interpenetration of knowledge, controlled by definition of the situation, and cognitive competence, controlled by performance capacity, the *generalization of competence* and *specification of knowledge* come to light.

L ⟷ I   From the interpenetration of knowledge, controlled by definition of

THE CONTINUITY OF THE DEVELOPMENT

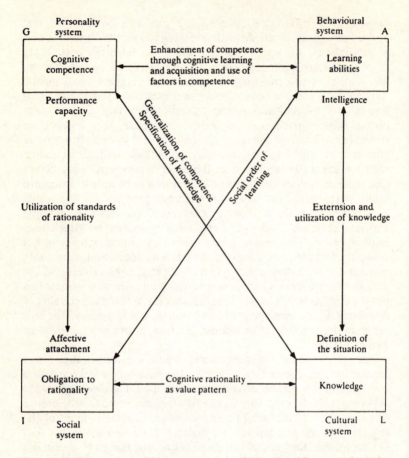

Figure 11 The zones of interpenetration of the cognitive complex, the cultural-adaptive aspect of the action system (adapted from T. Parsons and G. M. Platt, *The American University*, Cambridge, Mass.: Harvard University Press, 1973, Figure 2.5, p. 57)

the situation, and the obligation to rationality, controlled by affective attachment, we obtain *cognitive rationality as a value pattern.*

G ⟷ A   From the interpenetration of cognitive competence, controlled by performance capacity, and learning capacities, controlled by intelligence, the *enhancement of competence through cognitive learning* and *the acquisition and use of factors of competence* emerge.

G ⟷ I   From the interpenetration of cognitive competence, controlled by

94

performance capacity, and the obligation to rationality, controlled by affective attachment, we get the *utilization of standards of rationality*.

I ⟵⟶ A   From the interpenetration of obligation to rationality, controlled by affective attachment, and learning capacities, controlled by intelligence, the result is the *social ordering of learning*.

Let us now examine the above reciprocal relationships using the paradigm of interchange media[76] (see Figure 12).

The reciprocal relationship between the *cultural* and the *behavioural* systems is the most important aspect of the cognitive complex. The *cognitive standards of validity and significance* are cultural presuppositions (controlled by definition of the situation) which enter the behavioural system as input factors. Without such standards rooted in cultural patterns, the intelligent creation of knowledge in the behavioural system is impossible. Conversely, *judgements of the relevance of cognitive standards* in the creation of knowledge are a factor input guided by intelligence, from the behavioural to the cultural system. The application of cultural standards requires the use of intelligence; instances of application must then be reintegrated into the cultural pattern. In terms of product, the *demand for different categories of knowledge* is a product output from the cultural to the behavioural system. The type of knowledge demanded is a matter of how the use of intelligence is engrained in the culture at large. Nevertheless the search for knowledge mobilizes behavioural mechanisms and is determined by intelligence. The converse product output, from the behavioural system to the cultural system, is *knowledge* itself. The involvement of knowledge in cultural patterns is in turn controlled by definition of the situation.[77]

In the context of the reciprocal relationship between the *cultural* and *personality* systems, identity and personal style develop according to expressive standards. *Patterns of personal style* in action are in this case the factor input from the personality to the cultural system, controlled by personal performance capacity. Personal styles of behaviour, in the cultural context, are in turn translated into behavioural styles generally defined by the culture. Conversely *expressive standards* are a factor input guided by definition of the situation, from the cultural and into the personality system. Expressive standards which are culturally defined and generalized are processed within the personality system into personal styles of behaviour. On the product level, the *establishment of identity* is fed as an output from the personality system into the cultural system. Identity can only be personally developed. In as far as it is embedded in a further cultural frame of reference determined

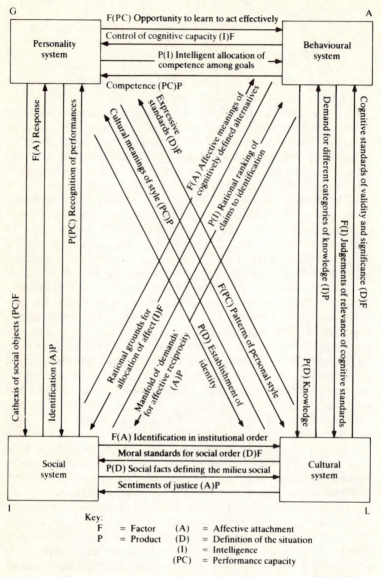

Figure 12 The input-output paradigm of the action system (based on T. Parsons and G. M. Platt, *The American University*, Cambridge, Mass.: Harvard University Press, 1973, Figure A.7, p. 439)

by definition of the situation, personal identity is subject to cultural definition and generalization. In the opposite direction, from the cultural to the personality system, *cultural meanings of behavioural styles* should be seen as product output. The generalizable meaning of behavioural styles is rooted in culture, and it is 'consumed' in personal action by the application of personal performance capacity in 'meaningful' personal styles of behaviour.

In the reciprocal relationship between *cultural* and *social* systems we find the foundations of a moral order. The institutionalization of normative culture belongs in this context. It is here, then, that the common *identification in an institutional order*, based on social solidarity, forms a factor input from the social to the cultural system, regulated by affective attachment. Thus the cultural pattern has a normative frame of reference set for it by way of the social context, which in turn can be generalized in the cultural context. Conversely, *moral standards for social order* should be seen as the factor input, regulated by definition of the situation, from the cultural and into the social system. The part played by culture in this case is the generalization of social norms into universal moral standards, which in the social context are translated into moral action. The first of the product outputs, fed from the social system to the cultural system, are *social facts defining the social milieu*. These social facts are 'consumed' by the cultural system in as far as they are 'culturally illuminated', that is culturally defined, on the basis of definition of the situation. Conversely, *sentiments of justice* should be seen as a product output of the cultural system for the social system. Sentiments of justice are based on cultural, normative definitions of the situation. In social action, they are 'consumed' by linking them to affective attachments, using them in every-day situations to reach decisions.

The essence of the reciprocal relationship between the *behavioural system* and the *personality system* is the organization of how action is actually carried out. In this context, *control of cognitive capacity* forms a factor input, guided by intelligence, from the behavioural to the personality system. The mobilization of cognitive capacities is a matter of intelligence, and in the personality system this is translated into goal-oriented action. Conversely the *provision of learning opportunities to act effectively* represents a factor input controlled by personal performance capacity, fed from the personality to the behavioural system. The extent to which an individual receives such chances depends on the dispositions of the personality and the goals it sets. On the product level, the individual's *competence* is the output provided by the behavioural system for the personality system. Competence depends upon intelligent learning, but personal performance capacity is a necessary factor for it to be translated into goal-oriented action. The equivalent product output in the other direction, from the personality to the behavioural system, is the *intelligent allocation of competence among different goals*. This is a question of the distribution of competence, in terms both of substance and of time, between the various goals; this distribution depends on personal dispositions and is then consumed in the execution of action by the use of intelligence.

The reciprocal relationship between the *personality system* and the *social system* should be regarded as a constituent element of social inclusion and the motivation of the individual. In this context it is the *cathexis of social objects*, the affectual attitude to social objects, which serves as a factor input from the personality system to the social system, and it is controlled by performance capacity. An affectual attitude toward social objects, that is toward other individuals or groups, but also toward values and norms, necessitates the personal activation of organically originated feelings, hence the need for the individual to apply his performance capacity. Conversely the *response* of the counterparts in social interaction to the individual's attitudes and actions forms the factor input from the social to the personality system, guided by affective attachments. Without this affectively based response from his counterpart, an individual is unable to develop confidence and hence begin to act competently. In production terms, the individual's *identification with others as the presumptive basis of solidarity* constitutes a product output from the personality system to the social system. The individual needs to activate his feeling and dispositions to be able to identify with other parties. This identification is consumed in social action, and is mobilized by general affective attachments. In the opposite direction, the *recognition* of an individual's *performances* by the constituents of his social environment should be seen as the product output of the social system for the personality system. To be confident in his action, the individual is reliant on this recognition, and 'consumes' it by mobilizing personal performance capacity.

The reciprocal relationship between the *behavioural system* and the *social system* is concerned with the allocation of rewards and with the affective basis of cognitive learning. Here *rational grounds for the allocation of affective attachments* signify a factor input from the behavioural to the social system, controlled by intelligence. The individual is not ascriptively tied to groups, but is able to choose membership of associations of any kind freely and on rational grounds; thus he enters rationally into new affective bonds. Conversely, *affective meanings of cognitively defined alternatives* are the factor input from the social system into the behavioural system, supported by affective attachment. In order to be relevant to and obligatory for cognitive processes, alternatives of action must have an affective significance for the actor which has a social basis. On a product level, the *manifold of 'demands' for affective reciprocity* are a product output fed from the behavioural to the social system. This focuses on the fact that a vast variety of types of behaviour can be mobilized from an individual's behavioural repertoire, and that these are translated by means of affectual support from the social environment into regular action. This social 'consumption' of the behavioural repertoire is determined by affective attachment. In the opposite direction the establishment of rational *ranking of claims to identification* should be interpreted as a product output from the social system to the behavioural system. The individuals, groups, ideas, etc. with which an individual chooses to identify, and the order of priorities emerging in the process, are a product of affectual attachment in social action. It is in cognitive learning processes, controlled by intelligence, that these identifications are 'consumed'.

In their investigation of the American university, Parsons and Platt use this method of analysing relations of interpenetration to explore the possibility of certain crises, either of inflation or deflation, which may afflict the various media.[78] In so doing, they demonstrate the aptness of this theoretical schema for clarifying dynamic processes. The modern educational institution can be viewed as an intelligence bank, and specific educational programmes can be viewed as firms in which intelligence can be invested, in order to increase the 'supply' of intelligence or to produce knowledge. Parsons interprets the crisis which struck American education in the 1960s, the high point of which was the student protests near the end of the decade, as the consequence of an inflationary phase followed by a deflationary phase which led to a new consolidation of the educational system. The period of student protest was preceded by a period of rapidly increasing investment of intelligence in the educational system. Intelligence was expended in a great undertaking to expand cognitive competence. This led to an overinvestment in cognitive rationality, creating expectations which educational institutions were unable to satisfy, particularly since these expectations had a moral and expressive component. This was an inflation of intelligence; intelligence lost its worth, in the sense that an increase in the supply of intelligence made available for cognitive ends was not accompanied by a corresponding increase in the ability to 'cash in' the increased expectations.

The consequence of the decrease in value of investments in cognitive intelligence was the withdrawal of invested intelligence from cognitive concerns and its 'deposit' in intellectual attitudes which met moral and expressive needs. This withdrawal of intelligence from cognitive undertakings was a deflationary phase, which manifested itself in decreased expectations of intelligence

THE CONTINUITY OF THE DEVELOPMENT

invested in cognitive concerns. This in turn led to a shortage of investments of intelligence in the cognitive undertakings of educational institutions. The characteristic expression of this deflationary phase was the student protest, in which the students withdrew their adherence from the university and invested their intelligence in moral and expressive undertakings. The ebbing of this phase led, in Parsons's understanding of it, to a consolidation which was marked by an increased investment in cognitive concerns and a new grounding of cognitive rationality in moral and expressive standards.[79] And it is only under such conditions as the increase in the long-term investment of intelligence – in which educational institutions play a special role as intelligence banks – that an increase in cognitive, moral and expressive products is possible and zero-sum conditions are overcome. An increase in cognitive rationality in such cases cannot exclude an increase in moral rationality. Inflationary and deflationary developments strengthen the incompatibility between these two symbolic orientations and create a zero-sum condition between them. The analysis made possible by the theory of media clarifies the conditions under which the threshold of incompatibility can be pushed back and zero-sum conditions can be overcome. Therefore the theory represents a real step forward in the working out of the fundamental ideas which were present at the very beginnings of the theory of action.

2.6.3 The interpenetration of the subsystems of the human condition: Action Theory and the Human Condition

In his last years, Parsons added the final building block to his theory of action: the extension of the theory in order to understand the interpenetration of the system of action with its environment.[80] The whole framework was now entitled the system of the human condition, in which the system of action performed the integrative function, the telic system performed the latent pattern-maintenance function, the system of the human organism performed the function of goal attainment (selection), and the physicochemical system performed the adaptive function. Again, evolutionary development signifies here the interpenetration of these analytically delimited subsystems, which is facilitated by generalized media permitting the accomplishments of one subsystem to be carried over into the others. The media of the systems which constitute the environment of the system of action are not symbolic in nature, but they are generalized mechanisms, and it is this property which allows them to impose form on the concrete material of the other subsystems.[81]

The analysis of the human condition is anthropocentric in its conception, that is, it is viewed from the standpoint of the human actor. The subsystems and their reciprocal relationships are analysed in terms of their significance for the human actor. We may now examine these subsystems in more detail.

The telic system is formed by the transcendental conditions of possibility of human existence. To this system belong, for example, space and time, the categories of human understanding, the categorical imperative, and the categories of judgement, in the sense which these terms have in Kant's transcendental philosophy. Here we also find the possible attitudes which man can take toward the world, attitudes which Parsons extracted from Weber's comparative sociology of religion and classified into four fundamental kinds by using the two axes of innerworldly–otherworldly and ascetic–mystical. What we are talking about here is a typology of attitudes which as transcendental conditions determine the specific mode of the meaningfulness of the world. We are not saying that it is necessary for human life to be guided by one or another concrete, existing religion. We are instead talking about the more general assumptions that humans have made about the meaning of life and about the striving for meaning which is one of the fundamental characteristics of human existence. When we see today in the realization of the normative idea of modernity the culmination of the meaning of social development, this gives a form of legitimation to our institutions through the giving of a specific answer to very general questions concerning the constitution of meaning as a transcendental condition of our existence.[82] The medium which is anchored in the telic system and makes possible the penetration of this system into the other subsystems of the human condition is transcendental ordering, to be understood as a generalized capacity to establish order which can be applied to any range of empirical objects whatever.[83]

The system of action consists of action which is intentional, oriented toward meaning. The medium localized in this system is meaning, and the structure of the medium is provided by language. Man's orientation to the world which surrounds him is determined by symbols. The penetration of the other subsystems of the human condition by this fundamental character of human action is made possible by the fact that meaning as a generalized medium allows form to be imposed on any matter whatsoever according to the standards of symbol formation.[84]

The *human organism* is to be understood as a goal-attaining system, the relation of which to its environment is controlled by cybernetic feedback processes. The medium which operates here is health, which is a generalized expression for very different characteristics of specific parts of the organism. Health can be acquired, increased and used up. It is the medium through which matter supplied by neighbouring subsystems can be given form in accordance with the needs of the functioning of the organism.[85]

Finally, the *physicochemical system* is the least ordered subsystem of the human condition. It functions as a source of resources for the entire systems and it is subject to the control of the other subsystems, which attempt to make its resources useful for themselves. This control is exercised through the media of the other subsystems. Through the transcendental constitution of order, there first emerges a recognizable order of nature; through meaningful categorization and treatment, nature is rendered comprehensible. Through the medium of health, physicochemical nature is adapted to the demands of the organism. The medium which effects the penetration of the other subsystems by the physicochemical system is the empirical ordering, in the sense of a reality governed by empirical causal laws which, as particular, specific laws, are to be distinguished from the transcendental order of space, time and causality.[86]

From the perspective of human action, the media of interchange in the system of the human condition are related to general categories of orientation, the fulfilment of which is measured by standards of evaluation:[87]

- *Empirical ordering* is linked to the category of *causality*, as the general frame of reference for empirical ordering. The relevant evaluation standard from the human point of view is the *adequacy of causal explanations.*
- *Health* is related to the orientation category of *teleonomy*, which represents a general frame of reference for the functioning of the organism. In this case the evaluation standard from the human viewpoint is *diagnosis*.
- *Meaning* is related to the orientation category of *generativity*. Generativity is the frame of reference for the creation of symbolic meaning and for language, which allows the creation within its system of an infinite variety of linguistic symbolization, all from the same basic linguistic elements. The relevant evaluation standard in this case is the *interpretation* (Verstehen) of expressions of meaning.
- *Transcendental ordering* is related to the orientation category of *transcendentality*. The latter is a general frame of reference for meaningful human existence. From the human perspective this frame of reference is the most general basis for natural order, organic order and order in action. The relevant evaluation standards from the human viewpoint comprise *transcendental argumentation* (or logic), in the sense of Kant's three critiques of reason.

In the light of this theory of the human condition, every empirical phenomenon is the product of the type of relationship pertaining between the subsystems. This relationship varies between one-sided accommodation, mutual isolation, reconciliation, interpenetration and one-sided dominance. Evolutionary upgrading necessitates mutual penetration between the differentiated subsystems, a mutual penetration regulated by the appropriate media. The securing of a functioning state of the human organism requires, for example, the penetration of the adjoining systems by the medium of health, which orients these systems toward the needs of the human organism. This control by the conditions of the human organism cannot, however, overcome the internal laws of the other subsystems. Instead, they relate to the functional needs of the organism as conditioning factors, so that causal laws, transcendental order and symbolization impose a form on the material of the organism through their respective media.

If we examine individually the reciprocal relationships between the subsystems of the human condition, we can identify the following zones of interpenetration (see Figure 13):

L ⟷ A From the interpenetration of transcendental conditions, regulated by transcendental ordering, and physicochemical processes, regulated by empirical ordering, we obtain the *constitution of natural order*.

L ⟷ G From the interpenetration of transcendental conditions, regulated by transcendental ordering, and organic goal orientation, regulated by health, the *purposiveness of organic life* is formed.

L ⟷ I From the interpenetration of transcendental conditions, regulated by transcendental ordering, and action, regulated by meaning, the *constitution of the order of action* results.

G ⟷ A From the interpenetration of organic goal orientation, regulated by health, and physicochemical processes, regulated by empirical ordering, we obtain the *mobilization of physicochemical resources for organic life*.

G ⟷ I From the interpenetration of organic goal orientation, regulated by health, and action, regulated by meaning, *the motivation of action* comes to light.

I ⟷ A From the interpenetration of action, regulated by meaning, and physicochemical processes, regulated by empirical ordering, *the meaning and cultivation of nature* is formed.

We can now take the step of examining the reciprocal relationships between the above subsystems from the perspective of the generalized media paradigm (see Figure 14).

The reciprocal relationship between the *telic system* and the *physicochemical system* is the subject of Kant's *Critique of Pure Reason*. The order of nature is a product of the interpenetration of the telic and physicochemical systems, and one can break this interpenetration down into an interchange of factors and an interchange of products. In the interchange of factors, the *categories of the understanding* penetrate the physicochemical order through the medium of transcendental ordering and, conversely, *sense data*

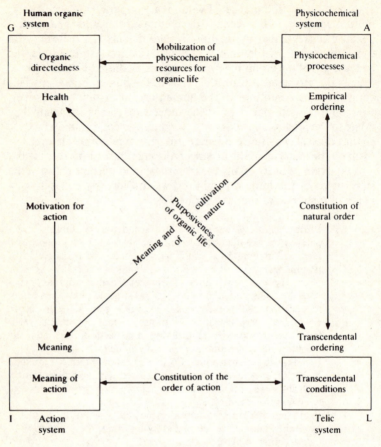

Figure 13 The human condition system's zones of interpenetration

penetrate the telic system through the empirical constitution of order. In the interchange of products, the *generalization of knowledge* as the achievement of the telic system penetrates the physicochemical system, but this generalized knowledgc is bound to the conditions of the empirical order of causal laws. Conversely, the *orderliness of nature* penetrates the telic system, but remains bound to the conditions of transcendental order.[88]

Parsons conceptualizes the relation between the *telic system* and the *system of the human organism* according to the model provided by Kant's *Critique of Judgement*. We are dealing here with the constitution of an organic order, with the goal directedness of organic processes within the framework of an encompassing order.

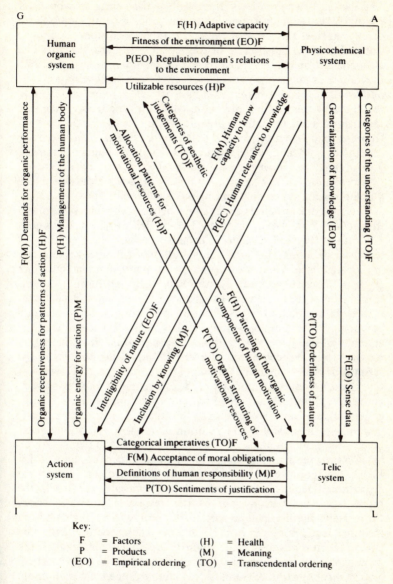

Figure 14 The input–output paradigm of the human condition system (based on T. Parsons, 'A paradigm of the human condition', in *Action Theory and the Human Condition*, New York: Free Press, 1978, Figure 5, p.407)

The factual organic order is the result of the degree to which, for example, human intervention in organic processes is integrated with or cuts against the grain of the constitutive conditions of organic order. From the perspective of the media paradigm, *categories of aesthetic judgement*, regulated by transcendental ordering, penetrate the human organic system as a factor input from the telic system. The *patterning of the organic components of human motivation*, regulated by the medium of health, penetrates the telic system as a factor input from the human organic system. As the product output from the telic system, *allocation patterns for motivational resources*, dependent on health, penetrate the system of the human organism. The organic *structuring of motivational resources*, dependent on transcendental ordering, represents a product output from the human organic system penetrating the telic system.

Parsons conceptualizes the relation between the telic system and the *action system* according to the model provided by Kant's *Critique of Practical Reason*.[89] The most fundamental conditions of the order of action, that is, the constitution of action as meaningful, are located here. The various rules that apply to human action are given a consistent meaning through their anchoring in this component of the human condition system. The obligatory character of the order of action results from its anchoring in the community component of the action system, that is at the 'I' extremity of the action system. The constitution of *meaningful order* in action requires the interpenetration of both 'L' and 'I' components in the system of the human condition. This is the general sense of Durkheim's thesis that morality requires a religious foundation and, conversely, that religion requires a moral foundation.[90] In this context also belongs Weber's thesis that the orderedness of action is determined essentially by the solution man has found at any given time to the problem of the constitution of meaning in the fact of the tension between a perfect ideal order and an imperfect real world.[91] From the point of view of the media paradigm, *categorical imperatives*, regulated by transcendental ordering, are the factor input from the telic system to the system of human action. Conversely the *acceptance of moral obligations*, regulated by meaning, is a factor input from the action system penetrating the telic system. *Definitions of human responsibility*, tied to meaning, are the product output from the telic system penetrating the action system. *Sentiments of justification* in action, tied to transcendental ordering, are the product output of the action system penetrating the telic system.

Henderson's conception of the 'fitness of the environment' provides the model for the relation between the *physicochemical system* and the *system of the human organism*.[92] Like all systems, the organism and physicochemical nature can stand in various relations to each other, of which interpenetration is only one. For the human organism, interpenetration with physicochemical nature means the active use of this nature, but not its exploitation. From the point of view of the generalized media paradigm, the *fitness of the environment*, as a factor input from the physicochemical system regulated by empirical ordering, penetrates the system of the human organism. And it is the *adaptive capacity* of the human organism which is a factor input from that system, regulated by the medium of health, penetrating the physicochemical system. The product output from the physicochemical to the human organic system is made up of organically *utilizable resources*, linked to the medium of health. The organic *regulation of man's relations to the environment* is a product output of the human organic system dependent on empirical ordering which penetrates the physicochemical system. This is the process of interchange between the organism and the physico-chemical composition of nature.

The interpenetration of the *action system* and the *system of the human organism* provides Parsons with a new access to the work of Freud.[93] Here we find the context for the organic element of the theory of socialization. The interpenetration of the structure of organic drives with intentional action is possible only through a successful socialization process, in the course of which the individual becomes capable of autonomous action as a personality. The personality, as a zone of interpenetration, is distinguishable both from the structure of organic drives, on the one hand, and from the material, social and symbolic environment, on the other. In the interpretation of the generalized media paradigm, *demands for organic performance* (for example, schooling in proper hygiene) are a factor input from the action system, regulated by meaning (articulated, say, through language), and penetrating the human organic system. Conversely, *receptiveness for patterns of action*, a factor input from the human organic system regulated by health, penetrates the action system. As the action system's product output, *the management of the human body*, a meaning-oriented system of guidance dependent upon health, that is upon the capabilities of the body, penetrates the human organic system. Conversely *the organic energy for action*, tied to meaning, is the product output from the human organic to the action system.

Out of the relation between the *system of action* and the *physicochemical system* there arises 'cultivated nature', nature as it has been shaped and formed by the human hand. To what extent in any concrete case order or lack of order is actually present depends on the extent to which man's treatment of nature is integrated into a consistent value system. As viewed by the media paradigm, *human capacity to know*, regulated by the interchange medium of meaning, is a factor input from the action system penetrating the physicochemical system. Conversely the *intelligibility of nature* for man, regulated by empirical ordering, is a factor input from the physicochemical system penetrating the action system. The product output of the action system penetrating the physicochemical system is *the human relevance of knowledge*, dependent on empirical ordering. The *inclusion* of nature in human action *by knowing* is the product output from the physicochemical system, tied to the medium of meaning, penetrating the action system.

This final theoretical development is another of Parsons's attempts to work out, in a new context, the conditions which underlie the attainment of continually higher degrees of the integration of freedom and order. In this instance the theory of action is integrated into the still more general theory of the human condition.

2.7 Applications of the theory of action

Talcott Parsons worked out the development of the theory which I have sketched here in a wide variety of contexts which we cannot look at individually here. Here belong, for example, the three essays on social stratification, the work on the development of modern society from an evolutionary perspective, and a larger number of studies on particular problems in the study of religion, the modern professions, politics, economics, socialization and other areas. All these works share the theoretical perspective I have set forth here, the core of which is the theory of interpenetration. This point is particularly worth making with regard to Parsons's work on the evolution of modern society and on social stratification, since this work is frequently misunderstood. It is this work which we will look at now.

2.7.1. *The theory of evolution as an application of the theory of action*

From the middle of the 1960s, Parsons increasingly applied himself to the task of incorporating the modern theory of evolution into his account of social-cultural evolution.[94] Although from 1964 on he devoted himself to the problem of evolution, he was far from committing the mistakes Spencer had made. In 1937, he had begun his critique of the positivistic-utilitarian theories represented by Spencer with the words 'Spencer is dead'.[95] It was not the theme of evolution as such, but the positivistic-utilitarian theory of Spencer against which Parsons had arrayed Weber, Durkheim, Marshall and Pareto. Parsons came around to the idea of evolution again on the basis of the voluntaristic theory of action in the 1960s. But one can understand what Parsons does with the notion of evolution only if one keeps the perspective of the general theory in mind. Evolutionary development is to be understood as the result of differentiation *and* interpenetration, through which limitations are overcome and more room can be opened up for the operation of various analytically differentiated subsystems, between which there existed sharper incompatibilities at the lower level of evolution. The characteristics of modern society – such as the market system, the modern bureaucracy, universalized law, democratic associations, or the modern professions – are not, as 'evolutionary universals', differentiated and isolated subsystems of society, but are instead products of interpenetration of inherently opposed forces, and in this form – on this point Parsons aligns himself with Weber – are found only in the West.

Within the framework of the voluntaristic theory of action, in which 'meaning' is the constitutive characteristic of human action and 'understanding' (*Verstehen*) is the corresponding method of explanation, sociocultural evolution, the evolution of action, cannot be understood as a quasi-naturalistic process.[96] Parsons had already refuted a version of such a theory in 1937, in his critique of Darwinism as a radically anti-intellectualistic variant of positivism.[97] Parsons held to this position up to the very end of his career. That means that we must give to the general categories of the theory of evolution a meaning consistent with the theory of action. Indeed, we can understand socio-cultural evolution as a sequence consisting of the constitution of genotypes out of a gene pool, the reproduction and variation of the genotypes, the construction and selection of phenotypes, and finally, the feedback effect of this process on the composition and structure of the gene pool.[98] But what is important here is that these terms be understood strictly in terms of the theory of action. So, by 'gene pool' we understand a value system, such as the modern Occidental value system rooted in Judao-Christian culture. The constitution of the genotypes corresponds to the *interpretation* of this value system, their reproduction and *variation* to the *traditionalization* and *socialization* of the interpretation and to *innovations* in it. The construction of phenotypes has to be conceived of as the application of value interpretations to specific subject matters. Their selection corresponds to the *institutionalization* of interpretations in social systems and their *internalization* in personality systems. As the theory of selection forms the core of every theory of evolution, so the theory of institutionalization and internalization forms the core of the theory of social-cultural evolution. That means that this theory of evolution grows out of a voluntaristic core[99] (see Figure 15).

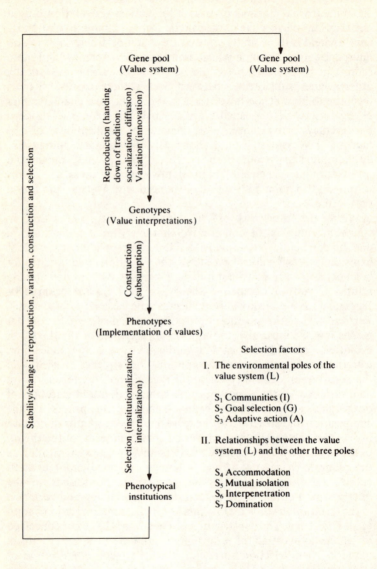

Figure 15 The gene pool, reproduction and variation of genotypes, construction and selection of phenotypes

More specifically, we can say that the selection of phenotypes in this system is determined by the kind of relation obtaining between the interpretations of the value system as the L-component of the four-dimensional action framework and the other three poles: community (I), goal attainment (G) and the articulation of interests (A). Selection is determined, in its content, by the content of the interpretations (L) and the content of the societal verities (I), goals (G) and interests (A) involved, as well as the relations between all of these, which may cover the full range of possible relations between potentially ordering and dynamizing systems: accommodation, reconciliation, mutual isolation, interpenetration, domination of one system by the other. Evolutionary development presupposes interpenetration, which leads to higher orders of complexity. The selection of a phenotype requires the communal anchoring of the interpretations of a value system, their rational specification to goals and the normative limitation of interests by the values, as well as the opening of the value system to the articulation of interests, the demands of goal attainment, and the rules which the societal community holds to be self-evident. From the perspective of goal-oriented societal collectives and personalities, which approach the G-pole of the action framework, evolutionary development means increased interpenetration with the material, social and symbolic environment. Corresponding to these three dimensions, one can understand the three concepts of 'adaptive upgrading' (G–A), 'value generalization' (G–L), and 'inclusion' (G–I) as so many specifications of interpenetration. The fourth concept, 'structural differentiation', refers to the product of this increasing interpenetration: this concept denotes a normatively integrated form of differentiation, the mechanism of which is the formation of continually expanding zones of interpenetration between the components of the action space.[100] We can see that a voluntaristic theory of evolution includes as essential components not only constellations of interests and power, but also the processes of the formation of community and the processes of the discursive grounding of norms. The kind of relation which obtains among these elements, how much weight each has and what effect each has on the others, can be discovered by using the model of possible relations between the subsystems of action.

2.7.2 The theory of stratification as an application of the theory of action

Social stratification is the result of a kind of relation between the economic, political, communal and cultural subsystems of social action. Social stratification as a system of legitimized inequality first arises from the mutual penetration of economic, political and

111

cultural dynamics and normative culture.[101] The arising of inequality, then, is ethically regulated and, conversely, the internal dynamics of inequality has an effect on the normative culture. Legitimate stratification arises in the zone of interpenetration between economic acquisitiveness, the acquisition of political power, the acquisition of professional competence, and communally grounded ethics. It can be explained neither purely economically, politically and professionally nor purely ethically, but only through the interpenetration of these spheres.[102] These are the terms of the problem which Parsons's theory of stratification set out to address from its very beginning (1940). This theory is a logical consequence of the voluntaristic theory of action; in this area of application, the very statement of the problem serves as a counterthesis to utilitarian or power-oriented theories of stratification. Parsons's theory is also distinguished, however, from all purely *functionalist* theories of stratification, such as those of Davis and Moore. Around the latter issue there has grown quite a long-standing debate.[103] Incomprehensibly, this debate has proceeded with those concerned taking for granted that the hypothesis of Davis and Moore would be a more precise version of the older hypothesis of Parsons. The hypotheses, however, do not appear in general to have anything at all in common.

Davis and Moore look for the cause of the universality of stratification, in the sense of differential rewards, in their functional value for the society, and they seek to explain concrete stratification structures in terms of the functional significance of roles for a society and the relative scarcity of people available to fill the roles. There are certain obvious objections to this theory. The consequences of concrete stratification structures, for example, the social conflict they engender, are not always functional, so that we cannot in general pronounce that stratification is always functional. The contribution of a given stratum to the persistence of a society can be determined neither by the actors involved nor by an observer. Therefore, the 'correct' distribution of rewards is inaccessible to human comprehension; its appearance in a concrete society would be a miracle which we could not even recognize. 'In summary, "unequal functional importance" is a complete unknown,'[104] George A. Huaco reminds us. The functionalist theory in this form is a modern version of the organic theory of society, which has the ideological consequence that everyone is perceived as in his place and as given the proper reward according to his contribution to the social whole. The existing structure of stratification is always the best possible for a given society.[105]

Now, Parsons's theory goes in a completely different direction. As an anti-utilitarian theory, it makes a basic distinction between quasi-naturalistic stratification structures (which simply *are*) and stratification structures which can make a claim to justification. A stratification structure can be justified only to the extent that its distribution of income, power, expertise, influence and prestige follows rules which are themselves incorporated in a generally shared system of values. Concrete stratification structures are not, according to this hypothesis, simply justified functionally by their existence. They *require* justification, and attempts at justification can succeed or fail. The entire debate over the functionalist theory of stratification has overlooked this central problematic of the voluntaristic theory of stratification. Instead, the debate has run itself into the dead end of two false alternatives: the organic theory of society on the one hand, and the positivistic theory based on power and conflict on the other.

Even the attempted synthesis which Lenski undertook does not address adequately the problem of order in stratification.[106] Any attempt to expand on Parsons's theory of stratification using 'power' as the determinant factor of stratification is setting out from a false formulation of the problem. No one would deny that power is a sufficient means for the enforcement of privilege, but the point which is challenged in the framework of the Parsonian theory is the thesis that power could ever bring about an enduring, legitimized *order* of stratification. On the contrary, the question must be answered as to how the use of power can itself be controlled.

The extent to which society contains a comprehensive community with a common normative culture, and to which the economic, political, administrative and intellectual spheres are integrated with this culture, becomes especially apparent in the character of the system of social stratification, in the degree of legitimacy accorded to it, and in the conforming or deviating reactions to it. In an extreme case, social stratification can result purely from the rules behind the distribution of economic, political and intellectual opportunity within economic, political and educational institutions, without any formative influence on these rules of distribution coming from common distributive *values* in a societal community. This can come about either because common values of distribution do not exist at all and society is instead divided into particularized communities which each have their own view of legitimate distributive values, or because the economic, political and intellectual institutions in their distributing function constitute separate spheres from normative culture, and these spheres do not mutually penetrate. If social stratification is attributable only to the distributive rules of the economic, political and intellectual institutions, it will soon conflict with the distributive values of individuals, of particular communities, or of a comprehensive societal community. Congruence between social stratification and distributive values can be expected only if there is interpenetration between distributing institutions on the one hand and distributive values on the other, that is between the economic, political and intellectual spheres and the comprehensive normative culture of a societal community. Only if this congruence exists will the social stratification be regarded as legitimate and attain acceptance. Conversely, incongruence between a given system of stratification and distributive values will lead to doubts as to the stratification's legitimacy, to alienation, deviation from institutionally issued rules on acquisition of opportunity, to protest, conflict, and also to change in the distributive institutions.

At this point we can tie across, in a generalized and qualified form, to Durkheim's connection of the theories of stratification and anomie in his study of suicide.[107] As Durkheim saw it, an actually existing stratification, reflected in the distribution of economic, political and intellectual opportunity, always represents a limited allocation of such opportunity compared with the amount of access to it which could, in principle, be conceived of. For such a distribution to be accepted by the individual, it requires moral justification, and for Durkheim this means it must be rooted in the normative culture of a societal community embracing all social strata. In particular, this justification requires the stratification, as established by the laws of distribution, to be congruent with the distributive values of the societal community. This congruence, in Durkheim's view, is suspended in circumstances such as an economic upswing, economic decline, or persisting prosperity, because under such conditions needs always run ahead of the allotted opportunities to fulfil those needs. However, one is compelled to make the more precise assertion that such a result could only come about if there were no countervailing influence upon both the autonomous nature of economic distribution and the unlimited, self-interested development of an individual's needs emanating from the establishment of distributive institutions, from distributive values, and from the universal anchoring of such values in the societal community. This limitation of Durkheim's thesis of economic anomie can be derived from his own premises.

In the absence of this shaping of both the rules of distribution and individual aspirations by common distributive values, and when the only common value is the unlimited development of individual aspirations – as Merton, continuing Durkheim's line, has postulated for American society[108] – then any deviation whatever from the unlimited level of aspirations naturally encourages the use of all possible means available, including illegitimate ones. In distinguishing between legitimate and illegitimate means, one must ask the question, to what extent are legitimacy and illegitimacy determined by distributive values, and to what extent are the latter anchored in a comprehensive societal community, rather than in particularized, perhaps dominant communities within society? Deviant behaviour in the form of the use of illegitimate means to gain access to economic opportunity is thus not a simple result of there being insufficient legitimate means relative to an unlimited level of aspiration. In as far as the functional connection can be observed empirically, one would have to state that the connection is conditioned by the absence of any anchoring of distributive values in a universal societal community, and the absence of a role for commonly binding distributive values in shaping both the laws of distribution and individual aspirations (see Figure 16).

The functional relationships illustrated can be more precisely explained in several stages. First of all, we must determine the various types of opportunity which are the dimensions of social stratification:

- economic opportunity (life opportunities), expressed in terms of income,
- political opportunity, expressed in terms of power,
- intellectual opportunity, expressed in terms of command over expertise.

We can attribute these opportunities to the appropriate economic, political and intellectual components of the social system in the analytical AGIL schema, without inferring that their distribution is determined by these components alone. The actual distribution of opportunity in a given society can be explained by the interaction of a number of sets of two factors. The first of each pair comes from the level of *economic prosperity*, measured by the per capita income of the population, the level of *political prosperity*, in the sense of how far the scope of political decision-making has been extended, and the level of *intellectual prosperity* in the sense of the availability of higher education to the population. The matching factors in these combinations come from the adherence to distributive laws on the part of the distributing institutions in the economic, political and intellectual spheres. Distributive economic institutions comprise market rules, property law and contract law, distributive political institutions are made up of the rules for collective decision-making, and the distributive intellectual institutions of the entry requirements for higher education and criteria for acquiring degrees and diplomas. The distribution of income, power and expertise can be determined either in one single dimension by the interaction of the degree of economic, political or intellectual prosperity with the respective economic, political or intellectual distributive rules, or it can be multi-dimensionally determined through the interaction of the

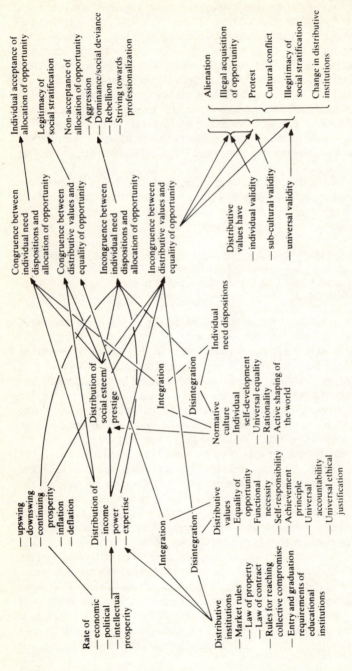

Figure 16 Social stratification and normative culture

appropriate form of prosperity with the interpenetration of the distributive institutions. In the latter case the distribution of income is determined not only by economic prosperity and economic distributive rules, but in addition by the rules governing collective decision-making as well as access to education and the acquisition of qualifications. The distribution of power does not follow simply from political prosperity and collective decision-making rules, but is additionally influenced by economic and intellectual distributive rules. Likewise the distribution of expertise is not the product solely of educational prosperity and the rules of entry and qualification, but also of economic and political distributive rules.

The extent to which the actual distribution of economic, political and intellectual opportunity which thus emerges also represents a legitimate social stratification depends on how far there can be said to be a comprehensive societal community with a common normative culture, and how far the distributive institutions and normative culture mutually penetrate each other. As Durkheim himself put it, the distribution must be accepted as just by those affected, no matter whether it implies inequality or total equality, if it is to maintain a certain stability, and not be continually disputed:

'A moral discipline will therefore still be required to make those less favoured by nature accept the lesser advantages which they owe to the chance of birth. Shall it be demanded that all have an equal share and that no advantage be given those more useful and deserving? But then there would have to be a discipline far stronger to make these accept a treatment merely equal to that of the mediocre and incapable.

But like the one first mentioned, this discipline can be useful only if considered just by the peoples subject to it. When it is maintained only by custom and force, peace and harmony are illusory; the spirit of unrest and discontent are latent; appetites superficially restrained are ready to revolt.'[109]

A prime consequence of the existence of a normative culture is a common and binding assessment of the possession of economic, political and intellectual opportunity through which a contribution can be made toward the implementation of the normative culture. A new dimension of stratification emerging from this assessment is *stratification according to social esteem, or prestige*.[110] Whether this comprises a unified prestige stratification which is accepted as legitimate, or whether it originates from the defining power of a social elite and stands in competition with other possible stratifications, will depend on the degree of universality of the community carrying the normative culture. The importance accorded to particular types of opportunity when prestige is being determined depends on the significance attributed to them in the framework of normative culture, and it is naturally of some import here whether the normative culture is based on a particular or on a universal carrier group. If normative culture is based on a combination of education and political decision-making authority – as was the case under Confucianism and to some extent under German idealism right into the twentieth century – then it will place little value as a component of prestige on access to economic opportunity; here the differentiation of prestige is more likely to be determined according to the congruence of the educational and the bureaucratic hierarchies. The combination of property, political decision-making authority and education is dismissive of those with the opportunity to make economic acquisitions in the market, and also of those who have obtained an education, if they do not also have property – this was particularly true of the European aristocracy before the bourgeois revolution. In contrast, the commercially-oriented bourgeoisie brought an emphatically economic culture into being and, in particular, managed to place a greater value on economic success in comparison to political influence and education. However, this bourgeois economic culture was again modified by democratization in both politics and education, in favour of a higher valuation of political decision-making authority and, even more so, of education. Modern normative culture is characterized by a revaluing of education, both in relation to the distribution of economic and political opportunities and in relation to the distribution of prestige, yet it has not pushed economic and political opportunity completely into the background. In this sense the modern order of prestige is based more than ever on the unification of different assessments of value in a single prestige hierarchy, but this is dependent on the development of a universal community to act as carrier of the prestige order, and this order does not achieve the same degree of universality in all modern societies.

The legitimacy and acceptance granted to a prestige-based stratification, as in the case of the stratifications according to income, power and expertise, is determined by its congruence or incongruence with normative culture. Inequality thus needs to be justifiable as functionally necessary for the implementation of a consensually born system of values. Certain types of inequality may be regarded as legitimate only in as far as they are preconditions for the later establishment of equality. An example of this is the greater decision-making authority of a teacher compared with his/her pupils, which is justified only in as far as it contributes to the process of increasing the pupils' qualifications so that they approach the expertise of the teacher. This is not to suggest that existing inequalities can in fact always be legitimized out of functional necessity, rather that any inequality must always be justified by a general consensus related to commonly-shared values, if they are ever to be legitimately institutionalized. This becomes all the more true with the greater acceptance of the commitment to reason as a fundamental value in modern society. In this way, normative culture is specified with regard to the distribution of opportunity, and hence indirectly with regard to the distribution of prestige. The more unified the process of institutionalizing modern normative culture, the more the specification of values responsible for determining whether or not stratification is just will be based on the particular qualities of the conjunction between individual self-development and universal equality, or between rationality and the active shaping of the world. In this respect the *distributive values* must incorporate these components and ensure they are reflected in the system of stratification. More specific distributive values may be found in the zones of interpenetration between the fundamental values which relate to all four components of the general action space (see Figure 17).

The *commitment to rationality* forms the 'L' component in the action space, with the *active shaping of the world* representing the 'G' component, *individual self-development* the 'A' component and *universal equality* the 'I' component. The following distributive values are derived from the zones of interpenetration between these basic values:

L $\longleftrightarrow$ A   From the interpenetration of rationality and individual self-development, rationally-guided *self-responsibility* emerges as the derived distributive value. This indicates that the only justified distributions of opportunity are those which can be attributed to a rationally acting individual's own responsibility, and not those based on external or internal compulsion.

L $\longleftrightarrow$ G   The derived distributive value in the zone of interpenetration between rationality and the active shaping of the world is the principle that the allocation of opportunity must be justified by *functional necessity* in relation to the rational and active shaping of the world.

L $\longleftrightarrow$ I   The combination of universal equality and rationality demands the *universal ethical justification* of the allocation of opportunity, that is the allocation must be justified according to rational rules of argument, with reference to the values of a universal community. The only justified allocations of opportunity are those which, after being rationally founded in a comprehensive community, can achieve universal validity.

G $\longleftrightarrow$ A   The zone of interpenetration between individual self-development and the active shaping of the world generates the *principle of achievement*. This distributive value requires opportunity to be

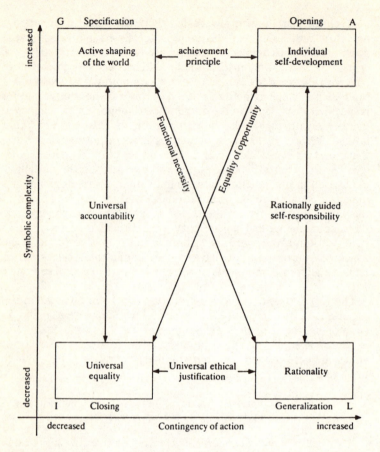

Figure 17 Distributive values in the zones of interpenetration of the basic components of modern normative culture

allocated according to the individual's contribution to the active shaping of the world.

G ⟷ I   The active shaping of the world and universal equality are brought together in the *universal accountability* of active formations of the world. What is meant here is that allocations of opportunity are justified not by each individual contribution to the formation of the world nor by each functional necessity, but only by those which imply an active shaping of the world with universal responsibility toward a comprehensive community.

I ⟷ A   The combination of universal equality and individual self-development produces the distributive value of *equality of opportunity*. This incorporates the two components in a special way, allowing universal equality in the *opportunity* for self-development. In this sense equality of opportunity is compatible with inequality resulting from the unequal realization of those opportunities, and the initiative in achieving this realization of opportunity is left with the individual. Equality of opportunity represents a distributive value in the sense that the only justifiable distributions of income, power, expertise and prestige are those based on equality of opportunity.

If we look at the normative culture of modern societies, then *concrete* inequalities require justification not just with reference to the values of active world-formation (the achievement-activism complex), but with reference to the entire system of values, if they are to be regarded as legitimate institutionalized inequalities. Parsons's argument on justified inequality is also only tenable in this general interpretation; his line is that inequalities must be justified by their functional necessity for the 'welfare' of society. This is how Parsons outlines the argument in his third paper on the theory of stratification:

In my two previous general papers on stratification theory, I have strongly stressed the importance of values as legitimizing differences of ranking. If the present interpretation that in the legal complex we are dealing with a pattern-maintenance function is correct, I should like to suggest that this valuational emphasis applies not only, as is obvious, to the factors of differential ranking, but also to equality – that the evaluative backing of constitutional law in this case constitutes the *specification* of the general value system of the society to the level of the *normative structure of the societal community*. It amounts to saying that the modern societal community shall be 'basically' a 'company of equals' and hence, so far as empirically possible, legitimate inequalities shall be 'won' from a base of equal opportunity and that the rewards which go to differential statuses and achievements shall be justified in terms of functional contribution to the development and welfare of the society.[111]

If we wish to avoid misunderstanding this argument as a variant of the functionalist theory of stratification, then we must replace the term 'welfare of society' to reflect a system of values which is ultimately rooted in a universal community. In doing so, we must emphasize that existing inequalities are in point of fact not *explained* by their functional contribution to the welfare of society, but are only *institutionalized* if they can withstand criticism in the light of a generally accepted system of values and attain justification. In any other case, though the inequalities may exist in reality, they are dependent on the constellation of power prevailing at any given time, are the constant object of conflict, and are not securely institutionalized. However, even an advantage toward the under-privileged is an insufficient justification in itself for inequalities. In this respect we have to contradict the second of John Rawls's two basic principles in his theory of justice. According to Rawls, the members of a community in which all have the same rights of participation, none of the members pursue interests directed toward others and all are guided by reason, would agree on the two following basic principles:

'First: each person is to have an equal right to the most extensive basic liberty compatible with a similar liberty for others.

Second: social and economic inequalities are to be arranged so that they are both (a) reasonably expected to be to everyone's advantage, and (b) attached to positions and offices open to all.'[112]

It should be pointed out that the second basic principle is subordinate to the first, and it is thus impossible to justify inequalities providing advantages for all if they impair equal access to basic liberties; yet the second principle contains fundamental features of utilitarianism. Advantage for all cannot in and of itself serve as a criterion for legitimate inequalities, as they can be institutionalized only after justification with reference to a shared system of values. If we attempt to establish the generally valid justification for inequalities, advantage for all could not be the appropriate criterion because its final reference point is always *individual* benefit, whereas a *generally valid* justification is only possible in connection with a system of values which is already generally carried. For each individual who is positively or negatively affected, a given inequality can produce a variety of actual advantages and disadvantages. This in itself makes it impossible, when seeking a justified basis for the inequality and using this criterion, to arrive at a result which could be seen as in any way stable or generally valid. The advantages, because they are dependent on interests, can constantly change, and because of their multiplicity they are impossible to comprehend. Universally carried values, on the other hand, are less unstable and multi-faceted, and in the light of them every advantage no longer necessarily provides a sufficient basis of justification for inequality. Such values can rule out even advantages which would accrue to all, declaring them illegitimate because the underlying desires and interests are forbidden. Inequality of knowledge concerning problems in political decision-making is quite often a result of the fact that those remaining ignorant have a greater interest in their own private affairs than in public affairs, always assuming that there are no restrictions on basic political freedoms and that opportunities of access are equal. In this case, inequality in political 'informedness' is an advantage to the uninformed. However this inequality will be seen as all the less justified, the more the advantages themselves contradict a generally accepted value such as the model of the active, responsible citizen pledged to participation in public affairs even if this may mean some sacrifice of private interests. A reduction of inequality in this case would require certain new sacrifices from precisely those citizens who had been least well-informed.

In modern societies the degree of legitimacy and acceptance accorded to the stratification system is determined more than ever before by the interpenetration between distributive values and distributive institutions, and by the degree of universal validity these distributive values owe to their anchoring in a universal community. The shaping of the distributive institutions by distributive values gives the institutions a frame of reference in which to fulfil their own requirements like, for example, functional necessities, without falling into a contradiction of the distributive values. Conversely it is only the shaping of distributive values by the distributive institutions which makes it possible to specify the values in the light of distributive demands. Normative culture must not be allowed to stay confined to an intellectual circle or any other particularized community, and the economic, political and intellectual institutions must be accessible to the carriers of normative culture. The less this applies, the more distributive values and distributive institutions will be disintegrated; this disintegration will in turn lead to an increasing incongruence between the stratification which exists in practice and distributive values. Under such conditions the existing social stratification is regarded more and more as illegitimate, and is no longer accepted. The more precise results of the incongruence between distributive values and the system of stratification depend on the extent to which normative culture is generally binding:

- If the distributive values used to assess a given case of injustice in allocation of opportunity are the values only of individuals, the results will be alienation and the attempt to deviate from institutionalized rules of distribution through the illegal acquisition of opportunity.
- If the values giving rise to feelings of injustice in the allocation of opportunity are not carried by an all-embracing societal community, but only by a particularized community, then the effects of alienation and illegal acquisition can be expected to be added to by subcultural protest and distributional and cultural conflicts.
- If the values actually are rooted in the comprehensive societal community, then the above-named reactions will quite probably be extended by a general definition of the existing stratification as

illegitimate, and the eventual transformation of the distributive institutions.

However, it is not just a question of congruence or incongruence between stratification and distributive values. If there is no simultaneous congruence between the allocation of opportunity in the social roles of the individual and the need dispositions of that individual then even if there is a congruence between the stratification and value systems, the existing allocation of opportunity will not be accepted. How far the former congruence actually applies depends on the degree of integration or disintegration between normative culture and individual need dispositions. Depending on the character of the disintegration between these two factors, a number of different reactions to the incongruence between allocation of opportunity and individual need dispositions might be expected: aggressive attitudes, and the dominance of need dispositions over social roles in the shape of social deviance, rebellion, or efforts toward the professionalization of the social role, which is felt to be undervalued.

If we examine the interrelationship we have just discussed in dynamic rather than purely static terms, then oscillations and variations over time in economic, political and intellectual prosperity must be seen as the primary dynamic factors producing corresponding oscillations and variations in the system of stratification. This process can take the form of economic, political or intellectual upswings, downswings, on-going prosperity, or of inflation or deflation of money, power, expertise or prestige. Such processes can generate not only incongruences between the allocation of opportunity and distributive values, but also between that allocation and individual need dispositions. The extent to which these incongruences emerge or prevail depends on how well the degree of integration between distributive institutions and values, or between individual need dispositions and normative culture, is capable of keeping them within bounds and then breaking them down.

2.8 The structure of the theory of action: Some controversial areas of discussion

Having thus far followed the development of the theory of action in Talcott Parsons's work, we may now deal with a number of particular problems which have given rise to controversial debate. Particularly worthy of discussion are the questions of the relationship between action theory and systems theory, the explanatory

programme, the formal structure and the normative basis of the
voluntaristic theory of action.

2.8.1 Action theory and systems theory

Contrary to a widely held view which has a number of variants following on from Robert Dubin, I do not see a break
in the development of Parsons's theory between the action
theory of the early years and a systems theory which has emerged
since the 1950s. Dubin draws a distinction between the action
theory-based Model I which he believes to be represented in
'Values, motives, and systems of action', and a systems theory-
based Model II which first appears in *Working Papers* and
which he constructs with reference to *Economy and Society*.[113]
As Dubin sees it, the actors in Model I are able to *choose* between
the orientations in action offered by the pattern variables, whilst
in Model II they have *particular* combinations of pattern variables *forced upon them* by the functional imperatives of the
social system. Thus those who have pursued Dubin's argument
frequently see in this transition a move away from the voluntaristic model of action formulated in *The Structure of Social
Action* in favour of a system-functionalist and quasi-naturalist
model of compulsion.

Dubin takes insufficient account of a distinction Parsons had
already expressly drawn in 'Values, motives, and systems of action' of
three analytical levels on which pattern variables have their effect on
action, and of the concrete level of human action which includes all
aspects within it. On the concrete level, the statement that individuals
may 'choose' between pattern variables actually means no more than
that the pattern variables should be attributed to the symbolic sphere
of human freedom rather than to the materially conditioned sphere
of necessity. In the symbolic sphere an ordering of action is
conceivable only as a definition by way of symbolic patterns to which
the human individual *at least in principle* commits himself
voluntarily. The pattern variables then represent types of ordering
for action. However, that is not to say that the voluntariness which
exists in principle means each individual can actually make a
completely free choice of patterns in every situation. The way in
which the action is shaped by the pattern variables depends on the
extent of their cultural validity as *cultural patterns*, their socially
binding authority as *role patterns*, and their motivational
internalization as *disposition patterns*. Through their interpenetration with each other as well as with adaptive behaviour, the
'choice' of the pattern variables is determined from three directions:
discursive procedures of justification, affective attachment and

125

motivational energy. Thus the pattern variables are neither alternatives chosen or rejected by the individual totally freely in a vacuum, nor patterns totally forced upon the individual from outside by 'system problems'. Both of these extremes, existentialist autonomy and collectivist conformity, are *possible*. However Parsons's action theory is intended to show how both extremes are avoidable in a voluntaristic order, by the interpenetration of the system levels and the pattern variables themselves. Dubin's proposal, on the other hand, regresses into the choice between existentialist autonomy and collectivist conformity. In this sense, the existentialist Model I as outlined by Dubin's classification has never actually existed in Parsons's work. Nor, however, can the collectivist Model II be found there. If it could, this would assume that only the social system could be considered as a system reference. On the contrary, Parsons sees the social system as only one among several reference points in systems analysis and believes any analysis of concrete action must take account of a number of system references and of a number of levels. This is also expressed in his own response to Robert Dubin:

'In many respects, this possibility of dealing with *multiple* system references and of keeping straight the distinctions and articulations between them, has turned out to be the greatest enrichment of theoretical analysis developed from Dubin's "Model II." A "flat" conception of a single system reference which must be accepted or rejected on an all-or-none basis for the analysis of complex empirical problems, cannot possibly do justice to the formidable difficulties in the study of human action.'[114]

Hence there can be no question of the individual actor being entirely subjected to external system-derived necessities in the development of Parsons's theory. In fact, the individual actor should be seen as the concrete object of the analysis whose action can be determined by various *analytically* distinguishable subsystems ranging from the environment which is cybernetically inferior to action, that is, that of physicochemical laws and the structure of organic drives, through the various aspects of action itself to the cybernetically superior environment, that of the problem of the meaning of life fundamentally peculiar to man.[115] For this reason it is also wrong to regard the individual action subsystems as actors in themselves.[116] Rather, action is always intentional and requires qualities which can be attributed only to *concrete* actors, and not to analytical subsystems of action. These subsystems are never more than aspects of action itself. The cultural system, for example, signifies the aspect present in every act – to whatever extent – of the *interpretation of meaning* of one's own action, that of others, or the world at large. The social-cultural system, as a subsystem of the social system, encompasses the aspect, again involved to a greater or lesser extent in all action, of *symbolic communication* among a number of actors. Nor, however, is the social system as a whole the concrete substrate of action. It too is only one aspect of action, namely the individual actor's orientation to the action and expectations of others; similarly the only aspect covered by the personality system is the determination of action by relatively general dispositions independent of situations; the behavioural system encompasses the aspect of the influence of stimulus and response learning on action. Which subsystems and which system levels determine action to what extent, and how these factors relate to one another, is not a question which can be decided *a priori*, but an empirical one dependent on varying preconditions.

A different interpretation from Dubin's of the supposed gap between action and systems theory in Parsons's work has been formulated by Jürgen Habermas.[117] Habermas's fundamental argument is that Parsons in the development of his theory only solves the conflict beween the life-world and the system, or between normative and conditional (functional) development by means of a compromise, and a compromise which he says has led to a surreptitious technicalization of the life-world, and to a pure apologism for *system* development without any kind of normative, critical counterbalance. He presents this argument in five steps:

1 Firstly, he argues that Parsons, while criticizing positivism in *The Structure of Social Action*, only achieved a monologic theory of action and did not succeed in developing a dialogic theory.
2 Secondly, he says, once Parsons was faced with the problem of dealing with society and not just individual actions, the fact that Parsons took up systems functionalism meant he replaced *social* integration with *functional* integration.
3 Thirdly, he purports to show that in Parsons's theory of the generalized media, the construction of the life-world media 'influence' and 'value commitments' according to the model of 'money' implies a systems oriented technical analysis of interrelationships in the life-world, thus subliminally legitimizing the growing technicalization of the life-world in modern societies as a necessary requirement in system terms.
4 Fourthly, he claims to prove that with his frame of reference Parsons can only conceive of the development of modern societies as an increase in systemic complexity and that *each and every* change of society in this direction was thus 'harmonized' and given a positive normative evaluation.
5 In the fifth step, Habermas attempts to demonstrate that even the attempt at re-Kantianizing Parsons's systems functionalism cannot purge the theoretical weaknesses and will ultimately lead to the development of

127

Western societies being falsely viewed as an unhindered realization of values while attention is turned away from the inner dynamic of systemic developments. The latter would then, as a result of pure apologism, take on the status of normatively legitimized institutions.

The difficulty here is that the theoretical inadequacies being exposed by Habermas tend to be matters of his own interpretation which do not find confirmation in Parsons's work. This is true even at the start with his presentation of Parsons's theoretical position in *The Structure of Social Action*. Habermas's claim begins by recognizing that Parsons makes a just criticism of positivism in his *Structure of Social Action* showing that, in so far as action is determined by autonomous will and is not totally subject to the laws of external causality, the only conceivable social order must be a *normative* order and hence the actors' goals must be limited and hierarchically organized by *voluntarily recognized normative standards*. However, Habermas contends that because Parsons follows Weber in choosing means-end rationality as a basic model for action, he cuts himself off from a solution to the problem of recognizing norms through 'communicative consensus formation'. Thus goal determination in action remains monadic in that it is confined to individual actors, without any connection with the *intersubjectively valid* definition of norms for action. Because of this, Habermas believes, Parsons was forced to introduce a systems-functionalist model for the analysis of society, which indeed proved to be the case in the 1950s. Yet in this functionalist model, his argument continues, the problem of social order is solved not on the basis of normative consensus, but by fulfilling the quasi-naturalistic functional requirements of maintaining the boundaries of social systems in relation to their environment. In the process, he says, the cultural system which in the first instance was always a separate system superior to action systems, now acquires the status of a subsystem alongside the other subsystems of action. The tension between the normative, consensual solution to the problem of order, which was originally aimed for but not achieved, and the quasi-naturalistic systems-functionalist solution is, Habermas believes, nevertheless evident in the still more prominent position given to the cultural system in the cybernetic hierarchy of conditions and controls. Ultimately though, this tension remained unresolved by Parsons. Habermas points out a similar source of tension in Parsons's theory of generalized media. This media theory was built around the model of money even though it is a medium relating to quasi-naturalistic interactive relationships, that is, the laws of the market. Of the other media, 'political power' could be described as the closest to this model, as the use of power also has a quasi-naturalistic character. However, according to Habermas, the model fails in the conception of 'value-commitments' and 'influence' as the respective media for the social-cultural system and the community system. These, he believes, are technical substitutes for communication.

In reality, however, Parsons neither presented a means-end-rational, 'monologic' theory of action in the early years, nor a quasi-naturalistic, functionalist systems theory in the later years. Both are constructions which cannot actually be found in Parsons's work. His fundamental thesis in *The Structure of Social Action* is that, in seeking to explain social order, we ought not to look upon action as solely determined by ends, means and given conditions; a *rule of selection* for ends and means must also be given. His further thesis states that this rule of selection cannot be merely the *standard of rationality* which would be represented by an individual actor choosing the most efficient combination of means, given conditions and ends, not if a non-naturalistic and non-accidental social order is to be established. Rather, an indispensable prerequisite for such an order is that the actors accept common and categorically binding norms. And the logical implication of this is that the norms should be consensually shared. It would contradict precisely Parsons's basic thesis against utilitarianism if one were to assume that the rules of selection were merely *individual* considerations of monadic, isolated actors: 'A society can only be subject to a legitimate order, and therefore can be on a non-biological level something other than a balance of power of interests, only in so far as there are common value attitudes in the society.'[118]

Habermas's interpretation of the solution to the problem of order in *The Structure of Social Action* is symptomatic of the approach taken in all his interpretations of Parsons's work.[119] He begins by discovering elements tending toward a normative, consensual solution, but then immediately sets about contradicting this by setting up constructions which cannot actually be found in Parsons's work. A striking example of this is the contention that Parsons understands the normative regulation of action as the value orientation of a single act performed by a single actor. In this case, norms would be reduced to individual ends, whereas Parsons himself speaks unequivocally of commonly shared values.

Habermas's representation of Parsons's *systems* theory is based on a concretization of analytical constructs far exceeding anything which can actually be found by referring to Parsons.[120] This process of concretizing analytical devices begins as soon as Habermas interprets the subsystems of action. In the programmatic paper 'Values, motives, and systems of action' the distinction is unmistakably drawn between the *concrete* action of individuals or collectives and the *analytical* nature of the social, personality and cultural systems which are involved in each act as it is performed in a particular constellation.[121] Parsons and Shils do also locate actors either in the social or the personality system, and this depends on whether the actor is a collective or an individual. The cultural system, on the other hand, always maintains the status of an analytically definable symbolic structure. In this case personalities and collectives need to be *empirically* sufficiently differentiated as to attain a delineated position in the context of action, hence forming the centre of action. It is only in this second sense that it is possible to speak of social and personality systems intentionally acting. That, however, would be to apply a duplicate meaning to the respective terms, and it runs totally counter to Parsons's aims if the second, intentional meaning in which the terms are used is carried over to the initial, analytical concept of the action subsystems. This, however, is exactly what Habermas does, immediately using the concrete concepts of 'culture', 'society' and 'personality' in place of 'cultural system', 'social system' and 'personality system', the terms used by Parsons to stress that these were essentially analytical differentiations. Without a doubt the original twofold use of the relevant terms leads to some confusion. But this is no reason to magnify the sources of confusion beyond the extent to which they appear in the original text. There are in fact clear distinctions which allow the confusion to be solved.

The distinction between concrete actors and concrete action on the one hand and analytic subsystems of action on the other is one which Parsons always adhered to quite unmistakably throughout the development of his theory. The twofold uses of the terms 'social system' and 'personality system' were also superseded in the later development. In *Working Papers in the Theory of Action*, the action system is expressly understood as an action space comprising analytically defined subsystems within which concrete action moves. Here again the actor in given roles, or with given need dispositions, must be distinguished from the analytic subsystems of interaction and of personality.[122] In 'Social systems', an article which appeared in the *International Encyclopedia of the Social Sciences*, there is an explicit distinction between the concrete individual or collective actor, the originator of intentional action, and the social system, which again is regarded as a level of analysis with a greater or lesser tendency to 'function' in its internal processes and its relationship of interchange with the environment:

'In dealing with social systems, one must distinguish terminologically between an actor as a unit in a social system and the system as such. The actor may be either an individual or some kind of collective unit. In both cases, the actor *within* a system of reference will be spoken of as acting in a *situation* consisting of other actor-units within the same system of reference who are considered as objects. The system as a whole, however, functions (but does not "act" in a technical sense) in relation to its environment.'[123]

The above arguments literally rule out the possibility of attributing intentional acts to social systems when viewed as subsystems of action, rather than as collective units and corporate actors. At no point in Parsons's work is there any justification for a claim that the actor could disappear as the concrete subject of action to be replaced by acting subsystems. And yet this is precisely the claim Habermas makes, without backing it up by reference to any formulation of Parsons which would point in this direction. This misinterpretation leads Habermas to embrace a conception of the relationships between the cultural, social and personality systems which has nothing at all in common with Parsons's own conception. Habermas reads an assertion into the relationship between the cultural, social and personality systems that the cultural system represents a superior, internal environment for the action systems, and yet is unable to act like an environment upon the action systems because it does not have the 'empirical qualities' of a systemic environment. The cultural system – which Habermas actually reifies as simply 'culture' – is in this model supposedly a substitute life-world 'objectivized' as a system. The 'transcendence of free-floating cultural meaning constructions' found in Parsons's concept of the cultural system is, according to Habermas, lacking in any kind of actualization of validity claims in contexts of action normally associated with the concepts of life-world and symbolic, discursive communication. Though he agrees Parsons's model demonstrates that social integration and the consistency of value patterns obey different standards from the functional integration which flows from the fulfilment of functional imperatives, he charges that the theory does not answer the question of how value patterns can effectively assert themselves when supposed by functional system developments. There is no barrier, he argues, to prevent the dissolution of the system of values by system developments. Such a barrier could only be established if social integration in the life-world were to be understood as a process of communication over claims of validity, and then brought into a relationship with the functional integration of society with its environment. Only in this kind of frame of reference would it become clear when functional integration could lead to instances of pathology. This would happen whenever functional integration were based on a delusion regarding the contradictions between the system of values and systemic developments, hence endangering communication-based social integration. However, this explanation of pathological elements is in Habermas's view impossible within Parsons's frame of reference because the cultural system is suspended in isolation and not linked to the systemic imperatives via the processes of communication.[124] Hence, action has no defence against being subjected to systemic imperatives.

In fact Habermas is only able to construct his argument in opposition to the appropriate concepts in Parsons's theory. The relevant passages in Parsons's work dealing with the subsystems of action referred to by Habermas deprive his argument of its foundation. Certainly, Habermas mentions the concepts which are crucial here, namely the institutionalization of normative culture in social systems and its internalization in personality systems, but he does not explain their meaning in the context of Parsons's theory. Instead, he reduces them to the level of a straightforward positivistic sanction mechanism.[125] In Parsons's theory, on the other hand, institutionalization and internalization are linked throughout to the formation of a consensus on values. Sanction mechanisms always require *consensual* support. This is a point which, as Habermas himself notes,[126] Parsons emphasizes even in his early interpretation of Durkheim in *The Structure of Social Action*, and continually restates in a variety of contexts.[127] Nor was Parsons unaware of the fact that language represents the underlying medium of consensus formation.[128]

Habermas also completely disregards Parsons's introduction, as he continued his system development, of the social-cultural (fiduciary) system between the cultural and social systems. In contrast to the symbolic structures of the cultural system, it consists of a particular type of social interaction, a type which cannot comprise anything other than symbolic communication, which is fundamentally different from communal, political or economic action. Within *communal action* it is discourse rather than the societal community, authority or exchange with fulfils the function not only of generalizing community norms, the norms of a self-evident life-world, but also of generalizing specific political and economic rules. What else, if not to distinguish these latter structures of social interaction, could be the point in differentiating between all the relevant social subsystems?

Parsons's systems structure allows us to distinguish unequivocally between the closing function of the life-world (or community) and the generalizing function of discourse; it also allows us to show clearly, in contrast to Habermas's approach of rationalistically hypostasizing discourse, where the limits of discourse lie as a normative basis for action, and where it needs to be embedded in an unquestioned life-world. Parsons insisted throughout his career that any kind of social order, even if it is located almost at the lowest level of instrumental action, must be anchored in a consensus on values. This in turn requires a twofold relationship: firstly, the system of values as a symbolic structure must be connected with the communal life-world via social-cultural discursive processes, and secondly, it must be equally intertwined via discursive processes with the instrumental level of action. In the former case, the value consensus arises as an affectively shared yet also discursively generalized world-view, and in the latter as an open and practically specified system of norms. The first relationship concerns processes of inclusion and public discussion, and the second concerns the discursive coupling of instrumental action to public discussion within special contexts of action related to particular problems. Pathologies are then generated in the event, firstly, of a failure to arrive at a value consensus on the level of public discussion and inclusion, and secondly, of a failure to justify concrete action by means of subsumption under common values. On the first level, intellectual discourse must be closely interlinked over several stages with forms of inclusive communalization, and on the second level, intellectual discourse must be similarly tied up, again in several stages, with problems of practical action. By virtue of this multiple intertwining, value consensus is in Durkheim's sense truly a product of immense cooperation, not simply of intellectual discourse. This was the model of *voluntaristic* order to which Parsons adhered right up to the construction of the various media-controlled relationships between empirically *differentiated* subsystems.

The thesis that the cultural system is left hanging in the air in Parsons's systems structure, with no effective link to the instrumental spheres of action, is Habermas's individual construction of the matter which collapses when one considers Parsons's actual writing on the relationships between the relevant action subsystems. This is no less true of Habermas's continuing argument. Setting out from his false premise that the cultural system is isolated in the 1951 systems structure, Habermas contends that Parsons's solution to the problem in his subsequent development is to reduce the cultural system to the status of other action systems so that it stands in a system-environment relationship with them. Despite Parsons's repeated emphasis that the action subsystems are analytical systems and must be distinguished from concrete individual or collective actors, Habermas assumes that all subsystems, including the cultural system, should be regarded as acting entities, and that the concrete actor as the subject of action has thus disappeared from the frame of reference. In the systems theoretical frame of reference the relationship between the cultural system and the other subsystems, he assumes, is reduced to a system-environment relationship.

However the only type of relationship which can exist between a system and the environment is a quasi-naturalistic conditioning relationship, and not a normative, regulating one. Therefore, he continues, even with the model of the hierarchy of cybernetic conditions and controls Parsons could not solve the problem of social integration, but rather social integration was meekly reduced to functional integration.[129] For this reason, according to Habermas, Parsons was also unable to reach an internal solution to the integration problem through a mechanism of communication, but resorted to the external solution of composing superior systems which performed a conditioning role from the top downwards; this extended to the building of the extreme example of the telic system, which would control the by now speechless subjects.[130]

Again, this sequence of argument owes much more to Habermas's own construction than it does to close textual interpretation. He reads Parsons's systems theory through the functionalistic spectacles of Luhmann. Even in the developmental stage of Parsons's systems theory the action subsystems are intended first and foremost as analytically delimited systems which are interlinked in many different ways in concrete action. Parsons never allows any doubt to arise on this question. What must be distinguished from the above is the analysis of media-controlled reciprocal relationships between *empirically* differentiated systems. But even this set of relationships is never conceived in the original texts as if they involved teleonomic processes of adaptation to an overly complex environment, as Habermas supposes when he applies Luhmann's approach. The consequence of this is that the relationships between the cultural system and the other subsystems in particular are not viewed in naturalistic terms as reciprocal adaptation processes. Parsons has covered the content of these relationships between subsystems in countless essays. At no stage in any of these does he argue from this naturalistic system-environment perspective.[131] It is therefore always possible for Parsons, in contrast to Luhmann, to avoid using the jargon of systems functionalism.

Anyone attempting to foist a systems functionalist perspective on Parsons virtually has to ignore everything Parsons has written on the subject of the relationships between action subsystems. To illustrate this, let us simply take one relationship as analysed in the theory of media: that between the social-cultural and economic systems, as empirically differentiated systems. Their differentiation demands the institutionalization of appropriate normative codes (discourse and exchange) and the media attributed to them (value commitments and money).[132] The social-cultural regulation of economic action by way of value commitments means in this instance that general value commitments are the means by which *normative limits* are set for economic calculation, and that economic action receives a positive normative orientation. In that they are institutionalized in a discursive social-cultural order, value commitments are kept apart from the calculation of utility, and in that they are transmitted to economic action, they attach the latter to norms. The processes require the building of discursive, practical bridges between the purely social-cultural and the economic contexts. These bridges are provided by, for example, practical discourse directed toward economic problems. Should such practical discussions not take place, or remain confined simply to the ideal or to the economic plane, then social-cultural and economic action will grow apart. This is where pathological phenomena then come to light. Conversely money is the carrier-medium which mobilizes economic resources for cultural purposes. If the universities have little access to economic resources, they will also not be very culturally productive. Further, every social-cultural institution, if it is to develop, must have a market for its ideas. How little the growing bureaucracy of the university system actually contributes to scientific and to general cultural creativity can, for example, be seen in day-to-day life in the German universities.

As the above example shows, in no way does Parsons's consideration of the relationships between action subsystems in the light of media theory involve quasi-naturalistic system-environment analyses; rather, it involves approaches to solving the problem of the connection between social and functional integration. Conclusions can also be drawn for media theory, which by no means implies the mechanization of the life-world which Habermas claims.[133]

Given that Parsons begins to construct a theory of action which is 'dialogic' in the above sense, and that he excludes all quasi-naturalistic solutions to the problem of order from the outset as inadequate to meaningful human action,[134] he can hardly have any reason to seek just that type of quasi-naturalistic solution by way of systems functionalism. This would be a regression back beyond Parsons's voluntaristic action theory and would represent a special version of radical anti-intellectualistic positivism[135] – an approach his work superseded – within which the problem of order is not solved in a normative, consensual manner, but by using quasi-causal functional laws. Moreover, Parsons never did propose systems functionalism in such a form,[136] but in fact himself protested that his approach was labelled in this way.[137] A consideration which immediately rules out a quasi-naturalistic systems functionalism is that, throughout his life, Parsons based his work around the *meaningfulness* of action as an object of action theory and around the fundamental significance of *interpretation (Verstehen)* as an adequate explanatory method. Quasi-naturalistic systems functionalism is equally ruled out by the persisting significance of institutionalization and the internalization of normative culture as constitutive conditions for society and the individual. Both of these conditions are an expression of the fact that any order, if it is not a naturalistic one, must be normatively and consensually based. This lies at the heart of voluntaristic action theory, and emerges in later formulations in the shape of the higher cybernetic priority accorded to social-cultural and communal aspects of social action in contrast to the economic and political aspects. The sign of that higher priority is that only the institutionalization of norms can allow order in economic or political action to develop on the level of meaningful and non-naturalistic action, norms which are justified not only because they are subsumed under a consensually shared system of values but also because value system and norms alike are anchored in collective solidarity. To illustrate, even the market cannot be conceived of as obtaining its order solely in a quasi-naturalistic fashion through the operation of external laws: in fact it has always been perceived as an institution rooted in normative culture. This does not prevent the market from representing a sphere of action which, within that normative frame of reference, is characterized to a relatively large extent by quasi-naturalisitic behavioural laws. The same applies to money as a medium of communication: it is only because of the order of property, an order which must be *normatively* justified, that money is defined as the only permissible means by which goods and services can be obtained. This again means that it must be subject to control by the media that have a higher ranking in the cybernetic hierarchy. Indeed the function of these media, specifically value-commitments and influence, is just that, namely to sustain the binding power of any type of order to conditions other than the exchange of interests or use of power. In consequence, they are not subject to the same laws as money, nor to the same laws as political power.

Although Parsons used money as a model when he developed the theory of media, this does not mean that he establishes the cybernetically higher-ranking media in a similar quasi-naturalistic fashion to money.[138] Value-commitments, for example, which are the medium applying to normative cultural discourse, express the fact that norms can only be institutionalized on the basis of a commitment to shared values which must then be used to justify more specific norms. If Parsons is nevertheless seen to investigate quasi-naturalistic types of process, namely inflation and deflation, on these higher system levels too, these need not necessarily imply that he has relapsed into an *overall* quasi-naturalistic interpretation of the media of 'value-commitments' and 'influence'. Rather, the crisis theorem involving inflation and deflation draws upon the possibility that action which is primarily social-cultural and discursive can also show up aspects of exchange which are cybernetically subordinate. It is on this subordinate level that inflationary and deflationary processes take place.

These interrelationships may be clarified with the help of a simple model. Value-commitments involve a number of complementary aspects, namely one's right and one's duty to participate in the discursive justification of norms – subsuming them under the values to which commitment has already been pledged – one's obligation to accept these discursive justifications, and one's right to expect others involved to also accept them. Hence other ways in which norms could be enforced, such as the use of power, are themselves normatively ruled out. But even so, this commitment is also at least partly entered into because of an *interest* in personally participating in the consensual justification of norms. In this respect, an exchange takes place between the individual and the community. The individual's value-commitment means that he renounces the use of personal power or the personal enforcement of norms in return for the assurance that only norms which he too would support will attain binding power. An increase in such value-commitments can be seen, through developments like the spread of equal civil rights to cover more and more sections of the population, and the expanded content of the civil rights themselves, in terms of an overall increase in participation in social-cultural discussions. The actual amount of norm justifications consensually arrived at may increase, decrease or remain constant over a period of time. Also, value-commitments on the one hand and successful consensual norm justifications on the other may vary independently of one another. The upshot of this is that the value of value-commitments for the interested parties will fluctuate or, in other words, be subject to inflation or deflation. For instance, inflation occurs whenever a growing number of individuals take part in social-cultural discourse without any equivalent increase in the extent of consensual norm justifications. An individual, in his role as an *interested party*, will lose confidence in the institution of discourse and may then resort to other means available to him for enforcing norms, such as the mobilization of power. This is a case in which the inner logic of the pursuit of interests comes completely to the fore, that is to say that the cybernetic control exerted over lower system levels by the higher levels collapses under inflationary conditions. The voluntaristic core of the theory of action, therefore, it also retained in the above field of application.

Let us now examine Habermas's criticism of Parsons's analysis of the development of the modern world. Habermas's view on this is that the only way Parsons could account for evolutionary progress in the system-environment model is through an increase in the complexity of the systems. Hence he would have to interpret any differentiation leading to greater complexity, regardless of its content, as progress.[139] It is only possible to take this view by placing Parsons, despite all his formulations to the contrary, firmly amid Luhmann's systems functionalism. Particularly here we see that functional and evolutionary analysis of *empirical* systems does not, as Habermas postulates, automatically force a quasi-naturalistic conception of the system-environment relationship. An instructive example of this is provided by the four evolutionary mechanisms of adaptive upgrading, specification (in place of structural differentiation), inclusion and the generalization of values. We can analyse a society as an empirical social system. A number of completely different conditions must be fulfilled for its development according to the nature of its internal and external environments. Requirements for the various evolutionary mechanisms arise as follows: in relation to the physicochemical environment, the necessary mechanism is adaptive upgrading through the mobilization of instrumental and technical resources; in relation to the environment of conflicting goals, it is the specification of action by means of the building of decision-making structures; in relation to the environment of particularized groups, it is their inclusion into a solidarized community and, in relation to the environment of ideas and values, the mechanism needed is symbolic generalization via discursive procedures. The evolutionary mechanism of value generalization points out the fact that as a cultural environment spreads out wider and wider, there is an increasing compulsion to discursively establish that norms of action can be proved to be universally valid. Thus the normative horizon of a concrete society undergoes a process of generalization. In this sense the society increasingly extends into the generalizing component of the action space.

Any instrumental, technical attempt to solve the problems of solidarity and of normative legitimation in this connection is, contrary to Habermas's assertion, ruled out by Parsons, as indeed it always was. Looking at the problems internally, the approach is once again to link together the various differentiated structures by interpenetration. For the interlinking to take place, structures must be institutionalized in the zones of interpenetration between subsystems: for example, practically applied discursive procedures must mediate between purely intellectual discourse, the community and political and economic action. In this sense, and in this sense only, it can be said, that a greater differentiation of systems is the result of interpenetration, signifying a higher stage of development for individual autonomy, change, social order and cultural universality. In this case the outer zones of the action system are, on the one hand, advanced in their development and, on the other, interlinked with each other to a greater extent, and in several stages. This interlinking is equivalent to an increase in the number of empirically differentiated but nevertheless integrated subsystems of action. This process must not be confined to the level of the social system. It must also extend to the general level of action and the level of the human condition. The only feature this concept of differentiation has in common with a purely technical, instrumental differentiation of society in response to an overly complex naturalistic environment, is that it actually contains the latter approach as its adaptive component. However, this is true only of the relationship to the naturalistic environment, not of that to meaning structures and social groups. The point of reference for the analysis is modern society, and the problem being treated is the realization of the idea of modernity, an idea which is being expanded in its scope of meaning, rather than being bisected by systems functionalism.

Thus we can see that a positive assessment of each and every systems differentiation really does not underly Parsons's theory of evolution, because it does not bring about the reduction of societal development to a quasi-deterministic functional differentiation which Habermas claims to see. The person Habermas is really looking at is Luhmann, and not Parsons. In the instances where Parsons, due to his American optimism which is alien to Europe's critical intellectuals, does arrive at such a positive view of the future of modern societies (the USA in particular), his view is not a necessary outcome of his theory but the result of personal, empirical judgements. Furthermore, the empirical judgements are not simply related to the various dimensions of functional systems dif-ferentiation, but equally, to inclusion and value generalization. Whether or not Parsons has judged rightly in these matters is irrelevant to the assessment of his theory.

Finally, let us turn to Habermas's critique of the revitalization of the Kantian core in Parsons's theory of action, a process which, in Habermas's opinion, is incompatible with Parsons's systems functionalism and must ultimately lead to the thesis that values are realized without any resistance as all contradictions between the system of values and systems developments fade away.[140] The prime objection to this is that the systems functionalism Habermas reads into Parsons's work does not even exist. What tendencies there might be in that direction do not have the significance attributed to them by Habermas. By far the greater part of Parsons's concrete work provides evidence against a systems-functional interpretation. The 're-Kantianization' of Parsons' action theory – also including systems and evolutionary theories – thus means no more than evolving its structure with a view to the shape in which it is objectively tenable. There is no added implication that the theory is now being stood on its head, leaving behind no more than an idealistic theory of culture. This again is Habermas's own construction as he looks at the idealism of neo-Kantianism instead of Kant's own combination of empirical realism and transcendental idealism. It is impossible to say that, in a voluntaristic theory of action, the inner dynamic of instrumental systems is undervalued. On the contrary, it is precisely this frame of reference which allows us to show the complexity of the presuppositions governing the intertwining of values, discursive procedures and instrumental action through interpenetration, or the number of different analytical levels on which the problem needs to be treated, or, conversely, how easily developments can lapse into the pathologies of one-sided dominance, accommodation, over-steering, under-steering, isolation or reconciliation.

In response to Habermas's five-stage critical analysis of the relationship in Parsons's work between action theory and systems theory, we can establish the following:

1 The starting point in *The Structure of Social Action* is not a monologic, but a dialogic theory of action involving a consensual solution to the problem of social order, in conjunction with instrumental action. This is the essence of the voluntaristic theory of action.

2 The integration of systems theoretical elements into the preceding action theory does not alter the voluntaristic position. This can be seen in the treatment of the two concepts of institutionalization and internalization, and in the analysis of the relationships between the subsystems of action.

3 In the theory of generalized media the voluntaristic position is expressed in the particular order of priority given to the media 'value-commitments', 'influence', 'power' and 'money'.

4 Evolutionary advance in the framework of the voluntaristic theory of action is not synonymous with the functional differentiation of systems: rather, the theory aims at a more widespread interlinking of 'social' and 'functional' integration.

5 Reconstructing Parsons's action theory from a Kantian perspective does not mean it will be re-idealized, only that the development of the *voluntaristic* core in the later theoretical developments – traces of which have been buried less by Parsons himself than by his critics – will be rediscovered.

One hardly needs to dispute that there are tensions in Parsons's work between idealism and positivism, and between a sociology of the life-world and systems functionalism. Indeed one could expect no different of a theoretical programme which has the express aim of integrating these opposing positions. Integration does not mean the dominance of one position over another, nor their reconciliation, nor yet their mutual isolation – it means their interpenetration. Both polar positions then retain their special status. Neither of the poles is done away with, but they are included in a wider frame of reference, that is, they are 'dialectically' replaced and preserved on a higher level. Integration through interpenetration signifies the successful development of a *common*, all-embracing categorical frame of reference, rules for linking the categories together, empirical hypotheses and practical applications. It would no doubt be an over-estimate of any author's ability if one were to expect him/her to fully achieve this integration at all stages of theoretical development. Thus, while in *The Structure of Social Action* it is the conflict between hermeneutic interpretation (*Verstehen*) and causal explanation which is most strongly in evidence, in later developmental stages the tension between idealism and positivism comes to light mainly in the conflict between action theory and systems theory. The solution to this conflict cannot lie in sacrificing one to the other, but only in finding better ways of integrating the two components by following the programme of a *voluntaristic* theory of action, a theory which can be reduced neither to the idealistic premises of life-world sociology or rationalistic developmental logic, nor to the positivistic premises of systems functionalism or orthodox materialism. The fact that Parsons was unsuccessful in completely integrating these divergent theoretical positions should by no means suggest that he has not made some substantial strides in the right direction. And even the moves Parsons has made can teach us more than an ambivalent theoretical position which, though it recognizes 'the differentiation of the systems from the life-world' as a stage of societal development from which we cannot go backwards, does not, because of its idealistic captivation, actually possess any *theoretical* concept for the integration of systems and life-world, and contents itself with mere normative postulates demanding a rolling back of the mechanization of the life-world so that we may regain it. However he tries to recognize the separate status and differentiation of systems, Habermas remains imprisoned by the dualism of German idealism, the inherent anti-modern tendencies of which cannot be shaken off easily. In this frame of reference then, the idea of a system is still something alien with which the life-world cannot be integrated.

Habermas also lacks the analytical instruments needed for an appropriate grasp of the conditions for integrating system and life-world. The two are separate spheres of action and separate paradigms are used to examine them. Any particular sphere of action may either be set free from the life-world, or may remain within it; it may stay outside the life-world or be reincluded in it. There are no theoretical instruments to analyse the relationship between system and life-world, and there is no place for any graduation of action spheres. Habermas is not prepared to 'banish' the life-world to the confines of an analytic subsystem within a broader frame of reference. Instead, he works with the concrete concepts of 'culture', 'society' and 'personality'; all these components can either float in the waters of the life-world, or perish if those waters are drained away.[141]

The analytical system structure of the voluntaristic theory of action sets itself apart from the above empiricist-concreticist perspective in that it constructs an action space in which concrete action moves through various fields and, conversely, in which the appropriate subsystems of action account for greater or lesser proportions of each concrete act, and interlink to a greater or lesser extent with one another. The life-world is the subsystem of communal action, always permeated by affective ties, and again, the subsystem can have a greater or lesser influence on concrete action, and can cast its net more or less extensively over the spheres of ordered exchange, authority and discourse to reach economic and adaptive action, political and personal action, and symbolic communication and definition of the situation. Here we have at our disposal a set of instruments for analysing the relationships between the life-world and systems in several dimensions and on several levels, which one would seek in vain in Habermas's approach.

In contrast to the voluntarist concept of linking communal action to instrumental and rational action, Habermas is unable to offer an adequate solution to the problem of order in modern societies. He excludes the affectual component of solidarity from the life-world, expecting the validation of norms to stand solely on the frail rationalistic support provided by a discursive process of ethical rationalization. The rationality of discourse is the sole basis of normative order. But how can one be sure that individuals will also recognize the laws of discourse, and the laws of the universal justification of norms? In order to escape the pitfall of an infinite regression, or vicious circle, other bases for norms, or at the very least for the rules of discourse, are necessary. In the voluntaristic frame of reference it can be shown with the help of Durkheim that such an appropriate basis for universal rules can develop only if they are anchored in the affectual solidarity of a universal community. Communication only becomes possible once a community has been formed. It is evident in the approach to this crucial question that Habermas, compared to the more comprehensive voluntaristic theory of action, falls back on a rationalistic reduction of action theory which tries in vain to subject material rationalization to the control of idealistic rationalization. But the crucial theoretical component of a developed theory of solidarity is lacking. The fact that Habermas's access to the latter area of theory is blocked manifests itself especially in his treatment of Durkheim's sociology; he strips it of all its affectual components, allowing it to culminate in the rationalistic idea of turning the sacred into secular speech. In no way should this be seen as a denial of the significance of discursive, argumentative procedures in establishing a value consensus; indeed Durkheim made a clear demonstration of this. What we are concerned with is simply that these procedures have the function of *securing the identity* of society through generalization and are not able to fulfil the further function of *attachment* to values and norms. Commitment to values and norms demands particular attachment to them arising out of a general quality of affectual attachment within a community. Under modern conditions this cannot be a particularistic community, but only an inclusive one. In this respect, inclusive processes are a special precondition for the attachment to universal norms, and they also have preconditions of their own. They cannot be substituted for by processes of discourse and argumentation. Inclusion cannot be reduced to the generalization of values. However, the alternative to the more comprehensive voluntaristic action theory offered by Habermas is an action theory bereft of this dimension of inclusive processes and human affectivity, and reduced to the rationalism and unresolved dualism represented by an idealistic developmental logic of the life-world and a positivistic developmental logic of systems – reduced, in other words, to a rationalistically 'bisected' theory of action.[142]

2.8.2 The explanatory programme for the theory of action

The pure interpretation of meaning (*Verstehen*), as an explanatory method of action theory, naturally applies only to the purely intentional, meaning-bearing aspects of action. On the level of the general action system, the method is applicable in its pure form only to the aspect of action at the extremity of the L-component. The greater the involvement of aspects of action from the other components, the more these components will have their own part in shaping the interpretive explanatory method, which thus takes on additional characteristics.[143] Hence considering the poles which regulate behaviour we can distinguish different methods of explanation: normative-rational (L-I), affectual (I), means-end-rational (G) and situtional interpretation (A). The more consideration we need to give to action's embeddedness in its broader environment, the more our explanation will assume a transcendental (L), causal (A) or teleonomic character (G). This makes readily understandable the fact that the explanatory approaches of disciplines such as economics and behavioural psychology, both of which relate to the adaptive (A) component of human action, have the strongest tendency among the sciences of action to display a quasi-causal character, whereas explanations in the humanities come closer to the explanatory type of hermeneutic interpretation.

Sociology is a science which lies in the zone of interpenetration of the various explanatory dimensions of action, and must therefore incorporate all their differing characteristics.[144] There is thus no question of playing off the various types of explanation one against the other; rather, they must be unified in a meaningful and useful way. This is particularly true for a *general* theory of action.[145]

We need not commit ourselves to a purely hermeneutic (*verstehende*) theory of action, to a purely functionalistic or teleonomic systems theory, or a purely deterministic theory of behaviour, or indeed any other particular theory and its respective explanatory model; on the contrary, we can assign an appropriate place to each of these theoretical approaches and explanatory strategies within the frame of reference of a comprehensive theory of action.[146] It is on this basis that voluntaristic action theory aims to bring about an integration on the metatheoretical level between positivism and idealism[147] (see Figure 18).

The action of an individual or collective actor can be explained through *interpretation (Verstehen)*. Here we presume that the actor orients what he does to a certain principle of action (the principle of realization (G), optimization (A), consistency (L), or conformity (I)), logically deriving and choosing the most appropriate goal-realizing, optimal, consistent or conforming action according to the relevant principle and to given initial conditions. The connection between the initial given conditions and the eventual action is not in this case a causal connection, but a logical one. In explaining the action, we then duplicate the actor's logical deduction in our interpretation. Beginning with the principle of action and the initial conditions subjectively perceived by the actor, we interpret the act as understandable in its subjective symbolic meaning because it is logically deducible from its premises. Depending on the field of the action space in which the action takes place, and the principle by which it is ruled, our interpretation from the actor's point of view will be subjectively means-end-rational (principle of realization), economically rational, situationally meaningful (principle of optimization), meaningful and consistent (principle of consistency), or normatively rational and affectual (principle of conformity). The principles of action clear the way for an interpretation which can be generalized.

On the level of individual, intentional action, we can assume there is a fundamental indeterminism. On the other hand, when we come to the level of structural relationships we encounter a quasi-determinism. This is true, for example, of the relationship between particular structural qualities in an individual's personality system and the frequency of certain patterns of individual action (for

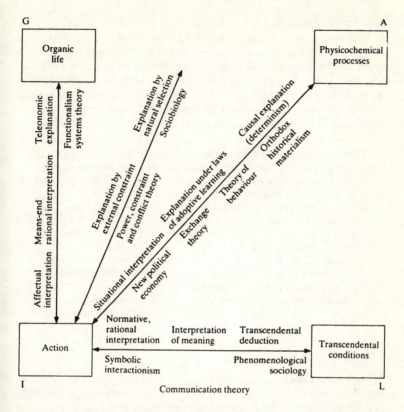

Figure 18 Dimensions of explanation and the explanatory limits of theoretical approaches within the frame of reference of the theory of action

example, aggressiveness), as it is also true of the relationship between structural qualities in a society's social system and the frequency of particular patterns of social action (for example, the violation of norms). The relationship between principles of action, the conditions of their application and individual or collective action is purely *logical* in character. There is no problem here in empirically verifying the relevant statements about these relationships. Should an actor not act as predicted, this is because he either has acted according to a different principle from the one the observer expected, has perceived the conditions for applying the principle in a different way, or has acted logically inconsistently. However, the relationship between structures, or between structures and aggregate actions, is a quasi-deterministic relationship. Statements made in this connection do therefore require *empirical* examination.

We explain structural features of an empirical and concrete action system or aggregate actions in a *quasi-deterministic* fashion by referring them back to other structural features of the system. In this case the theory of action is applied to the structural level in order to generate structural statements. The following structural statements can be formulated for the four fields of action, related to the structural features of an empirical, concrete political system:

- The more argument and discourse are strongly developed, and integrated via interpenetrative mediating systems with political decision-making, the broader will be the frame of reference for decisions viewed by the actors as justifiable, and vice versa.
- The more commitments to a universal community are strongly developed and integrated via interpenetrative mediating systems with political decision-making, the more political decisions will be accepted as collectively binding, and vice versa.
- The more incentives and exchange are strongly developed and integrated via interpenetrative mediating systems with political decision-making, the more frequently political decisions will be revised, and vice versa.
- The more power and authority are strongly developed and integrated via interpenetrative mediating systems with exchange, discourse and communal association, the more political decisions will be put into practice and accepted as justifiable and binding whilst remaining revisable, and vice versa.

In making a quasi-deterministic explanation we take, in our role as observer, a structural statement of this kind resembling a physical law, along with the relevant initial conditions, and logically deduce the appropriate structural feature for a system. In this case the connection between the initial conditions and the structural feature of the system being explained is a quasi-deterministic one.

If we wish to explain the structural qualities an empirical, concrete system must have in order to realize particular goals, we can apply the theory of action in order to provide *functional* explanations. The important point here is the completeness of the functional components which have to contribute to the realization of the goal. A functional explanation, if it is complete in this sense, presupposes an appropriate closed theoretical frame of reference from which the contributions needed to realize the goal can be derived. As an example, let us examine the selection, enforcement and carrying out of collectively binding decisions as the goal of a concrete political system. We can deduce from action theory that the necessary functional contributions toward achieving the above goal are the establishment of power and authority and its integration with processes of exchange, discursive procedures and comprehensive communal ties via interpenetrative mediating systems. To achieve this the theory of action has to identify all relevant factors, and their particular ordering and interdependence. Functional explanations of this type are technological recommendations for the achievement of goals, and can be distinguished from the process of applying the same frame of reference the other way round in *functionalistic* explanations. In the latter process the functioning of a system (or the realization of goals) is the premise from which the existence of the structures established as necessary components can be logically deduced.

If we are dealing with an empirical, concrete system with qualities close to those of an organism, the theory of action can be used to provide *teleonomic* explanations. This is particularly relevant to formal organizations. The explanation begins by establishing an organization's goals, the given environmental conditions, and a theoretical system for the structural and processual preconditions for realizing the goals in the environment, and uses them to account for certain regular activities within the organization as processes which, in the event of disruption originating in the environment, can repair the organization to its former goal-realizing state. Let us presume, for example, that new members join the organization. As newcomers they will jeopardize the sense of community of the organization's members. Thus special initiation ceremonies or the adoption of new members by colleagues who invite them home can be explained as activities designed to re-establish the sense of community under the new circumstances. This type of ceremony may indeed be set up by the organization's leadership with this express purpose. In this case the theory of action must provide us with a complete picture of the ordering and interdependence of all the subsystems of an empirical, concrete system.

We can use action theory both to explain the *stability* of an act or systems structure irrespective of time and to explain *changes* in it over the course of time. Different theories are not needed for the two purposes, as is often mistakenly claimed. The stability of an act or structure flows from the constancy of its initial conditions, and its change over time from variations in the initial conditions. Going beyond this simple exposition of the explanations for stability and change, action theory's frame of reference provides us with more precise answers if we note the way in which factors in the action space exert their effect. Exchange, incentives and learning are all factors which have an opening and transforming effect on symbolic structures and structures of action. The effect of broadening the structure of action and hence extending the scope for innovation is produced by argument and discourse. The obligation to norms and the commitment to a community have a stabilizing effect on symbolic structures and structures of action. Power and authority bring about the enforcement of actions and structures of action, but without stabilizing symbolic structures.

By social change we would normally understand not just the dissolution of structures, but the replacement of old structures by new ones. Thus the explanation of social change must have recourse to the explanatory variables of both factors which act to transform structures and those which act to stabilize them. Structure-stabilizing factors are relevant to an explanation both of the instability of the old structures and of the stability of the new. The instability of the old structures must not be attributed solely to the effect of structure-transforming factors, but the absence or inadequacy of structure-stabilizing factors must also be taken into account. The continuity of the new structures is naturally dependent on structure-stabilizing factors.

A special type of social change is the sociocultural evolution of societies. Here we have two tasks, one of clarifying the meaning of evolutionary advancement, and the other of interpreting the categories of evolutionary theory using the theory of action. In the action-theoretical frame of reference we can read evolutionary advancement in terms of an increased development of action unfolding simultaneously in all fields of action, with the integration of action preserved. The precondition for evolutionary advancement is the increasing interpenetration of society, environment and subsystems. This definition of the concept of evolutionary advancement can be conceived of as a translation of the central normative ideal of modernity into action-theoretical terms: the integration of individual autonomy of action with social order. This is only a definition of evolutionary advancement which cannot claim that the development of society actually is proceeding, or may proceed, along those lines. We can apply the theory of action in order to set out the conditions for this evolutionary advancement.

The use of action theory in providing evolutionary explanations must allow for three types of outcome: evolutionary advancement, stagnation or regression. Within such an explanation, the existence of an evolutionarily stable and successful phenotype is traced back to an underlying latent genetic code of a species, which by way of reproduction and variation, provides the basis for genotypes. From the genotypes, phenotypes are formed which are ultimately subjected to the process of environmental selection. Phenotypes which are successful in this environment and survive then determine for their own part the composition of the species' latent genetic code.[148] If these evolutionary categories are interpreted in the light of the theory of action, then the species is represented by a cultural community of societies, related to each other through cultural reproduction. The latent system of values of this cultural community should be seen as the genetic code. Interpretations of values form genotypes which are transmitted on by way of socialization and altered by innovation. The application of the value interpretations to concrete situations brings institutions into being, that is phenotypes, which in their turn determine the continuing composition of the system of values. Within the action space the institutions take on a structure determined on the one hand by rational specification from the general genetic code (L), and on the other hand by the influence of factors from the other three poles in the action space, namely communities and their self-evident life world (I), goals (G) and interests and learning processes (A). Finally, it is the type of relationship between these poles of action which shapes the phenotypical institutions. This relationship can range from one-sided accommodation, through reconciliation, mutual isolation, or interpenetration, to one-sided domination. Interpenetration is the precondition for evolutionary advancement.

A hallmark of the theoretical approaches generally offered as alternatives to the voluntaristic theory of action is the one-sided reduction in both their overall scope and their programme of explanation to particular fields of action and particular types of explanation. Hence the explanation of action is reduced by *symbolic interactionism* and *communication theory* to pure interpretation of meaning, by the *new political economy* to situational interpretation, by *exchange theory* to a combination of the latter with explanation by the laws of adaptive learning, by *behaviour theory* to these laws alone, by *orthodox historical materialism* to causal (deterministic) explanation, by *power and conflict theory* to a combination of situational interpretation and explanation by natural selection, by *functionalistic systems theory* to teleonomic explanations, and by *sociobiology* to the rules of natural selection. The limits of valid applicability in these approaches can be immediately recognized in the light of Parsons's more comprehensive theory of action. His theory of action determines the areas of application where these approaches would be confirmed, but equally determines those where they would be refuted. By thus eliminating their false content and maintaining their true content, the theory of action achieves, relative to the above approaches taken individually, what Popper has termed a closer approximation to truth, and hence an advance in knowledge.[149]

2.8.3 The formal structure of the theory of action

The theory of action does not consist of a conceptual scheme, as has been frequently asserted. The theory has its roots in the most basic problem of modern science and philosophy: How is the analytic order of the world possible? This problem is itself rooted in an anthropological constant: human life is possible only as meaningful life. And the meaningfulness of human life is, for the *modern* mind, closely tied to a belief in a conceptually comprehensible order of the world, an order which can be grasped by human understanding.[150] Parsons is indebted to Whitehead's analytical realism for this metaphysical belief. The instrument through which this belief is applied to reality and is made fruitful is the paradigm of ordering and dynamizing forces. This paradigm is the distilled result of the development from the duality of normative and conditional factors through the A–G–I–L schema to the cybernetic hierarchy and the theory of the generalized media of interchange.

Because of the extremely inclusive character of the action theory paradigm, which ultimately encompasses the whole human condition, the propositions which constitute its theoretical core must be formulated abstractly enough so that they can be given different interpretations on different system levels and in relation to different components on the same level. This means that the epistemological interpretation of the paradigm can vary from the hermeneutic to the causal, and from transcendental to teleonomic methods of explanation, depending on the field to which the paradigm is being applied. The paradigm consists of a theoretical calculus, theorems, and interpretations for the various levels:

1   *Theoretical calculus*
1.1   The degree of orderedness of the world (or of action) is defined (for man) by the degree of predictability of the external and internal world.
1.2   The degree of orderedness of the world (or of action) is determined by two diagonally crossing axes: opening and closing, and generalization and specification.
1.3   The degree to which structures of the world (or of action) display the effect of opening *vs.* closing or generalization *vs.* specification depends on the relation between the complexity of antecedents (symbols) and the contingency of consequences (actions).
1.3.1 Increased complexity of antecedents (symbolic complexity) → increased contingency of consequences (contingency of action) (relation of ambiguity-ambiguity).
       → Opening of action.
1.3.2 Decreased complexity of antecedents (symbolic complexity) → decreased contingency of consequences (contingency of action) (relation of univocity-univocity).
       → Closing of action.
1.3.3 Decreased complexity of antecedents (symbolic complexity) → increased contingency of consequences (contingency of action) (relation of univocity-ambiguity).
       → Generalization of action.

1.3.4 Increased complexity of antecedents (symbolic complexity) → decreased complexity of consequences (contingency of action) (relation of ambiguity-univocity).
→ Specification of action.

2 Theorems

2.1 The degree of orderedness of the world (or of action) is a function of the relative development of the structures listed above.

2.1.1 An excess of opening structures tends toward the dissolution of order.

2.1.2 An excess of closing structures tends toward immobilization.

2.1.3 An excess of specifying structures tends toward an order which is precise but in the long run unstable, because it is always susceptible to being overthrown by new specifications.

2.1.4 An excess of generalizing structures tends toward the continuity of an order which is very unspecified with regard to individual cases.

2.2 The degree of orderedness of action is a function of the relation of these structures to one another.

2.2.1 The accommodation of the ordering structures to the dynamizing structures tends toward the dissolution of order.

2.2.2 The reconciliation of the ordering and dynamizing structures tends toward a limited order, with gradations of more and less highly ordered spheres.

2.2.3 The mutual isolation of these structures tends toward the coexistence of spheres with a very high degree of order and spheres with no order.

2.2.4 The constriction of the dynamizing structures by the ordering structures tends toward the establishment of a very narrowly delimited order.

2.2.5 The interpenetration of dynamizing and ordering structures tends toward the unification of change and continuity, and of individual autonomy and social order.

2.3 Social change as the emergence of a new order is a function not only of dynamization but also of control, through generalizing, closing and specifying structures.

3 Interpretations

The interpretation of the calculus and the theorems is carried out by defining particular structures which are specific variants of the abstract structures on the different levels. This is how the various system levels with their respective structural components are derived. In this process, the farther the structural components move inwards from the outermost poles of action control toward the centre, the more it proves to be the case that, even though they always maintain a certain type of effect upon the ordering of the world (upon action) because of their greater proximity to one pole, the nature of their effect is nevertheless also determined by elements of the neighbouring poles. The most general levels of the system are:

3.1 the system of the human condition,

3.2 the system of action,

3.3 the social system.

All further elements of the theory of action are part of the interpretation of the calculus and the theorems. That includes the use of the pattern variables to characterize the structural components, the theory of socialization, the theory of media and the theory of evolution. The calculus, the theorems and the general interpretations on the three system levels are necessarily extremely abstract, and not accessible to *direct* empirical testing. Direct empirical testing first becomes possible when we reach the level of such assertions as: 'The level of fulfilment of role obligations in a collective increases as the emotional solidarity among the members of the collective increases.' However, it is always possible in principle to break the paradigm down to such assertions. We can read the foregoing empirical assertion as a specification of the controlling function of solidarity, a structural hallmark of the I-component, in relation to the G-component of carrying out roles in goal-oriented action in a collective.

2.8.4 The normative basis of the theory of action

It remains only for us to address the question of the normative basis of the voluntaristic theory of action itself. This is the question of its 'self-thematization'. The first consideration here has to be the obligation to cognitive rationality which is an aspect of the value pattern of modern Western culture, whose American variant Parsons has labelled 'instrumental activism'.[151] Cognitive rationality is the specification which this value pattern has received in the sphere of learning and knowledge, just as it has been specified as, for example, 'institutionalized individualism'[152] for the relation between the individual and the community. The integral parts of this value pattern are obligation to reason and to the active, normatively grounded shaping of the world, individual self-realization and universal solidarity.

Cognitive rationality as a specification of this value pattern implies that the assertions of any discipline concerning even normative developments should be cognitive, that is, free of value judgements, in Weber's sense of the term. That does not mean, however, that the discipline itself is not to be connected with the other components of the value pattern on the plane of its own normative basis. Clearly, we are dealing here with a view that owes a good deal to Weber's conception of the cultural significance of science and learning, and of their relation to values.[153] In this sense, the voluntaristic theory of action is inextricably bound to the idea of modernity, to the value pattern of Western culture. The kinds of questions the theory asks and the kinds of problems it confronts are inevitably affected by this. The central position of the concept of interpenetration has to be seen in this context. It is a generalized conceptualization of the central question rooted in Western culture alone: How is it possible to unify individual autonomy of action and social order?[154] The solution to the problem which the voluntaristic theory of action proposes consists of the constant construction of zones of interpenetration between opposed components of the human condition system: the telic constitution of the meaning of human life and organic needs, human community and nature. In the evolutionary-comparative specification of the theory of action, this solution is represented by the mechanisms of adaptive upgrading, inclusion, value generalization, value specification and normatively integrated structural differentiation. These mechanisms indicate the individual dimensions of the interpenetration of the human organism, the extreme point of the G-component of the human condition system, with the organic, material, social and symbolic environment. Evolutionary advancement in this sense is oriented to a *normative* guide, it is oriented to the 'idea of modernity'.[155] The sociological explanation of societal change however works with a wider framework which has to embrace even the most extreme deviations from this model by, for example, distinguishing between different kinds of relations between subsystems.

Our *commitment* to our cultural value pattern expresses itself above all in the *kind* of questions we ask. This commitment itself is not only rooted in rational argumentative justification, however. We can show in the model of voluntaristic action theory itself that its argumentative foundations lead to a potentially endless regress of the questioning of every position. Our commitment to our cultural value pattern expresses itself in a basic agreement among the participants in Western culture to exclude from discussion any alternative to our fundamental value which does not combine individual self-realization and social order. This is a fundamental value, to which one can give a particular distinction, such as 'the embodiment of the idea of rational man'. But in Western culture, to question it in any way is simply morally forbidden. For us it is a self-evident truth which is not subject to question. However, it is a value which should not permit any form of cultural imperialism toward other cultures, since the consensual basis of this value must be, in the final analysis, the human community, the human race itself. And it is this thought which may allow us to pardon ourselves for taking the idea of modernity as the potentially most universalizable normative idea.

Closing remarks

Talcott Parsons possessed a deep faith in the fundamental institutions of American society. This faith showed itself most clearly in his concrete analyses. These analyses bear witness to a great faith in the ability of those institutions to regenerate themselves in the face

153

of crisis. We can see this in his analyses of the political system, the integration of blacks, adolescents, the family, the structure of personality, the educational system. And, not infrequently, one can recognize the model of American society in Parsons's analytical theory construction also. For example, the purely controlling function which Parsons ascribes to the cultural system is a product of the interpenetration of intellectual culture and the white Anglo-Saxon Protestant societal community which is typical of American society. In continental Europe, however, the two spheres have remained quite distinct, with the result that a pure intellectual culture has appeared, and this culture has been able to have a much more dynamic effect.[156] Another example of empirical influence bearing upon the analytical construction of concepts is that the medium of influence is conceived as belonging to the community system, though in fact it lies in the zone of interpenetration between culture and the community – hence Parsons's preference for applying it to the professional-client relationship, which is located in this zone.[157]

The 'American biases' within Parsons's sociology do not hinder us from separating analytical theory from empirical assertion and from deriving from both a set of results such as has been yielded by no other sociology since Weber and Durkheim. There is no comparable theory in sociology today which has established such a depth and breadth in the understanding of change, conflict, power, authority and other areas of study which have been favoured by 'critical' sociologies. All attempts to oppose Parsons with a theory based on conflict or with some other form of 'critical' theory fail from the start; these attempts only go to show how little Parsons's criticism of the positivist tradition has been understood, because they imply nothing other than a Hobbesian variant of positivism.[158] And all attempts to argue against Parsons's normative theory of order from the standpoint of 'modern' economic theory look like attempts to criticize Kant from the standpoint of Hume's empiricism.[159] By the same token, modern systems functionalism does not offer more than Parsons, but less. The attempt to turn sociology into the hermeneutics of the life-world simply reduces it to a process of recounting everyday stories. In truth this is just one small part of what a general theory of action needs to take in. Nor does a combination of idealistic and positivistic developmental logic lead beyond Parsons – it returns us behind the level of development in action theory he had managed to attain, and has implicit within it a rational bisection of action theory.

Parsons's theory of action is the perspective which has allowed the most fruitful interpretation of the classics of the field: Durkheim, Weber and Freud.[160] This is especially true in the case of Max Weber. While a substantial number of readers of Weber try to extract from his works the correct understanding of the 'dialectic' of ideas and interests and his 'individualistic' theory of action, and to oppose this Weberian position to what they take to be the sociological reductionism of Parsons, Parsons developed long ago a theory which unites the contributions of Weber, Durkheim and Freud in a general theory of action. Parsons also managed to make substantial progress beyond the achievements of Durkheim, Weber and Freud.[161]

3 From positivism and idealism to the voluntaristic theory of action*

Introductory remarks

As early as in *The Structure of Social Action* (1937) Talcott Parsons pointed out the advances in sociological knowledge made by voluntaristic action theory over the two competing theories of positivism and idealism.[1] Voluntaristic theory integrates the essence of the other two approaches in a new paradigm and defines the limits of their validity. This insight, so decisive for the later development of action theory, will now be re-examined in the light of present-day voluntaristic action theory.

3.1 Voluntaristic action theory: The frame of reference

In *The Structure of Social Action* Parsons brings in the concept of the frame of reference of action. It is made up of the basic elements contained in action of any kind.[2] Even the smallest unit of action has to be seen as the particular concretization of these basic elements just as physical processes can only be conceived of in the framework of time, space, substance, causality, action and reaction. Thus, the categories of the frame of reference of action are to the sciences of action what Kant's categories of understanding (*Verstand*) are to physics. The categories that enable us to conceive of action are:

1   All action is directed toward *ends* (E) and moves from a point in time t_1, at which an end is distant, to a point t_2, at which this end is reached.
2   All action is located in *situations* (S) determined by
    (2.1) unalterable factors and *conditions* (C) and by
    (2.2) the means (M) available for the realization of ends.
3   *Norms* and selective standards (N) determining which ends and which

means may be chosen in general, and which means may be chosen for particular ends, have a regulating effect on the course of all action.

In this frame of reference we can say that all action is a function of ends, situations (conditions, means) and norms (see Figure 19).

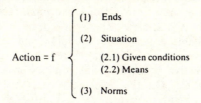

Figure 19 The action frame of reference

All action occurs within the action space defined by these categories. Action begins at a distance from a particular end (E_1) at point t_1, approaching this end (E_1) by point t_2. It is controlled by norms (N_1) and dynamized by situations comprising conditions (C_1) and means (M_1) (see Figure 20).

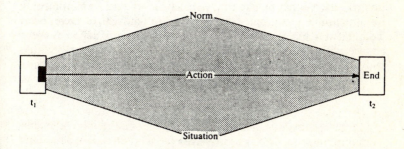

Figure 20 The action space comprising end, situation and norm

The movement of action in the action space formed by ends, situation and norms can be compared to the movement of physical bodies in space. Within the action space, the individual factors can affect the course action takes to a greater or lesser extent. It can be impelled in a particular direction from t_1 to t_2 by an end, thereby attaining a particular directedness. Action has to adapt to external factors by mobilizing means and has to be able to vary according to situation. Norms give action a regularity that remains the same regardless of situation.

One can, within the action frame of reference, imagine extreme theoretical positions from which action is seen predominantly in the perspective of one of the components of the action space. These positions also attempt to explain action in terms of a particular factor, for example, ends, situations (positivistic theories) or ends and norms (idealistic thought). On the level of object theory, *positivism* sees action as a function of *conditional* factors, that is, situation and ends. On the metatheoretical level it has a more *abstract* branch that stresses theory building and the deductive process, and a more *empiricist* branch based on the collection of data and the inductive process. What it aims at is the *causal explanation* of action. On the level of object theory, *idealism* conceives action as being motivated by *normative* factors, that is, norms and ends. On the metatheoretical level, it inclines either to *abstract* developmental logic or to *empiricist* historicism and attempts to *interpret* action. Explaining action has to be conceived as parallel to the interpretation of written texts. Beyond these characterizations positivism and idealism have to be viewed as positions moving between the extreme poles of their own separate axes that is for positivism between determinism and chance and, for idealism, between conformity and autonomy (Figure 21).

Positivism's one extreme pole is the complete causal determination of action either by extremely structured external conditions, or by immutable, external factors such as ends that have been assimilated to biological factors. The other extreme is action as sheer chance with indefinite conditions and no restrictions on possible ends. Norms, as controlling factors, are totally eliminated or reduced to the sole norm of means-end rational choice. Social order is

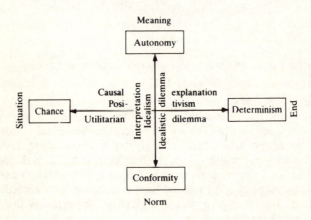

Figure 21 Dilemmas of action theory

therefore either a causally determined or a coincidental factual order. Utilitarianism, as a position, attempts to occupy the middle ground between the two extremes of determinism and chance. It postulates the possibility of social order as more than just sheer chance despite the great range of possible ends and the changes that may occur in external factors. However, this postulate only leads to the *utilitarian dilemma*, in which every theoretical position based on positivistic premises runs the risk of ending up at either of the extremes of sheer chance (anarchism) or totally causal determination (radical positivism). The reason for this is that it is almost impossible for the conditions attached to the middle-ground position to be satisfied. Where actors are free to choose any end they like and the only norm is that of means-end rational choice, order is only possible in small interactive units. Where interaction takes on a wider radius, order is determined by the extreme structuring of external factors and by severe restrictions on ends such as their reduction to innate drives like the survival instinct. This kind of order can only be deterministic and action is guided, in extreme cases, solely by external conditions. The utilitarian frame of reference does not allow for deviation from the rationality norm as a result of other norms but only through a lack of information arising from situational factors or through errors caused by the same factors. No distinction is made between the non-rational and the irrational. Consequently, rationality can have neither a normative basis nor can there be normative restrictions on it. Rationality and irrationality can only be factual and primarily determined by biology. The more the conditions of rationality are fulfilled, the more action can be seen as the intelligent adaptation to external factors. On the other hand, a naturalistic selection process adapts action to external circumstances all the more the less the above conditions are met, the greater the gaps in our knowledge or our ignorance due to lack of intelligence. Positivism thus reaches from anarchism, where everything is a question of chance, through utilitarianism and radical rationalistic positivism to radical anti-intellectualistic positivism, in which all order is totally determined by external conditions:

- *Anarchism* sees action as the product of sheer chance.
- *Utilitarianism* sees order developing spontaneously from an unlimited number of possible ends and changing situations.
- *Radical positivism* regards action as determined by unaltering ends and extremely structured external conditions as in the environment or hereditary organic dispositions.
- *Radical rationalistic positivism* perceives action as rational adaptation to external conditions.

- *Radical anti-intellectualistic positivism* sees action as a process of biological selection through external conditions.
- In *individualistic positivism*, rational adaptation or selection occur spontaneously.
- In *sociologistic positivism*, rational adaptation or selection occur as a result of collective pressure as an external condition.

Idealism ranges from a position of the total conformity of action with regard to norms to one of total autonomy and openness where the actor's sole orientation is toward the constitution of meaning through reason. This frame of reference excludes the effects that ends and external conditions can have on action. They are, at most, set against ideal factors. Social order appears as either purely conformistic or purely ideal and the *idealistic dilemma* is therefore to be found in the antithesis of conformity and autonomy.[3]

- *Conformism* (normativism) views action as the fulfilling of norms, as the desire to conform to norms, without taking account of ends, conditions and means.
- *Existentialism* (the theory of reason and culture) conceives of action as purely the constitution of meaning, independent of ends, conditions, means and specific norms.

What distinguishes the voluntaristic theory of action from all these extreme positions is that it takes all the components of the action space into account in its description and explanation of action. In doing so it advances beyond the more limited approaches. On the metatheoretical level it combines aspects of causal explanation with interpretive aspects. On the level of object theory voluntarism can be defined as follows:

- *Voluntarism* sees action as resulting from the nature of the relationship (interpenetration) between *conditional* factors (situation) and normative factors (norms) in an actor's goal orientation. Action is based on the pursuit of ends from a point, t_1, at which an end is distant, to a point, t_2, at which it is reached and on the selection of *means* for the realization of ends. It occurs in a situation consisting of conditions and means, and also within a normative frame of reference that serves to limit the choice of ends, means and combinations of the two.

In the voluntaristic frame of reference, action is marked by the tension between the conditional and the normative-meaningful poles. Between these one can imagine various intermediate positions. Using them we can define the external relations and the internal structure of human action step by step[4] (Figure 22):

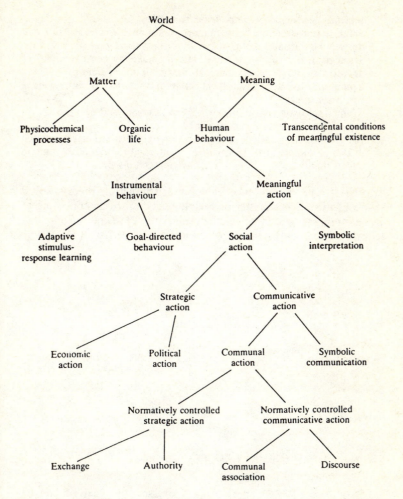

Figure 22 External interdependencies and internal structure of human
action

- On the general anthropological level of man in the world, action takes
  place in the tension between *matter* and *meaning*.
- Matter can be divided into *physicochemical* processes and *organic* life,
  while meaning can be divided into *human behaviour* and the
  transcendental conditions of meaningful existence.
- Human behaviour can be seen as either more conditional, *instrumental
  behaviour* or as *meaningful action*.
- Instrumental behaviour ranges from *adaptive* learning of the stimulus-
  response type to *goal-directed* behaviour, meaningful action from

161

- *social action* to purely *symbolic interpretation.*
- Social action oscillates between more conditional, *strategic action* and more symbolic/meaningful, *communicative action.*
- Strategic action occurs along a line bounded by the two poles of adaptive *economic action* and goal-oriented *political action.*
- Communicative action runs from *communal action* to purely *symbolic communication.*
- Communal action takes place between *strategic* and *communicative action*, both under *normative control.*
- Normatively controlled strategic action includes the area between *exchange* and *authority*. Normatively controlled communicative action covers that between *communal association* and *discourse.*

In the frame of reference of voluntaristic action theory, social action as the subject matter of sociology is defined as consisting of the addressing, receiving and deciphering of expectations and actions between two actors, ego and alter[5] (Figure 23).

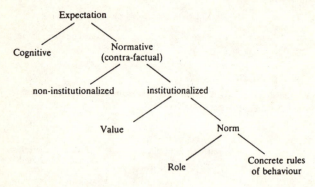

Figure 23 Types of expectation in action

The nature of the expectations addressed or received can be cognitive or normative. The non-fulfilment of cognitive expectations leads to their reassessment. Normative expectations are even upheld *contrafactually* where they are not fulfilled. To what extent ego and alter can actually cling to unfulfilled expectations depends on the degree to which these expectations are institutionalized in a particular social context. If their institutionalization is to have temporal, factual and social continuity it cannot be based just on superior power or an exchange of interests. When normative expectations go unfulfilled, ego and alter can only be sure of their institutionalization if they can count on the support of any other member of the same social group and on his support for sanctions designed to uphold those normative expectations. The last possible basis for the institutionalization of norms is a normative consensus. If this were not the case, there would always be the danger of the war of all against all, of anomie, the opposite of social order.

For their part, normative expectations can narrow or broaden the scope of action. Values define a wider frame of reference; they allow for a number of different actions. Norms define action more specifically within the frame of reference. In extreme cases, they demand one definite and particular action. Within norms, social roles represent general normative expectations. They can be made restrictive by concrete rules of behaviour.

The voluntaristic institutionalization of normative expectations is neither utterly conformistic nor totally anomic, neither deterministic nor coincidental but located somewhere between these extremes. There are a number of different orientations that action can take on with regard to institutionalized norms:[6]

- subjectively intended and objective conformity,
- subjectively intended conformity, objective deviation leading to consensually based sanctions,
- subjectively intended deviation, objective conformity,
- covert, subjectively intended and objective deviation followed by consensually based sanctions,
- overt, subjectively intended and objective deviation followed by consensually based sanctions.

The degree to which normative expectations are institutionalized decreases, as does the degree of voluntaristic order, and society is closer to a state of anomie if deviation increasingly goes unsanctioned and the consensus on sanctions gets smaller.

We have used the conceptual frame of reference introduced by Parsons in *The Structure of Social Action* to demonstrate voluntaristic action theory's superiority over the more narrow approaches of positivism and idealism. We will now move on to do the same for the frame of reference of the four-function paradigm in the abstracted form of the action space constituted by the two dimensions of symbolic complexity and contingency of action. The earlier frame of reference of action (ends, situations, norms) first has to be translated into the new frame of reference (symbolic complexity and contingency of action). In the earlier frame of reference, 'norms' had two different functions: closing and symbolic generalization. In order to characterize the idealistic dilemma and its two opposing poles it was therefore necessary to introduce *meaning* (or the *symbolic frame of reference*) as an additional category clearly distinguished from norms. Action is thus viewed as a function of ends (E), situations (S) (means (M) in the light of existing conditions (C)), the symbolic frame of reference (F) and norms (N), and these categories can be relocated in the action space frame of reference of symbolic complexity and contingency of action.

Symbolic complexity and contingency of action constitute the basic dimensions of an action space with four extreme positions, each having a particular effect on action:[7]

A – Highest degree of both symbolic complexity and contingency of action (Opening).

G – Highest degree of symbolic complexity, lowest degree of contingency of action (Specification).

I – Lowest degree of both symbolic complexity and contingency of action (Closing).

L – Lowest degree of symbolic complexity, highest degree of contingency of action (Generalization).

Within this frame of reference of the action space, the two positivistic and the two idealistic extremes can be integrated into one single system of interdependent variables. This was not possible in the earlier end-situation-norm frame of reference. Thus the four-function scheme of complexity and contingency takes our knowledge another step beyond the original frame of reference. Positivism lies between opening and specification, idealism between generalization and closing. Positivistic anarchism occupies the A-extreme of the action space, radical positivism the G-extreme, idealistic existentialism the L-extreme and idealistic conformism the I-extreme. The model allows us to analyse all six possible horizontal, vertical and diagonal relations and gradations between the extremes. We no longer have two separate axes on which action ranges from chance to determinism or from autonomy to conformity, but a unified system in which action moves between the four *interdependent* poles of opening (A), specification (G), generalization (L) and closing (I). If we now transpose the external interrelations and the internal structure of human action into our model, fourfold differentiations are obtained in place of the two sets of twofold differentiations yielded by the old model (Figures 24 and 25).

-   On the level of the *human condition*, action is exposed to the tension between the poles of physicochemical processes (A), organic life (G), human behaviour (I) and the transcendental telic conditions of meaningful existence (L).
-   On the level of *human behaviour*, action occurs in the tension between adaptive (A), goal-directed (G), social (I) and symbolic-interpretive action (L).

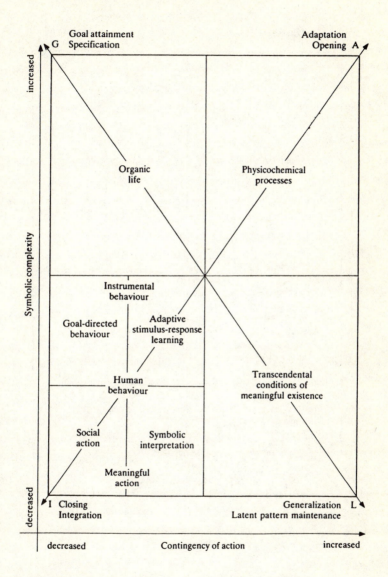

Figure 24 Action in the action space of the human condition

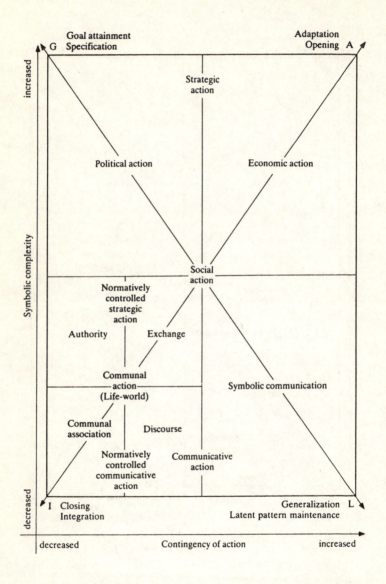

Figure 25 The inner structure of social action within the action space

- On the level of *social action*, action is subjected to the tension between economic action (A), political action (G), communal action (I) and symbolic communication (L).
- On the level of *communal action* (life-world), action is exposed to the tension between exchange (A), authority (G), communal association (I) and discourse (L).

The categories defined by Parsons and Shils in 1951 in 'Values, motives, and systems of action' can also be translated in terms of the more generalized frame of reference. In the 1951 frame of reference, action occurs in a *situation* toward which an actor *orients* his action.[8] The *situation* can be perceived as the environment of an action system and the less the action system is integrated with it the more this environment assumes the character of an external condition. In the complexity-contingency model, the *orientation* of action has to be differentiated into different modes of interpenetration with the environment whereby the basic differentiation is identical with the four extreme types of the symbolic–action model. A fourfold differentiation completes the threefold differentiation of the frame of reference. We can, with the extended model of symbolic complexity and contingency of action, integrate the 1937 and the 1951 frames of reference of action and the frame of reference of the A–G–I–L scheme with its basic classification into external and internal, instrumental and consumatory orientations (see Figure 26).

- We interpret the situation of action as an environment that, in line with the model's dimension, can be differentiated into the physical, organic, social and cultural-telic environment (= conditions).
- The orientations of action are as follows:
  A. External, instrumental orientation (increased symbolic complexity and increased contingency of action).
  Adaptive orientation of the behavioural system (new) (= means)
  A. cognitive (new)
  G. cathectic (new)
  I. evaluative (new)
  L. meaningful and constitutive (new)

  G. External, consummatory orientation (increased symbolic complexity and reduced contingency of action).
  Motivational orientation of the personality system (= goals)
  A. cognitive
  G. cathectic
  I. evaluative
  L. meaningful and constitutive (new)

  I. Internal, consummatory orientation (reduced symbolic complexity and reduced contingency of action).

167

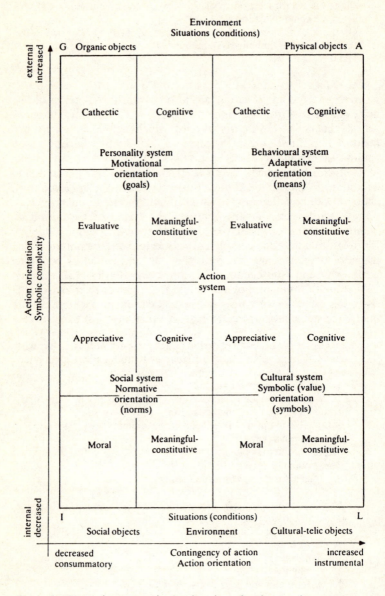

Figure 26 The action system in the situation of action (environment)

Normative orientation of the social system (= norms)
A. cognitive (new)
G. appreciative (new)
I. moral (new)
L. meaningful and constitutive (new)

L. Internal, instrumental orientation (reduced symbolic complexity and increased contingency of action).
Symbolic (value) orientation of the cultural system (= symbols)
A. cognitive
G. appreciative
I. moral
L. meaningful and constitutive (new)

Let us now examine a little more closely the movement of action in the action space of symbolic complexity and contingency of action. This occurs between four *fields* of action – *directedness* (increased symbolic complexity with reduced contingency of action), *adaptivity* (increased symbolic complexity and increased contingency of action), *identity* (reduced symbolic complexity with increased contingency of action) and *structuredness* (reduced symbolic complexity and reduced contingency of action). In the field of adaptivity action is open and can change from one situation to the next. In the field of directedness it is specified to definite and particular action regardless of situations. In the field of identity it retains certain constant features despite countless variations. In the field of structuredness it is closed and invariant even if situations change. The respective poles of the action space guide action into these fields. *Ends* give it directedness; adaptivity results from the application of *means* to the *conditions* pertaining in a situation; identity derives from a general *symbolic frame of reference* while structuredness is defined by *norms*. In its directedness (d), adaptivity (a), identity (i) and structuredness (s), action is thus a function of ends (E), means (M), symbolic frame of reference (F) and norms (N) under particular conditions (C):[9]

$$A_{d, a, i, s} = f(E, M, F, N)C$$

The extent to which action is guided into one of these four fields and determined either by ends, situation, frame of reference or norms depends on the formation of *principles of action* (P):

- Action can be determined by the *optimization principle* (P(op)). As logically deduced from ends, power and particular initial conditions.
- Action can be determined by the *optimization principle* (P(op)). As such it is the logical product of means and conditions in a situation with the optimum of preference realization being calculated, this in particular initial conditions.

- Action can be determined by the *consistency principle* (P(cp)). It is then logically subsumed under a general frame of reference in particular initial conditions.
- Action can be determined by the *conformity principle* (P(np)). In this case it follows as a logical deduction from norms and commitment to these norms in particular initial conditions.

The extent to which action is guided by one or other of these principles depends in turn on the strength of various structures and media as factors guiding action.

- Definite need dispositions, performance capacity, well defined decision-making structures and power lead action into the field of directedness with realization as the guiding principle.
- Learning processes, intelligence, exchange processes and incentives (money) lead action into the adaptive field with optimization the guiding principle.
- Symbolizations, definitions of situation, discourse and argument lead action into the field of identity with consistency the guiding principle.
- Affectual attachment to norms, affectual bonds, community formation and commitments lead action into the field of structuredness with conformity the guiding principle.

How strongly these structures and media affect action depends on their degree of development as well as on the degree of development and the structure of the mediating systems between them which tend toward the extreme poles of the action space or combine several aspects:

- If mediating systems do not exist, structures and media that are only poorly developed will be dominated by those that have reached a high degree of development. This oversteering of action is not quite as great if mediating systems exist between the more highly and the less developed structures and media. The greater the structural similarity between the mediating systems and the dominant structures, the more this process occurs.
- If the degree of development of all structures and media is low and there are no mediating systems between them, action is malintegrated and its scope is limited. The formation of mediating systems integrates action but its scope remains limited.
- If all structures and media are highly developed and no mediating systems exist the result is conflict. Where mediating systems have developed action is integrated and its scope is large. In this case the subsystems of action interpenetrate.

We can sum up by saying that:

- Action moves between the fields of directedness, adaptivity, identity

and structuredness.
- This variation is a function of ends, means, frames of reference and norms in particular conditions. The relevance of these factors depends on the strength of the principles of realization, optimization, consistency and conformity.
- The strength of the principles of action is a function of various structures and media of action and of the relationship between them. This relationship can be one of malintegration or integration with a low development of structures and media. If development of structures and media is high, the relationship is one of domination, oversteering, conflict or interpenetration.

3.2 Power and conflict theory, economic theory, the idealistic theory of culture and normative theory in the voluntaristic frame of reference

We can, within the frame of reference of voluntaristic action theory, define the conditions in which action is guided either by one of its four principles or by an integrated or unintegrated combination of principles. What, in contrast to these restrictions, typifies specialized approaches is the assumption that a particular principle underlies action as a whole and that it applies in all four fields of action. Following on from the four principles of action we can distinguish four, analytically separate, theoretical approaches – two variants of positivism and idealism respectively. Utilitarianism and *economic theory* represent a version of positivism in which action is guided by the randomness of situation and the optimization principle. In *power and conflict theory*'s positivism, action is determined by the extreme structuring of situations, the distribution of power, for example, by the domination of specific goals and by the realization principle. The *idealistic theory of culture* (or rationalistic idealism) conceives of action as being guided by a general frame of reference and the consistency principle. The other version of idealism, *normative theory* (or normativistic idealism), sees action being determined solely by norms and the conformity principle. The actual extent of each of these theoretical approaches will now be demonstrated by using the frame of reference of the voluntaristic theory of action.[10] The descriptions of the theoretical approaches are of course analytical constructs. These exist not just in a pure form but also in various combinations, some more integrated than others. A very common unintegrated combination links abstractive and rationalistic idealism with abstractive, rationalistic elements of positivism. Its explanatory tools are reduced to a combination of ethical rationalizations of culture with instrumental, systemic rationalization of the economic and political spheres. The historico-empirical level and the component of a theory of solidarity are thus excluded[11] (Figure 27).

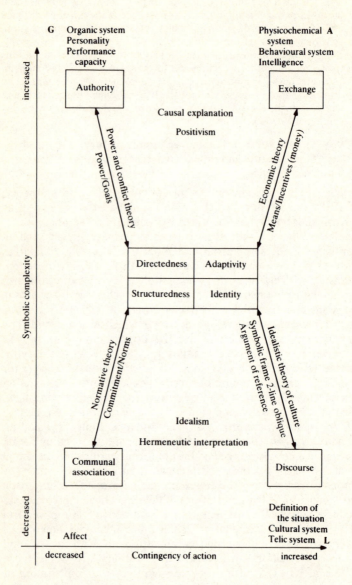

Figure 27 Spheres of action and theoretical approaches

3.2.1 Power and conflict theory

Let us first of all consider the realization principle. Action based on the *realization principle* involves the mobilization of power for goals and is a product of the power available to actors for the pursuit of particular goals. Action is deduced from the power to pursue particular goals. In extreme cases these push action in a specific direction regardless of situation, norms and frames of reference. At the level of the social system, action follows from the goals of those actors who are able to mobilize the most power. Explanatory interest is focused on the *execution* of actions that relate to goals. An actor can only carry out actions successfully if he has sufficient power. If, for example, we wish to explain why government B succeeded in realizing particular policies when its predecesor government A did not, we often put it down to government B having more (parliamentary) power at point t_2 than government A at point t_1.

The realization principle (P(rp)) is the fundamental principle of action in positivistic *power and conflict theory*.[12] It overstates the principle's validity by postulating all action (A) as a function of power mobilized for particular ends (E) relatively regardless of means (M), frame of reference (F), norms (N) and conditions (C):

$$A = f\ P\ (rp)\ (E(M,F,N))\ C$$

The realization principle, as propounded here, applies totally and in all the fields of action. However, the realization principle is only valid in the field of the directedness of action. It can certainly explain *goal realization* in action without having to take circumstances into account. Thus, an actor with sufficient power and performance capacity can take the *most direct route* to his goals whereas an actor with insufficient power often has to take the long way round. However, the realization principle ceases to provide satisfactory explanations as soon as action enters other fields of action. It cannot explain action that comes about despite actors having no power or only very little. And neither can the principle explain the acquisition of power unless this is based on already existing power. In order to obtain more power an actor would, according to the theory, have to have more power than other actors before he even started. The theory of power fails whenever learning processes enable actors to adapt more successfully to their environment, in other words, in the field of adaptivity. Processes such as the success of actors with no power and actors who at first have less power acquiring more than other actors are, for power and conflict theory, anomalies. They have to be explained with the help of ad hoc hypotheses and residual categories that do not form an integral part of its frame of reference. Its basic hypothesis is as follows:

Of two actors, the one with more power will realize his goals.

This hypothesis is falsified whenever a more powerful actor fails to realize his goals and less powerful actors realize theirs. It is fair to assume that this happens rather frequently especially when, as a result of learning processes, increased adaptivity and variability of action, less powerful actors successfully by-pass other actors' power or obtain power. David's defeat of the more powerful Goliath is an example of this.

Let us assume that our falsification of conflict theory is not based on mistaken assumptions as to the actual power of the two combatants, that is, that David really is less powerful than Goliath. In that case, there are two courses open to adherents of the theory: to expand the concept of power or to introduce ad hoc hypotheses and residual categories. They can stretch the concept of power till it covers every means toward the realization of goals and not just those means with which other actors' resistance can be overcome which is the usual sociological definition. One could of course include David's cunning and intelligence in an expanded sense of 'power' but this would make the concept of power very vague indeed. It would then be synonymous with 'ability to act' and would no longer contain the characteristic effect of power, which is that goals are converted into action in as *direct* a way as possible irrespective of situation, frames of reference and norms. This does not mean that power ultimately steers action in all its facets. When we say that David's cunning triumphed over Goliath's power we mean that it was not a simple case of superior power defeating inferior power but that another factor limits the effectiveness of power as a means of steering action. The fact that David has to make more detours than Goliath before he can act shows that this other determinant steers action in a different way to power. David's action does not take place in the field of directedness assisted by the power to achieve his aims but in the field of the adaptivity of action. Here action displays more openness (variability). In the field of directedness it is assumed that an actor has a number of primary goals and that these are realized by using the power at his disposal. Only a comparatively minor variation of action is called for. In the field of adaptivity, on the other hand, goals and means vary much more. Action is primarily oriented toward optimizing goal realization in a given situation. In the light of experience, the order of priority of goals can vary constantly so that action develops no clear directedness. The fox that has learned that the grapes are too high for it to reach quickly abandons this particular goal and turns its attention to more realizable goals. These two very different steering factors would be supplanted by the extremely imprecise determinant of the 'ability to act' if we were to extend the concept of power to cover the field of adaptivity. If we keep to a more precise definition of power and falsify the theory, the only thing left for its adherents is to introduce residual categories and ad hoc hypotheses. Such residual categories would not be integrated into the frame of reference, while the ad hoc hypotheses containing them would not be integrated into the system of theoretical statements. An example of a residual category would be the concept of the ability to learn and a suitable ad hoc hypothesis would be the assumption that an actual case of a less powerful actor being more successful than a more powerful actor could be explained by his cunning and intelligence.

The theory of power and conflict is not in a position to explain actions that have their roots in learning processes and that allow actors to find a way round the obstacles confronting them and to act regardless of how much power is available to them. If the theory held true, the more powerful actors would also have to be always the more cunning. With the general theory of action we can explain why the theory of power and conflict breaks down here. According to its assumptions the realization principle can only explain action that occurs in the field of absolute directedness, the realization of goals by the most direct route. The premises of the theory of action state, however, that when action is oriented toward the optimization principle the directedness of action and the effectiveness of power are limited. This is all the more likely at the social level the more developed the use of incentives (money) and exchange have become as institutions and the more the character of the mediating systems between exchange and power is one of exchange. In parliamentary democracies, the free articulation of interests and the search for political support perform this opening function. The more these are institutionalized, the more opening processes counteract the effects of power and reduce the directedness of action. Action shifts increasingly into the area of adaptivity and this varies more easily. At the general level of action, learning processes have the same effect. Their development and mediation with the exercise of power also reduces the directedness of action resulting from power. All political actors are forced to proceed in a more roundabout way and political decision-making becomes a very varying, very indirect and often arduous process. On the other hand, power is all the more likely to be effective in determining action the less incentives, exchange and learning processes are institutionalized. Thus the voluntaristic theory of action can be used to define the conditions in which the theory of conflict applies or does not apply.

The theory of power and conflict not only fails in the field of adaptivity. It is similarly unsuccessful in the field of the identity of action. This is particularly true in the case of innovations. Power and conflict theory leads us to expect only those innovations to be successful for which more power can be mobilized than for their predecessors or rivals:

Of two actors, the more powerful of the two will succeed in putting his innovations into practice.

This hypothesis is contradicted when less powerful actors succeed in putting their innovations into practice and more powerful actors do not. We can assume that this happens quite frequently. The theory of power and conflict has therefore been falsified again.

If we exclude attempts to expand the concept of power, proponents of the theory are again reduced to introducing residual categories and ad hoc hypotheses. They could point out that the less powerful but successful innovator succeeded in proving that his action was in fact more in line with accepted, more general goals than previous ways of acting. This amounts to admitting that, in certain conditions, power and conflict theory does not apply and that actions can also be realized without power. The condition for this is that a change in action can be subsumed under more general and accepted goals. Thus in this case it is the field of identity in which power and conflict theory is falsified. If power were the basic determinant of action, there could be no changes or innovation in action unless there had first been power struggles and shifts in the distribution of power. This is quite obviously wrong and increasingly so the more actors in a given social context share a common, general, symbolic frame of reference under which they can subsume a larger number of actions acceptable to all of them. General symbolic frames of reference enable action to vary greatly while keeping its identity. Thus, rational argumentative subsumption under a commonly accepted, general, symbolic frame of reference, not enforcement through power, is the factor here which allows innovations to be put into practice. The general theory of action shows us that this is more likely the greater the institutional development of discursive procedures and the more discursive mediating systems limit the effectiveness of power as a determinant of action. On the other hand, where argument, discursive procedures and discursive mediating systems are less institutionalized it has to be assumed that power plays a greater part in the implementation of innovations. The general theory of action thus demonstrates which conditions power and conflict theory is valid in and which not.

The field of the structuredness of action is another field of action in which conflict theory produces incorrect prognoses. Regularity of action can, according to the theory, only be explained if certain actors permanently enjoy more power and if regularity permanently serves the realization of their goals. If regularity loses this function, we can expect the more powerful actors to abandon it:

If an actor can mobilize more power to change a regularity than other actors can to uphold it, and if the regularity has lost its function for his goals, the change will be effected.

This hypothesis is contradicted by the everyday experience of how regularity of action is maintained even though it would be more functional to the goal realization of the more powerful actors if that regularity were abandoned.

Democracy implies that the party or parties that win an election do not misuse their power to overturn all the rules of action that they think are a nuisance. Their motive for not doing so is perhaps prudence, which means that they are acting not in the field of directedness but of adaptivity. In the more stable democracies, commitment to the democratic institutions is undoubtedly another motive. If we again rule out observational error and any extension of the power concept, power and conflict theorists once more have to resort to residual categories and ad hoc hypotheses if anomalies like this are to be explained. They could point out that traditions tend to have long lives. While this hypothesis is beyond power and conflict theory's frame of reference we can, with the frame of reference of the general theory of action, explain why it is only true in certain conditions that the maintenance of, or change in, regularities are functions of the power that can be mobilized for such ends. We can also show that the permanence of regularities is proof that action is to a certain degree immune to distributions of power. The functionality of regularities for an individual actor's goals varies much more than the regularities themselves. In the frame of reference of action theory, this feature, the structuredness of action irrespective of situations and goals, is explained by reference to more permanent factors. These are the degree to which actors feel part of a larger community, and the commitment to shared norms that results. These in turn are based on an affectual sense of belonging. They restrict both power and the use of power as a means of steering action. Action can therefore only be seen as the product of mobilizable power if rules of action are not maintained irrespective of goals and situations as a result of community formation, commitment, obligation to norms and communally structured mediating systems. As far as political action is concerned, commitment to the democratic community and its norms limits the effectiveness of power as a determining factor.

Summing up we can say that in the action theory frame of reference the validity of power and conflict theory's realization principle has to be qualified as follows: It only explains absolute *directedness* of action toward goals. This assumes that need dispositions, performance capacity, the use of power and authority are all clearly developed and that learning processes and intelligence, exchange and incentives (money), symbolizations and definitions of the situation, discourse and argumentation, affectual attachment to norms and affectual belonging, communal association and commitment to shared norms are not. This also assumes that mediating systems are clearly developed according to authority relations or that they are entirely missing. Where these features apply the political system oversteers other subsystems or it dominates them. The effect of the clearer development of the other subsystems and the non-political structuring of the mediating systems is to limit the effectiveness of power. Action then moves much more into the fields of adaptivity, identity and structuredness and these are not bound by the realization principle. What follows is a formalized definition of the validity of power and conflict theory as qualified above:

Action is more and more a function of an actor's goals and the power he can mobilize, irrespective of means, frames of reference, norms and conditions; it is all the more clearly directed and has less and less adaptivity, identity and structuredness, the clearer the development of performance capacity/need dispositions, power/authority and the less clear the development of intelligence/learning process, incentives (money)/exchange, definitions of situation/symbolizations, argumentation/discourse, affectual belonging/affectual attachment to norms, commitment/communal association and the less clear the development of mediating systems or the more their structure is one of power/authority.

3.2.2 Economic theory

Our examination of the individual principles of action continues with the *optimization principle*. When action is guided by the optimization principle, actors choose to perform those actions for which they expect an optimum of goal realization. Action evolves logically from the principle and the initial conditions prevailing in a situation. In the purest example of optimization the determining force of goals is dependent on the calculation of the optimum in the particular situation. Similarly, symbolic frames of reference and norms are in a state of flux. The optimization principle covers goals, frames of reference and norms so that their effect on action varies depending on means and conditions in each particular situation. If the pursuit of a particular goal has a negative effect on other goals, its priority is lowered. Action, therefore, lacks a clarity of direction. Its location is the field of adaptivity. Here the variability and openness of action are at their highest. The main determinant of action is *situation*.

The optimization principle (P(op)) is *economic theory*'s principle of action.[13] It uses this principle to explain action as a whole and not just adaptive action. In other words, it regards all action as adaptive action. Directedness, identity and structuredness are non-existent because they cannot be perceived in a perspective of this kind. Action (A) is merely a function of the optimization (P(op)) of ends (E) through the use of means (M) in particular conditions (C). Symbolic frames of reference (F) and norms (N) are on a par with the other factors. They are equally a part of the optimization calculation and are therefore open to infinite variation:

$$A = f \ P(op) \ (M(E,F,N)) \ C$$

This extension of the optimization principle's object domain leads to incorrect predictions as soon as action enters the fields of directedness, identity and structuredness.

We shall consider the field of directedness first. The optimization principle says that action changes whenever situations or means and conditions change:

If, with a change of situation from y_1 to y_2, the optimality of action x_1 changes in favour of action x_2, the actor will switch from action x_1 to x_2.

This hypothesis is contradicted if, in the relevant conditions, actors do not switch to action a_2 but persist with action a_1. Their action is then less dependent on situations and more clearly directed than economic theory assumes.

As there are numerous examples of this kind of goal-directedness, we can regard economic theory as falsified as far as the field of directedness is concerned. Actors do not vary their action as often as they would have to if they only applied the optimization principle. Rational choice theorists could of course attempt to prove that persisting with action a_1 represented greater utility than action a_2. They could point to the effects of action a_2 on the actor's other goals. When these goals are taken into account a_1 appears to have better achieved the optimum than a_2. This method of subsequently introducing new goals is one frequently used to shield economic theory against falsification. This usually means the theorist re-constructs the situation until it makes 'economic sense' again. This way the theory can always be saved from falsification by the introduction of new goals. Economic theory thus becomes a completely elastic tool quite unsuitable for the making of precise predictions.

Action is all the more undetermined, and even fully open, the more goals an actor has with regard to which his action can be optimized. Theoretically action cannot possibly be goal-directed in this case. This assumption is, however, refuted by the fact that action often displays a continuous orientation toward goals. It is here that optimization theorists are forced to resort to residual categories and ad hoc hypotheses beyond their own frame of reference. The relevant residual category is the assumption that action is optimized within *strictly defined* goals whereas actors maximize their action with reference to a limited number of goals. Whether they can accomplish this in a changed situation without a change in action depends on how much power is available to them.

In contrast, these factors are integrated into the frame of reference of the voluntaristic theory of action. It only predicts the complete non-directedness and rapid situational variation of action if exchange processes, incentives (money) and learning processes have fully evolved and actors have neither superior goals nor the necessary power to realize them. At the level of political action, this state of affairs exists when the societal collective as a corporate actor fails to specify superior political goals or when clear decision-making structures and the corresponding power have not developed. In this case, political action consists of adaptive learning on the part of competing individuals and has no clear directedness.

Economic theory can also be falsified in the field of identity of action. According to the optimization principle, action only varies if optimality conditions change as a result of changes in situation, that is, in means and conditions. Variation in action is always nothing more than the result of learning processes or new incentives. This also means that actors have to learn to deal with every new situation and have to find an optimal course of action. Action can be expected not to change if conditions remain the same and actors do not acquire new means (through learning processes). If conditions alter, actors can only be expected to alter their action after fairly long learning processes and after acquiring new means. If action is a constant search for the optimum it ought to remain the same in unchanged situations and be marked by a time-consuming search in changed situations:

If, for an actor, the situation remains the same, his action will remain the same. If the situation changes, new action only appears after some time.

The first assumption is refuted when action varies although the situation remains the same and the second when action does not alter with situations. It can be assumed that this happens quite often and that the theory's predictions will therefore be refuted.

The husband who knows how to please his wife and who does not give her flowers every day but does one thing one day and another thing the next is an example of how action can vary although conditions remain the same. The student who has grasped the principles of geometry and who can therefore answer a whole range of questions does not have to alter his action with each change of situation. He does not first have to master new time-consuming learning processes before he can answer new questions. A government that shares a normative frame of reference on the democratic decision-making process with other political actors can act in different ways in identical situations. In new situations, it can continue to act in its normal way without first having to engage in a long search for the optimal course of action.

To explain the anomalies that these examples represent to it, economic theory has to use residual categories and ad hoc hypotheses. The concept of the general symbolic frame of reference is one such residual category and the assumption that action is altered in identical situations and not altered in new situations if it can be subsumed by means of rational argument under a general symbolic frame of reference represents an ad hoc hypothesis as far as economic theory is concerned. In the latter case actors have the ability to use general features of action as a means of orientation under which they can subsume a number of more specific actions and which they can apply to a variety of situations. While this hypothesis lies beyond economic theory's frame of reference it does form part of the frame of reference of the voluntaristic theory of action. Furthermore the latter theory can also determine the conditions in which it is valid. These are well developed discursive structures and the widespread use of rational argument. On the other hand, action is more likely to remain the same in identical situations and to require new adaptive processes in new situations if discursive structures and the use of rational argument are not particularly widespread and action is dominated by exchange, incentives and trial and error. If a husband and wife do not talk to each other very much he will hardly be able to vary the way he acts. He will have to learn by experience on every occasion. The same is true for the mathematics student at school and, in a political context, for governments. The less democratic decision-making processes are the subject of discourse and the greater the role of pure interest politics, the more the making of political decisions becomes a matter of trial and error and a constant search for the optimum.

Economic theory has just as much trouble with the field of the structuredness of action. The theory states that action can be expected to vary whenever situations, conditions and means change because, as a rule, conditions of optimality vary with changes in situation. If it has just been raining and using an umbrella was optimal, keeping it up is just an unnecessary waste of energy if the sun is now shining unless one wants to exercise one's arm muscles. The economic hypothesis in question can be formulated as follows:

If in situation y_1 action x_1 is optimal and action x_2 in situation y_2, and the situation changes from y_1 to y_2, actors will alter their action from x_1 to x_2.

The retention of action a_1 in situation b_2 represents a refutation of the hypothesis. As this can be observed quite frequently, we can consider economic theory falsified in this particular field of action.

It is of course true that we put our umbrellas away if it stops raining, that we sell our cars if they become too expensive to run, that we buy new shirts if we do not like our old ones and that we look around for a new theory if our old one is causing too many problems. But it is just as true that we often find it hard to give up something that has become useless and costly and to take up something new that would bring us closer to an optimum of goal realization. We often turn down the chance of personal profit because of things and people dear to us. We do not change our wives, husbands, friends, students and clients from one day to the next like shirts, trousers and jackets just because life with them has become harder, more costly and demands more sacrifices than before. And when we act this way our action can, as far as achieving optimum goal-realization is concerned, be most irrational.

To explain this type of action using economic theory one would have to prove that sticking to old forms of behaviour even though there had been a change in situation was the optimum course of action with regard to other goals. However if we take the economic approach to its logical conclusion, there cannot possibly be any lasting goal except for the optimization principle itself. The economically minded act in strict accordance with the optimization principle, that is, they choose to perform those actions that promise optimum return. If the scrap metal trade is more lucrative than philosophy and pop music more lucrative than jazz, they will switch from philosophy to scrap metal and from jazz to pop. Only those goals that can be realized as fully as possible without impinging upon other goals are selected as a basis for action. Optimizing actors have no fixed goals except for the optimization principle and rush from one activity to another. Their action is devoid of continuity. Continuing with certain forms of behaviour is out of the question since this would always involve lost opportunities and losses elsewhere. One could go as far as to say that particular action ranks so highly that benefits always outweigh costs. One would then have to describe as economically rational the action of a manufacturer who continued producing goods that nobody bought until he starved to death as a result. In a case like this, starvation must have been so high-ranking a goal that producing unwanted goods was the most economic course for the manufacturer to take. Explanatory strategies of this sort, however, contradict the optimization principle, which does not allow for action to be so one-sided and continuous in orientation toward a single goal without the effects on other goals being taken into account. Since conditions of optimality are changing all the time it is quite impossible for a particular goal and a particular mode of action to establish themselves at the expense of other goals.

It is at this point that economic theorists have to resort to residual categories and ad hoc hypotheses not inherent in their approach. In most cases these are tradition and the affectual attachment to things, people and actions. They are said to prevent actors from acting economically and rationally. Someone who has always bought his newspaper at the shop around the corner will not suddenly switch to a subscription even if it is preferable economically. Someone who has always had coffee in the morning will not become a tea drinker just because coffee has become much more expensive than tea. If someone loves philosophy, he will not swap it for a lucrative scrap metal business. If a man loves his wife he will not replace her as soon as their life together becomes more difficult. Someone who loves a sports team will continue to support them even if they lose fairly often. Someone who loves democracy does not turn his back on it just because he has lost the democratic competition for power. For economic theory, these assumptions are ad hoc hypotheses from beyond its frame of reference whereas for voluntaristic action theory they are special assumptions within its frame of reference. Voluntaristic action theory states that highly structured action cannot follow from principles such as the optimization principle that imply the constant adapation of action to new situations, but only from principles that immunize at least certain aspects of action against situational changes. This is the function of norms and affectual attachments of the actor to those norms, mediated by the affectual attachment to a community as the carrier of the norms. The more these have evolved, the greater the structuredness of action and the less it will vary according to optimality calculations. On the other hand, where exchange, incentives and learning processes dominate, and commitments and affectual attachments to norms and communities are lacking, action follows optimality calculations and varies from situation to situation. It is increasingly easy to change things, people and modes of action the less affectually attached we are and the more accustomed we are to exchange in general.

Summing up, we can say that economic theory's optimization principle only explains modes and aspects of action in the field of adaptive action, that is, modes of action that vary from situation to situation. Economic theory breaks down in the fields of the directedness, identity and structuredness of action. It is only valid in the following conditions:

Action is all the more a function of the optimization of actors' goal realization, with situation a decisive factor and with goals, frames of reference and norms being submitted to the optimization calculation, and is all the more adaptive and displays less directedness, identity and structuredness, the clearer the development of intelligence/learning processes, incentives (money)/exchange and the less clear the development of performance capacity/need dispositions, power/authority, definitions of situation/symbolization, argument/discourse, affectual bonds/affectual attachment to norms, commitments/communal association and the less mediating systems have evolved or the more they are structured along incentive/exchange lines.

3.2.3 The idealistic theory of culture

We shall now examine another principle of action, the *consistency principle*. When action accords with the consistency principle it is subsumed under a general symbolic frame of reference and is logically deduced from the frame of reference and the respective initial conditions. As the frame of reference can establish symbolic meaning, can be normative, expressive or cognitive in character, it and the respective initial conditions give rise to particular 'meaning constructions', norm orientations, expressions and cognitions in action. The frame of reference enables action to retain its identity irrespective of goals, means, conditions and norms, which are themselves integrated into the frame of reference. Someone who views the world in economic terms will perform a whole variety of actions but his action will still retain its economic character. Someone who sees the world as an object of love will interpret all concrete action, for all its variation, as an act of love. The actor who sees the world as a struggle for power perceives all his action in terms of superior and inferior power. If the world is regarded as a process of communication, all action is seen as contributing to that communication. If all the actors in an interactional context perceive the world in the same frame of reference they always, when applying their own respective interpretations, see action in the same light. If, for example they see political action in terms of democratic compromise, they can always retain a basic higher-order characteristic no matter how much action may vary. Actors' orientation is thus toward maintaining the *consistency* of the frame of reference. Action is only allowed if it falls within the frame of reference. Thanks, however, to the scope of the frame of reference and its integrative power actors are able to vary their action considerably. Action retains its *identity* as consistently democratic action, for example, in spite of variation in the particular.

The consistency principle ($P(cp)$) is the only principle of action in the *idealistic theory of culture* or rational idealism.[14] It treats the totality of action as the result of the subsumption of particular actions under a general frame of reference by means of rational argument. Taking the social level, action is a product of processes of symbolic communication within a common general frame of reference:

$$A = fP(cp) \ (F(E,M,N)) \ C$$

Such an extension of the consistency principle as in the idealistic theory of culture is falsified in fields other than that of the identity of action.

We need only consider the field of adaptive action to realize the theory's weaknesses. It can only explain constant general features of action but not particular features that vary according to situation, nor can it explain changes in the frame of reference of action. Action is expected not to vary even in changing situations:

An actor with frame of reference z will continue to act according to z if situation y_1 changes to situation y_2.

This hypothesis is contradicted whenever frame of reference c is not applied in situation b_2. It is fair to assume that this is no infrequent occurrence and that the idealistic theory of culture is therefore falsified.

The requirements for falsification are met whenever a scientist's observations contradict his general theory or whenever an actor deviates from his general principles. As a rule such occurrences are attributed to learning processes. The scientist has learned from experience and the moralist has discovered that he can act 'more successfully' in certain situations if he departs from his basic principles. For the idealistic theory of culture, however, learning is a residual category, and learning hypotheses are ad hoc hypotheses. They lie beyond its frame of reference.

Another field of action in which the consistency principle produces invalid predictions is that of directedness. According to the principle, action cannot be expected to be directed at the level of specific actions. At this level action is indefinite and is not directed so that relatively accidental situational changes are to be expected. For those acting consistently in a general frame of reference, how they act in a particular concrete instance is of no interest. This is true of the innerworldly mystic, for example. He is not concerned with concrete action as long as he maintains his oneness with God. In changing situations, identical action cannot be expected at a level more specific than the frame of reference. If a situation contains a number of alternatives, an actor with only one frame of reference is unable to take decisions. His action is likely to vary randomly:

If actions x_1 and x_2 are alternative realizations of frame of reference z for an actor, the choice of x_1 or x_2 is a random one.

This hypothesis is contradicted whenever an actor with frame of reference c does not choose randomly between alternative actions a_1 and a_2 but directs his action to one of these alternatives. As this is quite often the case the consistency principle does not enable accurate forecasts to be made.

The scope of action allowed by a constitution is wider than that realized by political legislation. Nevertheless, legislation is binding. It therefore narrows the scope of action although other forms of action are conceivable under the constitution. It is power that makes this narrowing down possible. Where action is goal-directed despite the existence of alternatives, the idealistic theory of culture is forced to resort to residual categories and ad hoc hypotheses. Deviation from the principle of randomness has to be explained in terms of the fixed goals and the power available to an actor. These do not, however, form part of the idealistic theory of culture's frame of reference.

The consistency principle can also not be successfully applied in the field of the structuredness of action on the comparatively concrete level of repeatedly performed actions. Its frame of reference would again lead us to expect much greater variation in concrete actions than is in fact the case. The consistency principle states that actors have a relatively wide frame of reference allowing for relatively large variation in concrete actions:

An actor with frame of reference z will be found to perform actions x_1 and x_2 if they can be subsumed under frame of reference z.

This hypothesis is contradicted by the continuity of action a_1 even though frame of reference c also allows action a_2. The fact that this occurs frequently falsifies the idealistic theory of culture in this particular field.

For scientists, the search for truth is a general frame of reference. It allows statements to be tested not only empirically and statistically but also hermeneutically. In spite of this, most scientists do not alternate between the two methods but adhere firmly to just one of them. Their concrete action is substantially narrower than their general frame of reference. Similarly, other values such as the principles of freedom and equality allow far more scope than is realized in concrete action. In nineteenth-century liberal society the view of equality as mere civil equality before the law was self-evident. The extension of the concept of equality to political, social and cultural participation was achieved only very slowly although scope for this extension had always been inherently present in the principle of equality. In order to explain such restrictions that are regarded as self-evident one would have to bring in the affectual attachment to norms through community formation. These are factors that lie beyond the frame of reference of the idealistic theory of culture and have to be introduced as residual categories in ad hoc hypotheses.

Summing up, we can say that the consistency principle of the idealistic theory of culture only explains action in the field of the identity of action, in other words the consistency of action in relatively high variability. The theory breaks down in the fields of the adaptivity, directedness and structuredness of action. It is valid under the following conditions:

Action is to a greater degree a function of the consistency principle, maintains its identity to a greater degree and displays less and less adaptivity, directedness and conformity the clearer the development of definitions of situation/symbolization, argument/discourse, and the less clear the development of performance capacity/need dispositions, power/authority, intelligence/learning processes, incentives (money)/exchange, affectual bonds/affectual attachment to norms, commitments/communal association, with mediating systems poorly developed or discursive in structure.

3.2.4 Normative theory

We finally turn to the *principle of conformity* as a general principle of action. For an actor acting according to the principle of conformity, action is always a fulfilment of norms in concrete situations. The action results as a logical deduction from the commitment to norms and concrete conditions for the application of the norms. One norm for example rules out the use of officially forbidden aids at examinations. If candidates resist any temptation in this direction, their action can be logically derived from this norm and the situation of the examination. In this case, the principle of conformity explains particularly such acts of conformity to norms which are performed without any expectation of gain or any fear of sanctions. The decisive variable here is the commitment to norms which is based on the affectual attachment to the norms produced by communal association. The principle of conformity explains action which remains structured and shows a certain regularity in different situations even in the absence of stable external conditions, calculations of utility and threatening sanctions. The believer who goes regularly to daily prayer through rain, hail or storm, the Puritan who always approaches economic action with total honesty, even under unfavourable conditions, both act according to the principle of conformity.

The principle of conformity (P(np)) serves as an exclusive principle of action to *normative theory*, to normative idealism.[15] An implicit normative theory often underlies works of phenomenological sociology, of ethnomethodology, objective hermeneutics, and symbolic interactionism. They conceive action as the interpretation of a general frame of reference, for example of a normative shared life-world, of a milieu, or of an objective meaning structure. However, on the level of complex societal interconnections, action within such a frame of reference is relatively indeterminate, the most varied specifications of the frame of reference then become possible. The basic values of modern societies do not immediately result in concrete institutions and actions. It is therefore no coincidence that works taking the above-mentioned approaches are confined to relatively closed social contexts like the family, within which the symbolic frame of reference unequivocally determines action, and where a one-to-one definite relationship between symbol articulation and action exists. Here, action is interpreted as the fulfilment of norms. The representatives of these approaches do not generally recognize that they thus succumb to a hypostatization of the principle of conformity and do not possess a frame of reference for the *theoretical* integration of non-normative factors. These have to be introduced surreptitiously, partly unnoticed, as residual categories. In this sense, a large part of the literature regarding itself subjectively as belonging to idealistic culture theory can also be related to normative theory in its objective consequences. This brings to light the idealistic dilemma of the contradiction between autonomy and conformity. In terms of normative theory, every action has to be explained as a deduction from norms and their conditions of application:

$$A = f P(np) (N(E,M,F)) C$$

Such an extension of the principle of conformity to all fields of action however leads to falsifications outside the action field of structuredness.

In the action field of adaptivity, action varies from situation to situation contrary to the principle of conformity. Nevertheless, according to normative theory, any situation occurring in which the initial conditions for a certain norm are given can always be expected to produce the appropriate norm-conforming action:

If the conditions of applying a norm are realized in several situations, the norm will be fulfilled by action in every situation.

Every action in one of the above situations which does not fulfil the appropriate norm contradicts this normativistic hypothesis; every variation of action to suit a new situation opposes the hypothesis. This state of affairs always arises when situational deviations from norms occur; hence normative theory is falsified in these cases.

Acts contradicting the normative hypothesis can be explained by the fact that other actions are more useful in certain situations and that the individuals learn how to manage situations better by departing from normatively prescribed paths. These categories however constitute residual categories for normative theory which have to be introduced by ad hoc hypotheses. They lie outside its frame of reference.

Normative theory also faces problems of explanation in the field of directedness of action. According to its premises unchanging action can only be expected where the actors cannot imagine other alternatives, because of the normative confinement of their horizons of expectation which has already taken place:

If no norms determine action, it varies from situation to situation.

Every case where the directedness of action extends over different situations without a preceding normative confinement of the imaginable alternatives of action contradicts this hypothesis. Normative theory is falsified by this frequently occurring fact.

Every political act of law-making enforces a particular prescription for action extending over different situations without a preceding normative limitation of the alternatives of action. Here the relevant factor is power which has to be brought in by an ad hoc hypothesis, because it lies outside the frame of reference of normative theory.

Finally, the field of identity is a further field of action within which the principle of conformity turns out not to be successful. According to the principle of conformity, an innovation, that is, a change in the course of action though the situation remains the same, is impossible without the dissolution of the respective norms:

If a norm is valid for a certain situation, one and the same action can always be expected in that particular situation.

Every change of action without a preceding change of norms contradicts this hypothesis. As this is the case frequently enough, normative theory can be considered falsified in this context too.

The above conditions always arise when action is guided by general normative principles without further specifications, leaving ample scope for actors to make innovations without preceding changes of norms. This holds true for contract law and for norms of professional action in a particularly telling way. The most different contract models are possible within the frame of reference of contract law, the most different solutions to professional problems within the frame of reference of professional ethics. Innovations have to be explained in this context by discursive argumentation which proves a particular action may be subsumed under a general norm. However, discursive argumentation reaches beyond the frame of reference of normative theory and has to be brought in as a residual category by an appropriate ad hoc hypothesis.

We can sum up as follows: The principle of conformity is capable of explaining action in the field of structuredness, but not in the fields of adaptivity, directedness, and identity. Normative theory has therefore to be qualified in the following way:

The more affectual ties/affectual attachment to norms, commitments/communal association are clearly developed, and the less clearly performance capacity/need dispositions, power/authority, intelligence/learning processes, incentives (money)/exchange, definitions of situation/symbols, arguments/discourse are developed, and the less mediating systems are clearly developed or the more they are communally structured, the more action is a function of the principle of conformity, the more it is definitely structured, and the less it shows adaptivity, directedness and identity.

Concluding remarks

We have so far seen that the more comprehensive frame of reference of voluntaristic action theory can point out the conditions which must be fulfilled before the individual action-theoretical approaches can be regarded as valid. This holds true for each of the four approaches considered here; each of them has its validity confined to one action field in the action space of symbolic complexity and contingency of action. Economic theory and power and conflict theory, as variants of positivism, and culture theory and normative theory, as variants of idealism, are all theories whose validity is confined to a particular action field. Voluntaristic action theory succeeds in including the residual categories and ad hoc hypotheses of specific approaches in its conceptual and theoretical frame of reference by specifying the limiting conditions of validity of the individual approaches and by surpassing them in its applicability. In this way, it achieves an advance in knowledge compared to the other theoretical approaches. It excludes the false content of the older approaches, retains their true content and hence surpasses them in its total content.

Concluding considerations: 'Dialetically' replacing positivism and idealism with the voluntaristic theory of action

Since the beginning of modern science Western thought has been marked by the competition of two fundamental traditions – the idealism of the intellectual disciplines, the humanities, on the one hand, and on the other, the positivism of the scientific and technical disciplines. Both schools of thought exist in two more or less extreme or diluted forms, depending on their orientation toward analytical abstraction and/or empirical concretion. Idealism thus varies from pure rationalistic idealism, the greatest exponent of which was René Descartes, to historicistic idealism, which reached its peak in the German historicism of the second half of the nineteenth century. Positivism ranges from rationalistic positivism with emphasis on scientific theoretical abstraction and the deductive process, to empiricist positivism that takes empirical perception as its starting point and aims at induction.

The quality which really is peculiar to modern Western thought is that these opposing schools of thought are not completely separated from each other and allocated to different spheres, but that they compete, discuss and influence each other, penetrate the direction of each other's thinking, making possible a higher-level integration of the two fundamental traditions in a new, more comprehensive paradigm. This is not to deny that conflict still exists between the two traditions. Attention has, however, to be drawn to the fact that modern Western science contains a considerable number of approaches aimed at overcoming the gap between the two schools of thought. It is this tendency that so fundamentally distinguishes Western science from that of non-Western cultures.[1]

Outside the modern West both schools of thought do exist, but they are separated from one another, or one particular school dominates over the other. There is a highly developed technological-practical thinking in the sense of an empiricist positivism in China, but abstracting rationalism is much less developed, and as far as it exists at all, rationalism is divided from empiricism. Abstract thought, rationalistic idealism, has advanced extraordinarily far in India, and one can also find impressive empiricistic-positivistic thinking, but both are distributed to completely separated spheres and carrier strata. Nowhere has rationalistic idealistic thought succeeded as it did in Hellenistic philosophy; and antiquity also left witnesses of a highly developed technology based on empiricistic-positivistic thinking, but both are hierarchically graduated and thereby related to particular spheres. The two schools of thought conjoined to a considerable extent in the scientific communities of the Italian Renaissance in the sixteenth and seventeenth centuries and each had equal rights for the first time. Here, a far reaching mutual penetration takes place, the first and qualitatively new result of which is the *rational* experiment which has to be distinguished from purely empirical trials. This development continues in the scientific communities of seventeenth-century England and spreads through Europe and the USA in the following centuries.[2]

In the field of philosophy, Immanuel Kant achieved the first and most consistent integration of idealism and positivism. Kant showed that modern science is characterized by the combination of regulated orderedness with openness for experience, and of theoretical general validity with empirical specification. These characteristics cannot be explained just from the collection of sensory perceptions, or from general categories, not from monistic ways of seeing the world, whether positivistic or idealistic, but through a dualistic view, namely through the interpenetration of categories of understanding and sensory perceptions.[3] The same holds true for the emerging modern Western social orders, at least in tendency and in comparison to all pre-modern and non-Western social orders. Their peculiarity is the connection of normative orderedness with an openness to interest articulations and change, of universal validity with concrete specification, including the thus ever-present conflict between these extremes. We can explain this quality neither purely in terms of the aggregate of the selfish inclinations of particular individuals nor purely in terms of the validity of categorical imperatives, and neither purely from hypothetical imperatives nor purely from general principles. The interpenetration of these factors is required; we can also see the knowledge of this fact rooted in Kant's thought. Kant pointed out that the unchangeable regularity of social orders is dependent on the validity of categorical imperatives. But he also demonstrated that – whatever the variations in practical needs for regulation – only universally generalizable principles can possess categorical validity and maintain continuity in change. Empirical orders, however, cannot rely solely upon these basic factors of categorical and universal validity, because they would lack variability and practical concretion if they did. Here, the interpenetration of universally valid and categorical principles with needs, interests and hypothetical imperatives is necessary. The knowledge of this fact can clearly be derived from Kant's practical philosophy, even if Kant stressed mainly the categorical and universally valid character of moral orders.[4]

Modern sociology, in the shape it took around the turn of the century, has to be viewed as a science in which the integration of the two traditions of idealism (the humanities) and positivism (the natural sciences) has obtained particular significance. No other science faces so severe a conflict between the two opposing approaches. It can be assumed that the conflict itself gives rise to new integrative approaches:

'The social sciences must be treated as a fully autonomous category. They are not natural sciences in the sense of excluding the categories of subjective meaning, that is, they must consider knowing subjects as objects. Nor are they humanistic-cultural in the sense that the individuality of particular meanings must take complete precedence over analytical generality and such categories as causality. The emergence of sociological theorizing in the sense outlined crystallized this synthesis more sharply than any other intellectual event of recent times.'[5]

The synthesis of positivism and idealism is particularly apparent in the works of Max Weber and Emile Durkheim. In his classical study, *The Structure of Social Action*, Talcott Parsons sees these two thinkers converging in a general theory of action on which their respective sociologies are based. He refers to it as a voluntaristic theory of action as opposed to idealistic and positivistic theories.[6] Voluntaristic action theory resolves the idealistic-positivistic conflict in an integrated paradigm.

In the voluntaristic perspective, human action varies from naturalistic dynamic to individual freedom. On the metatheoretical level, the theory of action thus extends from empiricistic-positivistic or rationalistic-positivistic varieties of causal explanation, to rationalistic-idealistic or historicistic-idealistic forms of meaning interpretation. In the field of human freedom, action moves between the dynamizing pole of learning and the articulation of interests, the controlling pole of commitment to norms, the generalizing pole of discursive orientation toward general principles and the specifying pole of the attainment of particular goals through power. Depending on how absolute the emphasis is on a particular pole, the object theory varies from utilitarian positivism (utilitarianism)[7] to normative idealism (normativism),[8] from rationalistic idealism (theory of reason)[9] to power and conflict-theoretical positivism (power and conflict theory).[10]

As a rule, metatheoretical rationalistic positivism is associated with object-theoretical positivistic utilitarianism, empiricist positivism with positivistic power and conflict theory, rationalistic idealism with the idealistic theory of reason and historicistic idealism with idealistic normativism[11] (see Figure 28).

The intent of voluntaristic action theory is to integrate these specialized approaches, all of which have their different limitations, and to do so both on the methatheoretical and on the object-theoretical levels. The concern on the metatheoretical level is to link

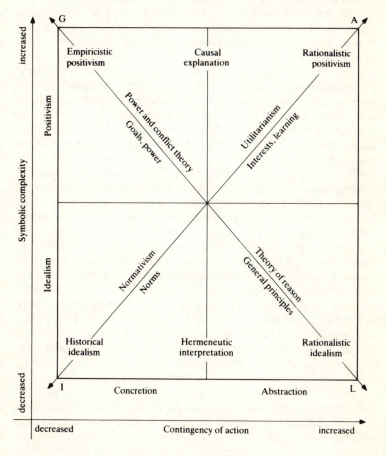

Figure 28 Variations of positivism and idealism

195

analytical abstraction and empirical concretion, and also idealism and positivism. Analytical abstraction necessitates a general conceptual and propositional framework which is applicable to any object at all, and farther-reaching than any empirical collection of data or generalizations. In Parsons's conception of the voluntaristic action theory it is the action frame of reference comprising end, situation (conditions, means) and rules of selection which initially carries out this function; later on it was expanded to form the A–G–I–L schema.[12] By using a general frame of reference, voluntaristic action theory differs both from empiricistic positivism and from historicistic idealism. For the general frame of reference to be properly applied, intermediate levels of analytical abstraction must be construed, and models developed for particular aspects of action such as economic, political, communal, cultural or professional action. Such a methodological approach differs from rationalistic idealism and positivism in that the above models must be derived not by way of pure deduction from the general frame of reference, but from the latter's interaction with empirical data and empirical generalizations.[13] Voluntaristic action theory distinguishes itself from positivism as seen in total by conceiving of human action as meaningful and hence understandable behaviour in the interpretive sense of *Verstehen*; it distinguishes itself from idealism by also including within its field of applicability the link between action's meaningful stratum and non-meaningful strata, and by also involving in its frame of reference quasi-causal structural laws such as statements regarding the connection between the degree of collective binding power in political decisions and the rate of deviance in political action. Another feature of this methodological approach is then the systematic testing of these quasi-causal structural statements using empirical social research procedures and causal analysis. This too is a distinction between the voluntaristic theory of action and pure meaning-interpretive idealism.[14]

On the object-theoretical level, the aim of the voluntaristic theory of action is to integrate the more specialized approaches already mentioned, namely positivistic utilitarianism and power and conflict theory together with idealistic normativism and rationalistic theory. The initial assumption in bringing about this integration is that action is determined by two opposing poles, one having a dynamizing effect (or function), the other an ordering effect (or function):

'Action must always be thought of as involving a state of tension between two different orders of elements, the normative and the conditional.'[15]

There are then action subsystems which correspond to these

opposing poles and can have differing relationships to each other, hence forcing action more into the field of openness and adaptivity, or more into the field of orderedness, closedness and conformity, or indeed leading it through both of these fields. One possibility is for the dynamizing subsystems to one-sidedly 'oversteer' the ordering subsystems, which results in accommodation. The converse is, however, equally possible, and this leads to a one-sided dominance on the part of the ordering subsystems. Between these two extremes lie various forms of temporal and/or material separation, reconciliation or, finally, the interpenetration of the subsystems. Of all the types of relationship between subsystems, interpenetration is the one which allows action to develop more freely in all its spheres. It means that action can simultaneously gain in both adaptivity and conformity on a higher level.[16]

When the above dualistic model is expanded, two more opposing poles (subsystems) are brought into it, which, respectively, have a generalizing or a specifying effect upon action.[17] Thus, they either steer action into the field of maintenance of identity whatever the situation, or, on the other hand, into the field representing directedness toward goals, again regardless of the situation. Once again the relationship between the subsystems concerned can range from one-sided generalization through separation, reconciliation and interpenetration, to one-sided specification.

Whilst positivistic utilitarianism regards action as guided solely by the opening subsystem, positivistic power and conflict theory solely by the specifying subsystem, idealistic normativism solely by the closing and idealistic rationalistic theory solely by the generalizing subsystems, the voluntaristic theory of action incorporates a model capable of showing under which conditions action is forced into one direction or another, or indeed into any combination of directions. In this regard, the theory achieves an advance in knowledge in comparison with the monistic world-views of the separate approaches mentioned above. The advance of the voluntaristic theory of action compared to the more specific approaches to action theory becomes particularly apparent in their respective answers to the basic sociological question: What are the conditions under which social order is possible?

Utilitarian positivism can imagine order only under the restricted conditions allowing the spontaneous emergence of order out of the selfish inclinations of the actors. This will apply only if any deviation from the order-producing regularities immediately causes costs for the actors, surpassing whatever gain they make from the deviation. This holds true only for small interdependent social circles.

For power and conflict-theoretical positivism, social order is only possible if there is a one-sided distribution of power so that, in the pure case, a dominating powerful actor always succeeds in enforcing ways of acting upon all of the other actors. According to this theory social order necessarily breaks down as soon as the distribution of power changes. This is the authoritarian version of power and conflict theory. The liberal version conceives social order as possible only with a complete balance of power between the actors. This balanced order dissolves automatically when there are changes in the power distribution favouring one or several actors at the cost of the others.

Social orders explained by utilitarianism or by power and conflict theory are factual, quasi-naturalistic orders resulting from the fact that the individuals are oriented to particular situations and to other actors strategically facing them as they would be to natural conditions not changeable by communication. These orders emerge only from extreme structurations of the external conditions of action, either from complete interdependence within small circles or from one-sided power distribution or from a complete balance of power, as spontaneous and causal order or as compulsory order.[18]

A limited view also characterizes idealism. Normativistic idealism sees order as only possible in closed communities in which a complete commitment of every individual to the norms of the community dominates. Where, however, the circles of interaction assemble several communities and where the individuals' interactions extend over the borderlines of the communities, social order is precluded according to this theory. Social order is possible here only as a conformistic order wherein the individual does not possess any autonomy and self-responsibility but merges totally into the community. The actors do not in any way exist as individuals, but only as community members.[19]

For rationalistic idealism social order results from reasonable, discursive argumentation, that is, only if all of the actors bring in arguments and listen to arguments, and if consensus results from argumentation. This is only possible if the actors do not argue from particularistic positions. As soon as particularisms of this kind break in, consensus and therefore social order cannot emerge. In this frame of reference, social order is an ideal order and therefore an order far removed from reality and not very effective.[20]

How, then, does voluntaristic action theory's answer to the question of the conditions producing social order differ from the above limited views? Its peculiarity lies in the fact that, according to its perspective, a social order has to combine all of the attributes absolutized in the specific approaches. It has to show a certain closedness conditioned by communal association but this in turn must set down a relatively wide framework within which it is open for the situationally varying constitution of order according to interest constellations. A social order also has to possess a relatively general identity which emerges from discursively established consensus on general principles but not on specific rules. And lastly it requires the implementation and enforcement of specific decisions where conflict reigns, a process which must be backed up by power. These attributes can only be united in social orders by the interpenetration of the respective subsystems and by the emergence of respective mediating levels in the zones of interpenetration. Contract law gives an example of such a mediating level. To the extent that it possesses an obligatory character, it is rooted in communal solidarity. But, at the same time, it is a system of norms which leaves a wide scope for individual bargaining on mutual obligations according to interest constellations. Furthermore, in order to be anchored in consensus, it must be subsumed under general, commonly shared principles, like the principles of self-responsibility, freedom, equality and reasonableness in modern societies. In order to be enforced in the case of conflict it needs the application of power which has, however, to be controlled and to be opened by other subsystems; this power is generalized by rational legitimation (the constitution), determined by communal norms (the law), and opened by political exchange. In this case, contract law has to be explained by the mutual penetration of closing communal association and opening exchange, generalizing discourse and specifying authority, and it reinforces their continuing interpenetration as soon as it is established. We can call a social order emerging in this way a *voluntaristic* order.[21] It integrates a certain conformistic closedness based on affectual ties with the openness for individual inclinations and self-responsibility; and it combines a general identity relying on consensus, which it maintains independently of every specific change, with the ability to implement and enforce the order in concrete conflict situations. In this way positivism and idealism are 'dialetically' replaced with voluntaristic action theory's broader frame of reference.

Post scriptum

The programme thus far carried out has pursued two concurrent aims. The first was to introduce the reader to the theory of action's form of thinking, the second was, by working through to the Kantian structure and the voluntaristic core of the theory, to open up ways in which it can be further advanced. The main emphasis in this respect has been on elaborating the *general* perspective. The greater the degree to which the reader has taken up this perspective, the easier it will be for him/her to correct the subjective errors which have been committed here in the light of action theory's objectively tenable structure.

Notes

Chapter 1

* This essay on the basic structure of voluntaristic action theory in the work of Talcott Parsons is based on a revision and expansion of an article entitled 'Talcott Parsons und die Theorie des Handelns I: Die Konstitution des Kantianischen Kerns', which appeared in the original German in *Soziale Welt* 30, 1979, pp. 385–409. *Soziale Welt*'s editor commissioned the essay as an appreciation of Parsons's work shortly after his death in Munich on 8 May 1979. An English version entitled 'Talcott Parsons and the theory of action: I: The structure of the Kantian core' appeared in the *American Journal of Sociology* 86, 1981, pp. 709–39.

1 This dissertation, written in German, was never published. However, two essays on the subject did appear in the *Journal of Political Economy*: T. Parsons, 'Capitalism in recent German literature: Sombart and Weber, I', in *Journal of Political Economy* 36, 1928, pp. 641–61; and 'Capitalism in recent German literature: Sombart and Weber, II', in *Journal of Political Economy* 37, 1929, pp. 31–51.

2 T. Parsons, 'Wants and activities in Marshall', in *Quarterly Journal of Economics* 46, 1931, pp. 101–40; 'Economics and sociology: Marshall in relation to the thought of his time', in *Quarterly Journal of Economics* 46, 1932, pp. 316–47; 'Pareto', in D.L. Sills (ed.), *International Encyclopedia of the Social Sciences*, New York: Macmillan (1933) 1968, Vol. 11, pp. 567–8; 'Pareto's central analytical scheme', in *Journal of Social Philosophy* 1, 1936, pp. 244–62.

3 T. Parsons, *The Structure of Social Action*, New York: Free Press (1937) 1968.

4 T. Parsons, *Action Theory and the Human Condition*, New York: Free Press, 1978.

5 Representative literature: R. Dahrendorf, 'Struktur und Funktion. Talcott Parsons und die Entwicklung der sociologischen Theorie', in *Kölner Zeitschrift für Soziologie und Sozialpsychologie* 7, 1955,

pp. 491′591; 'Out of utopia: Toward a reorientation of sociological analysis', in *American Journal of Sociology* 64, 1958, pp. 115–27; C.W. Mills, *The Sociological Imagination*, London: Oxford University Press, 1959; A.W. Gouldner, *The Coming Crisis of Western Sociology*, London: Heinemann, 1971.

6 Floyd N. House, in his review of *The Structure of Social Action*, ranked the potential of the work for social theory very high. Although he confirmed this assessment when the second edition was published, he had to complain: 'It is unfortunate that it is so long and so abstruse in style; many American students of sociology who would profit by it will be deterred from reading it.' (F.N. House, 'Review of T. Parsons, *The Structure of Social Action*', in *American Journal of Sociology* 45, 1939, pp. 129–30; ibid., p. 130; 55, 1950, pp. 504–5). Similar difficulties of comprehension were voiced by Ellsworth Faris in his review of *The Social System*: 'It would be difficult to contend that the book is well written. Even his loyal disciples will often confess that there are parts that are very difficult to understand.' (E. Faris, 'Review of T. Parsons: *The Social System*', in *American Sociological Review* 18, 1953, pp. 103–6). And although Faris in his review sought to urge the author to use a more generally comprehensible language, one could hardly claim Parsons had taken his criticism to heart. The works which followed at times make even greater demands on the reader. House's concern that few would summon the discipline to read *The Structure of Social Action* undoubtedly also applies to his later writings. This is not so much the particular fault of a particular author, however, as it is that of the entire discipline. Any demanding sociological texts should be allowed time for their interpretation. It is impossible to simply dash through Marx, Weber, Durkheim or Parsons in one seminar course and to understand them, though this unfortunately is what is normally expected of and by sociology students. In philosophy this would be regarded as dilettantism. Yet sociology has been forced to change pace by the tremendous increase in demand from external practical fields, to the extent that the pace is now truly hectic. Faced with such an extensive and openly accepted demand for its services, it no longer has time to consolidate its *scientific* core.

7 The stereotype criticism of Parsons's work, including that of its poor style, is documented in E. Schwanenberg, *Soziales Handeln – Die Theorie und ihr Problem*, Bern: Huber, 1970, pp. 12–27.

8 A record of the charismatic power of Parsons's action theory is provided by a number of works published in his honour: A. Inkeles and B. Barber (eds), *Stability and Social Change*, Boston: Little, Brown, 1973; J.J. Loubser, R.C. Baum, A. Effrat, V.M. Lidz (eds), *Explorations in General Theory in Social Science. Essays in Honor of Talcott Parsons*, New York: Free Press, 1976. Enno Schwanenberg has made a fundamental contribution to interpreting both the metatheoretical and object-theoretical basic structure of Parsons's action theory and its relevance to psychology: E. Schwanenberg, *Soziales Handeln – Die Theorie und ihr Problem*; 'The two problems of order in Parsons' theory: An analysis from within', in *Social Forces* 49, 1971, pp. 569–81.

More recently François Bourricaud and Jeffrey Alexander have provided important interpretations: F. Bourricaud, *The Sociology of Talcott Parsons (L'Individualisme institutionel)*, transl. by A. Goldhammer, Chicago: University of Chicago Press, 1981; J.C. Alexander, 'Formal and substantive voluntarism in the work of Talcott Parsons: A theoretical and ideological reinterpretation', in *American Sociological Review* 43, 1978, pp. 177–98. Then most recently of all Jeffrey Alexander has completed a comprehensive and extraordinarily significant reconstruction of action theory's development: J.C. Alexander, *Theoretical Logic in Sociology*, 4 vols, Berkeley: University of California Press, 1982-4. Slightly before that Jürgen Habermas's comprehensive work on action theory appeared, incorporating a detailed critique of Parsons's work: J. Habermas, *Theorie des kommunikativen Handelns*, 2 vols, Frankfurt: Suhrkamp, 1981 (Vol. 1 now available in translation: *Theory of Communicative Action*, Boston: Beacon Press, 1984). Although Habermas strives to achieve an integration of idealistic and positivistic positions in the above, he does not actually progress beyond an unintegrated combination of idealistic and positivistic rationalism. Affectual components, on the level of object language, and empirical/historical components, on the level of meta-language, are not accorded any systematic place value in his approach. This means that action theory is reduced to become an idealistic-postivistic rationalism. Despite the exhaustive discussion of fundamental aspects of Parsons's work, by misinterpreting his theory of action Habermas blocks his own access to a more thoroughgoing integration of idealism and positivism. He thus falls short of Parsons himself. Other writings I would like to give special mention from the interpretive literature on Parsons are: The contributions to M. Black (ed.), *The Social Theories of Talcott Parsons: A Critical Examination*, Englewood Cliffs. N.J.: Prentice Hall, 1961; W.C. Mitchell, *Sociological Analysis and Politics: The Theories of Talcott Parsons*, Englewood Cliffs, N.J.: Prentice Hall, 1967; H.J. Bershady, *Ideology and Social Knowledge*, Oxford: Blackwell, 1973; J.H. Turner and L. Beeghley, 'Current folklore in the criticism of Parsonian action theory', in *Sociological Inquiry* 4, 1974, pp. 47–55; J.H. Turner, *The Structure of Sociological Theory*, Homewood, Ill.: Dorsey (1974) 1978; J.H. Turner and L. Beeghley, *The Emergency of Sociological Theory*, Homewood, Ill: Dorsey, 1981; G. Rocher, *Talcott Parsons and American Sociology*, London: Nelson, 1974; F. Chazel, *La Théorie analytique de la société dans l'oeuvre de Talcott Parsons*, Paris: Mouton, 1974; B. Johnson, *Functionalism in Modern Sociology: Understanding Talcott Parsons*, Morristown: General Learning Press, 1976; K. Menzies, *Talcott Parsons and the Social Image of Man*, London: Routledge, 1977: I. Procter, 'Parsons's early voluntarism', in *Sociological Inquiry* 48, 1978, pp. 37–48; N. Luhmann, 'Talcott Parsons – Zur Zukunft eines Theorieprogramms', in *Zeitschrift für Soziologie* 9, 1980, pp. 5–17; S. Jensen, *Talcott Parsons. Eine Einführung*, Stuttgart: Teubner, 1980; W. Schluchter (ed.), *Verhalten, Handeln und System. Talcott Parsons' Beitrag zur Entwicklung der Sozialwissenschaften*,

Frankfurt: Suhrkamp, 1980; H.P.M. Adriaansens, *Talcott Parsons and the Conceptual Dilemma,* London: Routledge, 1980; J. Almaraz, *La teoria sociologica de Talcott Parsons,* Madrid: Centro de Investigaciones Sociologicas, 1981; N. Genov, *Talcott Parsons and Theoretical Sociology,* Sofia: Publishing House of the Bulgarian Academy of Sciences, 1982.

9 T. Parsons, 'On building social system theory: A personal history', in *Social Systems and the Evolution of Action Theory,* New York: Free Press, 1977, p. 68.

10 I. Kant, *The Critique of Pure Reason,* transl. by J.M.D. Meiklejohn, in *Great Books of the Western World, 42: Kant, Chicago/London,* etc.: Encyclopaedia Britannica, 1952, pp. 1-250.

11 T. Parsons, 'On building social system theory', p. 26, note 10.

12 Studies on this topic exist, but they remain preliminary and fail to construct a complete interpretive framework. A direct connection between the cognitive theories of Kant and Parsons has been asserted by H.J. Bershady (1973), who in my view, however, fails to grasp the essential nature of the correspondence. Bershady draws a parallel between Parsons's 'action frame of reference' of 1937 – conditions, means, ends and norms as *a priori* categories of every social science – and Kant's categories of the understanding, and he concentrates on the critical assessment of the claim that causal explanation according to the *covering law model* is possible only if it is based upon this frame of reference. Bershady does not see any continuous development of *content* in Parsons's elaborations of his theory after 1937; he sees them instead as related attempts to satisfy the conditions of generalization and causal explanation with one theoretical framework after another. In this, he is hampered by an overly narrow, purely functionalist interpretation of the action frame of reference, reducing Parsonian theory to an attempt to formulate *necessary* conditions for the existence or evolutionary development of social systems, an attempt which is forced to settle for functionalist explanations as a second-best solution, strict causal explanation always seeming to be out of reach. Also unsatisfactory is the quasi-teleological solution to the dilemma of causal explanation vs. ideography which Bershady, following V. Wright, puts forth. This is nothing but a relapse into historicism which sacrifices Parsons's greatest achievement, namely the constitution of sociology as a discipline which is not forced to understand itself in terms of either the models of strict causal explanation of the natural sciences or the pure ideographic methods of the study of the arts and other cultural products. In order to understand Parsons's basic perspective, we must draw a parallel, not between the action frame of reference and the categories of the understanding but between the action frame of reference and the structure and purpose of Kant's critical project as a whole, concentrating on the interpenetration between the categories of the understanding and sense data, between the categorical imperative and hypothetical imperatives, between the teleological principle and concrete judgements. Only thus does a perspective of interpretation begin to emerge in the theory of action,

allowing its full scope and explanatory power to be exploited. See H.J. Bersady, *Ideology and Social Knowledge*. On the relationship between the normative and the conditional spheres in the theory of action, see E. Schwanenberg, 'The two problems of order in Parsons' theory: An analysis from within'; *Soziales Handeln: Die Theorie und ihr Problem*.

13 I. Kant, *The Critique of Pure Reason*; *The Critique of Practical Reason*, in *Great Books of the Western World, 42: Kant*, Chicago/London, etc.: Encyclopaedia Britannica, 1952, pp. 291–361; *The Critique of Judgement*, in ibid., pp. 461–613.

14 Parsons was inspired to undertake this restudy by a series of discussions which took place at the University of Pennsylvania between 1974 and 1976: T. Parsons, 'A paradigm of the human condition', in *Action Theory and the Human Condition*, pp. 352–433; 'Death in the Western world', in *Action Theory and the Human Condition*, pp. 331–51.

15 T. Parsons, 'A paradigm of the human condition', pp. 355–6. In the first sentence of this quotation I have modified Parsons by reversing the pairs of terms. I have done this so that the first term in each pair will be the 'transcendental' term and the second the 'empirical' term. This makes the pairs of terms in the first sentence formally identical with those in the second sentence.

16 D. Hume, *A Treatise of Human Nature*, ed. by L.A. Selby-Bigge, Oxford: Clarendon Press (1739–40) 1973; 'An enquiry concerning human understanding', 1st edn, in *Enquiries Concerning the Human Understanding and Concerning the Principles of Morals*, ed. by L.A. Selby-Bigge, Oxford: Clarendon Press (1748/51) 1966, pp. 5–165.

17 D. Hume, *Enquiries Concerning the Human Understanding and Concerning the Principles of Morals*, pp. 11–17.

18 Ibid., pp. 20–45.

19 See the 'Transcendental aesthetic' and 'Transcendental logic' in I. Kant, *The Critique of Pure Reason*, pp. 108–14. For an attempt to use this Kantian perspective to elucidate some aspects of the controversy between critical rationalism, Marxism and critical theory, see R. Münch, *Gesellschaftstheorie und Ideologiekritik*, Hamburg: Hoffmann & Campe, 1973.

20 This is already a central idea in Weber's work. See M. Weber, *From Max Weber: Essays in Sociology*, transl., ed., intro. by H. H. Gerth and C. Wright Mills, Oxford/New York: Oxford University Press, 1979, pp. 141–2 (WL 596–7); *The Protestant Ethic and the Spirit of Capitalism*, transl. by T. Parsons, New York: Charles Scribner's Sons, 1976, pp. 13–14, 23–5 (RS I 1,10); *The Religion of China. Confucianism and Taoism*, transl. and ed. by H. H. Gerth, New York: Free Press, 1964, pp. 125–9, 147–54, 196–200 (RS I 414–16, 435–43, 481–4); *The Religion of India. The Sociology of Hinduism and Buddhism*, transl. and ed. by H. H. Gerth and D. Martindale, New York: Free Press, 1967, pp. 144–7 (RS II 143–7).

21 I. Kant, *The Critique of Judgement*, §22, §§61–8.

22 I. Kant, *The Critique of Practical Reason*, Part I, Book II.

23 Ibid., p. 305.

24 Ibid., p. 302.

25 See M. Weber, *The Religion of China,* pp. 147–50 (RS I 435–8): *The Religion of India,* pp. 144–6 (RS II 143–6).

26 T. Parsons, 'A paradigm of the human condition', pp. 370–1. There is an interesting parallel between this last theoretical essay from Parsons's pen and the last from Emile Durkheim's. Both are concerned with the anthropological level, the human condition, and both use Kant's dualism as a starting point. See Durkheim, 'The dualism of human nature and its social conditions', in *On Morality and Society,* Chicago: University of Chicago Press, 1973, pp. 149–63 (314–32). The difficulties readers may have in understanding the core of Parsons's action theory if they fail to recognize its Kantian nature is frequently evident throughout the responses to Parsons's work. Schütz, as one of the first to enter the debate, was already beset with these difficulties. He criticized Parsons from a subjectivistic and idealistic position. See their published correspondence: A. Schütz and T. Parsons, *The Theory of Social Action: The Correspondence of Alfred Schütz and Talcott Parsons,* ed. by R. Grathoff, Bloomington: Indiana University Press, 1978.

27 T. Hobbes, *Leviathan,* in *Collected English Works of Thomas Hobbes,* ed. by W. Molesworth, Vol. 3, Aalen, W. Germany: Scientia (1651) 1966, Chaps 13, 14, 17.

28 Cf. J.M. Buchanan, *The Limits of Liberty – between Anarchy and Leviathan,* Chicago: University of Chicago Press, 1975, especially p. 27. Buchanan, in strict conformity with utilitarian theory, attempts to explain 'how "law", "the rights of property", "rules for behavior", might emerge from the non-idealistic, self-interesed behavior of men' (p. 54). The advantages they can gain, believes Buchanan, are the motivation for individuals to agree to a set of rules. It is only the enforcement of those rules which must be placed in the hands of a superordinate state sanctioning body (pp. 64–70). However, the distinction between a liberal initial situation and a state-controlled situation in day-to-day life is really an artificial one. In reality, it must always be the case that individuals acting self-interestedly will attempt to evade the rules to pursue their own advantage. Hobbes's Leviathan, then, lurks beneath even the most liberal of utilitarian models.

29 T. Parsons, *Structure,* pp. 3–125, especially pp. 89–94.

30 T. Hobbes, *Leviathan,* Chap. 17.

31 T. Parsons, *Structure,* p. 93.

32 T. Hobbes, *Leviathan,* Chap. 18.

33 Ibid., Chap 14, 15.

34 Ibid., Chap. 17.

35 J.S. Coleman, 'Inequality, sociology, and moral philosophy', in *American Journal of Sociology* 80, 1974, pp. 739–64; cf. J.S. Coleman, 'Collective decisions', in H. Turk and R.L. Simpson (eds), *Institutions and Social Exchange,* Indianapolis: Bobbs-Merrill, 1971, pp. 272–86; *Power and the Structure of Society,* New York: Norton, 1974.

36 V. Vanberg, 'Kollektive Güter und kollektives Handeln. Zur Bedeutung neuerer ökonomischer Theorieentwicklungen für die Soziologie', in *Kölner Zeitschrift für Soziologie und Sozialpsychologie* 30, 1978, pp. 652–79.

37 Ibid., p. 671.
38 T. Parsons, *Structure*, p. 94.
39 This type of argument, characteristic of a number of critiques, is flawed at its very foundations. The following provide examples of the problem: D.P. Ellis, 'The Hobbesian problem of order: A critical appraisal of the normative solution', in *American Sociological Review* 36, 1971, pp. 692–703; V. Vanberg, 'Kollektive Güter und kollektives Handeln'; *Die zwei Soziologien. Individualismus und Kollektivismus in der Sozialtheorie*, Tübingen: Mohr Siebeck, 1975, pp. 161–94; H.G. Schütte, 'Handlungen, Rollen und Systeme. Überlegungen zur Soziologie M. Webers und T. Parsons', in H. Lenk (ed.), *Handlungstheorien interdisziplinär IV*, Munich: Fink, 1977, pp. 17–57. For more recent criticism of Parsons's theory of order see Parsons's dispute with T. Burger, 'Talcott Parsons, the problem of order in society, and the program of an analytical sociology', in *American Journal of Sociology* 83, 1977, pp. 320–34; cf. T. Parsons, 'Comment on Burger's critique', in *American Journal of Sociology* 83, 1977, pp. 335–9.
40 T. Parsons, *Structure*, p. 82. An interpretation of Parsons which more closely approaches this core of his theory can be found in: J.C. Alexander, 'Formal and substantive voluntarism in the work of Talcott Parsons'.
41 On this topic, see N. Luhmann, 'Interpenetration – Zum Verhältnis personaler und sozialer Systeme', in *Zeitschrift für Soziologie* 6, 1977, pp. 62–76; S. Jensen, 'Interpenetration – Zum Verhältnis personaler und sozialer System?', in *Zeitschrift für Soziologie* 7, 1978, pp. 116–29; N. Luhmann, 'Interpenetration bei Parsons', in *Zeitschrift für Soziologie* 7, 1978, pp. 299–302. According to Luhmann, the concept of interpenetration occurs 'only late' in Parsons's writing, while Jensen asserts that it is introduced in the mid-1950s. Both authors fail to see that already in *The Structure of Social Action* Parsons is putting forth a theory of interpenetration. Nor are they aware of the basic affinity of this conception with Kant's philosophy. Luhmann veers away from Parsons's theoretical programme before he has really understood it or sounded out the true scope of the theory. In my view, this scope is wider than that of the new conception offered by Luhmann.
42 T. Parsons, *Structure*, pp. 77–82. On the Kantian structure underlying Parsons's treatment of the problem of social order, see Parsons's own reference in T. Parsons, 'On building social system theory', p. 69, footnote 69.
43 I. Kant, *Critique of Practical Reason*, Book I, Chap 1 (pp. 297–314).
44 T. Parsons, *Structure*, pp. 76–7.
45 Examples of authors arguing along these lines are: D.P. Ellis, 'The Hobbesian problem of order'; V. Vanberg, 'Kollektive Güter und kollektives Handeln'; J.S. Coleman, 'Collective decisions'.
46 This indispensable precondition of the explanation of the generation of norms as the core of social change has been ignored by all those critics who have declared Parsons's theory unable to explain change. Consequently, all alternative theories exhibit an overly narrow

conception of the problem in question and are doomed to failure from the start. This holds true of all contributions in this context from Dahrendorf via Mills right up to Gouldner and others.

47 Only from this general perspective can we understand Weber's explanation of the development of modern Western society. This in itself goes to prove the explanatory potential of a theory of interpenetration. Cf. M. Weber, *The Protestant Ethic*; *The Religion of China*; *From Max Weber: Essays in Sociology*, pp. 267–322; *The Religion of India* (all together RS I, II complete).

48 See the interesting study by H.J. Bershady, *Ideology and Social Knowledge*, and also Parsons's positive review and Bershady's comment: T. Parsons, 'Review of Harold J. Bershady: *Ideology and Social Knowledge*'; H.J. Bershady, 'Commentary on Talcott Parsons' review of H.J. Bershady's *Ideology and Social Knowledge*'. Both of the latter subsequently appeared in: T. Parsons, *Social Systems and the Evolution of Action Theory*, pp. 122–34 and 134–41.

49 A.N. Whitehead, *Science and the Modern World*, New York: Macmillan (1925) 1967.

50 T. Parsons, *Structure*, p. 30. At this point Parsons directly takes up the work of Lawrence J. Henderson. Cf. L.J. Henderson, 'An approximate definition of fact', in *University of California Studies in Philosophy* 14, 1932, pp. 179–200. However, after his renewed study of Kant Parsons himself stressed that this was a fundamentally Kantian perspective: T. Parsons, 'Comment on R. Stephen Warner's "Toward a redefinition of action theory: Paying the cognitive element its due"', in *American Journal of Sociology* 83, 1978, p. 1354.

51 E. Durkheim, *The Division of Labor in Society*, transl. by G. Simpson, New York: Free Press, 1964, especially pp. 111–32, 200–29 (*De la Division du travail social*, Paris: Presses Universitaires de France (1893) 1973, especially pp. 79–102, 177–209).

52 E. Durkheim, *Sociology and Philosophy*, transl. by D.F. Pocock, London: Cohen & West, 1965, pp. 37–79 (*Sociologie et philosophie*, Paris: Presses Universitaires de France (1924) 1974, pp. 51–101); 'The dualism of human nature and its social conditions'.

53 E. Durkheim, *The Division of Labor*; *The Rules of Sociological Method*, transl. by W.D. Halls, London: Macmillan, 1982 (*Les Règles de la méthode sociologique*, Paris: Presses Universitaires de France (1895) 1973); *Suicide*, transl. by J.A. Spaulding and G. Simpson, London: Routledge, 1952 (*Le Suicide*, Paris: Presses Universitaires de France (1897) 1973); *Moral Education*, transl. by E.K. Wilson and H. Schnurer, New York: Free Press, 1961 (*L'Education morale*, Paris: Presses Universitaires de France (1925) 1974); *The Elementary Forms of the Religious Life*, transl. by J.W. Swain, London: Allen & Unwin, 1976 (*Les Formes élémentaires de la vie religieuse*, Paris: Presses Universitaires de France (1912) 1968); cf. T. Parsons, *Structure*, pp. 376–408; 'Durkheim's contribution to the theory of integration of social systems', in *Sociological Theory and Modern Society*, New York: Free Press, 1967, pp. 3–34.

54 E. Durkheim, *Suicide*, Chaps 2, 3, 5.

55 E. Durkheim, *The Division of Labor*, Preface to the second edition, pp. 1–31 (I-XXXVI).

56 E. Durkheim, *The Division of Labor*, p. 131 (101): 'Society becomes more capable of collective movement, at the same time that each of its elements has more freedom of movement.' In addition, cf. pp. 129–32 (98–101), 396–409 (391–400).

57 M. Weber, *The Protestant Ethic*; *The Religion of China*; *From Max Weber: Essays in Sociology* pp. 267–322; *The Religion of India* (all together: RS I, II complete); *Ancient Judaism*, transl. and ed. by H.H. Gerth and D. Martindale, New York: Free Press, 1952 (RS III).

58 M. Weber, *Economy and Society. An Outline of Interpretive Sociology*, 3 vols, ed. by G. Roth and C. Wittich, New York: Bedminster Press, 1968, Vol. 2, Part 2, Chap VI, viii-xv (W/G 2 V §§8–12); cf. T. Parsons, *Structure*, pp. 500–78; 'Introduction to Max Weber's *The Sociology of Religion*', in *Sociological Theory and Modern Society*, pp. 35–78.

59 M. Weber, *The Religion of China*.

60 M. Weber, *The Religion of India*.

61 Ibid.

62 M. Weber, *The Protestant Ethic*, pp. 33–284; *From Max Weber: Essays in Sociology*, pp. 302–22 (together: RS I 17–236).

63 M. Weber, *Economy and Society*, Vol. 3 (Part 2) Chap. XVI (W/G 727–814).

64 This is the explanatory line taken in M. Weber, *The Protestant Ethic and the Spirit of Capitalism*.

65 This aspect is emphasized by Weber in 'The Protestant sects and the spirit of capitalism'. Cf. M. Weber, *From Max Weber: Essays in Sociology*, pp. 302–22 (RS I 207–36).

66 See, above all, S. Freud, *The Ego and the Id*, authorized transl. by Joan Rivière, London: Institute of Psychoanalysis, 1927.

67 T. Parsons, 'The superego and the theory of social systems', in *Social Structure and Personality*, Glencoe, Ill.: Free Press, 1964, p. 19

68 T. Parsons, 'The incest taboo in relation to social structure and the socialization of the child', 'Social structure and the development of personality: Freud's contribution to the integration of psychology and sociology', both in: *Social Structure and Personality*, pp. 57–77 and 78–111; 'Family structure and the socialization of the child', 'The organization of personality as a system of action'; T. Parsons and R.F. Bales, 'Conclusion: Levels of cultural generality and the process of differentiation', all in T. Parsons and R.F. Bales, *Family, Socialization and Interaction Process*, London: Routledge, 1956, pp. 31–131, 133–86, 353–94.

69 Parsons, of course, by developing his thesis on the convergence of Durkheim and Weber into a voluntaristic position from their respective traditions of positivism and idealism, had already applied a theoretical perspective of interpretation in the process. It was this fundamental core in the two approaches which actually made it possible for the Kantian theory of interpenetration to be established; this is where the genius of Talcott Parsons's achievement lies. Among the attempts at

interpretation of these classic authors which have been developed at least in part in opposition to Parsons, not one has made possible a theoretical development as fruitful as Parsons's. Without exception these attempts lose themselves in certain aspects of the discussion and are unable to open up a perspective from which a general theory can be constructed. This is true of Bendix, who reduces the Weberian perspective to the single aspect of the struggle for power between different social groups, and who, in changing Weber from a sociologist into a historian, sacrifices sociology as a theoretical discipline: R. Bendix, 'Two sociological traditions', in R. Bendix and G. Roth, *Scholarship and Partisanship: Essays on Max Weber*, Berkeley: University of California Press, 1971, pp. 282–98. For Parsons's comments see T. Parsons: 'Review of Reinhard Bendix and Günther Roth: *Scholarship and Partisanship: Essays on Max Weber*, in *Contemporary Sociology* 1, 1972, pp. 200–3. Nor can Pope, Cohen and Hazelrigg offer an interpretation of Weber and Durkheim which is as constructive as Parsons's. They reduce Durkheim to a 'sociological realist' and Weber to a 'theorist of conflict and interests' and, in the same context, charge Parsons with approaching the classics with a predetermined interpretive scheme. But this is exactly the reason Parsons has been able to integrate both authors within an extendable theoretical framework, while the efforts of Pope, Cohen and Hazelrigg remain mere patchwork: W. Pope, 'Classic on classic: Parsons' interpretation of Durkheim', in *American Sociological Review* 38, 1973, pp. 399–415; W. Pope, J. Cohen and L.E. Hazelrigg, 'On the divergence of Weber and Durkheim: A critique of Parsons' convergence thesis', in *American Sociological Review* 40, 1975, pp. 417–27; J. Cohen, L.E. Hazelrigg and W. Pope, 'De-Parsonizing Weber: A critique of Parsons' interpretation of Weber's sociology', in *American Sociological Review* 40, 1975, pp. 229–41. For further elucidation see the discussion between Pope, Cohen, Hazelrigg and Parsons: T. Parsons, 'Comment on "Parsons' interpretation of Durkheim" and on "Moral freedom through understanding in Durkheim": Comment on Pope and Cohen', in *American Sociological Review* 40, 1975, pp. 106–11; 'Reply to Cohen, Hazelrigg and Pope', in *American Sociological Review* 41, 1976, pp. 361–5; J. Cohen, 'Moral freedom through understanding in Durkheim: Comment on Pope', in *American Sociological Review* 40, 1975, pp. 104–6; W. Pope, 'Parsons on Durkheim, revisited: Reply to Cohen and Parsons', in *Amercian Sociological Review* 40, 1975, pp. 111–15; W. Pope, J. Cohen and L.E. Hazelrigg, 'Reply to Parsons', in *American Sociological Review* 42, 1977, pp. 809–11; D.R. Gerstein, 'Durkheim and *The Structure of Social Action',* in *Sociological Inquiry* 49, 1979, pp. 27–39. Also directly relevant to this discussion are the article by R.S. Warner, 'Toward a redefinition of action theory: Paying the cognitive element its due', in *American Journal of Sociology* 83, 1978, pp. 1317–49, together with subsequent comments by Parsons and by Pope and Cohen: T. Parsons, 'Comment on R. Stephen Warner's "Toward a redefinition of action theory: Paying the cognitive element is due"', pp. 1350–8; W. Pope and

J. Cohen, 'On R. Stephen Warner's "Toward a redefinition of action theory: Paying the cognitive element its due"', in *American Journal of Sociology* 83, 1978, pp. 1359–67. The German interpretation of Weber's work deliberately talks around Parsons, partly by renouncing sociological theory altogether and constructing an ideal type of the inner development of ideas independent of the instructions of a 'sociological perspective' (as does Tenbruck), partly by maintaining that one can by-pass Parsons with a Weberian dialectic of ideas and interests (as Schluchter proposes). Both interpretations are interesting and informative, but neither is able to produce a systematic starting point for theoretical developments beyond Weber as Parsons did, and they patently lack any possibility of treading the path to Weber's theory of interpenetration which Parsons had opened up. See F.H. Tenbruck, 'Das Werk Max Webers', in *Kölner Zeitschrift für Soziologie und Sozialpsychologie* 27, 1975, pp. 663–702; W. Schluchter, 'The paradox of rationalization: On the relation of ethics and world', in G. Roth and W. Schluchter, *Max Weber's Vision of History*, Berkeley: University of California Press, 1979, pp. 11–64; 'Max Webers Gesellschaftsgeschichte. Versuch einer Explikation', in *Kölner Zeitschrift für Soziologie und Sozialpsychologie* 30, 1978, pp. 438–67; *The Rise of Western Rationalism: Max Weber's Developmental History*, transl. and intro. by G. Roth, Berkeley: University of California Press, 1981.

70 This has been explicitly pointed out as a theoretical problem by Luhmann in his most recent work, though he does not actually make systematic use of Parsons's achievements: N. Luhmann, 'Durkheim on morality and the division of labor' in *The Differentiation of Society*, transl. by S. Holmes and C. Larmore, New York: Columbia University Press, 1982, pp. 3–19; 'Soziologie der Moral', in N. Luhmann and S. Pfürtner (eds), *Theorietechnik und Moral*, Frankfurt: Suhrkamp, 1978, pp. 8–116; 'Interpenetration – zum Verhältnis personaler und sozialer Systeme'; 'Interpenetration bei Parsons'; see also S. Jensen, 'Interpenetration – Zum Verhältnis personaler und sozialer Systeme?'.

71 The materialist position has, at least in many of its versions, become a crude functionalism, which is satisfied that it has explained a phenomenon as soon as any kind of positive functional relation, no matter how abstract, with the system of capitalism is discovered. It might be said, therefore, that authors like van den Berghe are directing their arguments in the wrong direction: P.L. van den Berghe, 'Dialectic and functionalism: Toward a theoretical synthesis', in *American Sociological Review* 28, 1963, pp. 695–705.

72 This is the true meaning, for example, of Benjamin Nelson's conception of the development 'from tribal brotherhood to universal otherhood' as the main line of development of the process of civilization itself: B. Nelson, *The Idea of Usury. From Tribal Brotherhood to Universal Otherhood*, Chicago: University of Chicago Press (1949) 1969. Weber had himself worked within a similar conception.

73 T. Parsons, *The Social System*, Glencoe, Ill.: Free Press, 1951. The development is taken further in: T. Parsons and R.F. Bales, *Family, Socialization and Interaction Process*.

74 T. Parsons and E.A. Shils (eds), *Toward a General Theory of Action*, Cambridge, Mass.: Harvard University Press, 1951.
75 T. Parsons, R.F. Bales and E.A. Shils, *Working Papers in the Theory of Action*, New York: Free Press, 1953.
76 T. Parsons and N.J. Smelser, *Economy and Society*, New York: Free Press, 1956; T. Parsons, 'On the concept of political power' (1963), 'On the concept of influence' (1963), 'On the concept of value-commitments' (1968), all in *Politics and Social Structure*, New York: Free Press, 1969, pp. 352–404, 405–38, 439–72.
77 T. Parsons and G.M. Platt, *The American University*, Cambridge: Harvard University Press, 1973; T. Parsons, 'Some problems of general theory in sociology', in *Social Systems and the Evolution of Action Theory*, pp. 229–69.
78 T. Parsons, 'A paradigm of the human condition'.

Chapter 2

* This chapter comprises a reconstruction of the theory development in the work of Talcott Parsons, and is derived, with thorough revision and extensive additional material, from the follow-up to the essay on voluntaristic action theory upon which Chapter 1 was based. The original, much shorter version appeared in German under the title of 'Talcott Parsons und die Theorie des Handelns II: Die Kontinuität der Entwicklung', in *Soziale Welt* 31, 1980, pp. 3–47. An English version with minor revisions then appeared as: 'Talcott Parsons and the theory of Action II: The continuity of the development', in *American Journal of Sociology* 87, 1982, pp. 771–826.

1 I. Kant, *The Critique of Pure Reason*; *The Critique of Practical Reason*; *The Critique of Judgement*.
2 M. Weber, *Economy and Society*, Vol. 2, Part 2, Chap. VII, viii–xv (W/G 314–81); T. Parsons, 'Introduction to Max Weber's *The Sociology of Religion*'.
3 On this point, see the following: J.C. Alexander, 'Formal and substantive voluntarism in the work of Talcott Parsons'; F. Bourricaud, *The Sociology of Talcott Parsons*; I. Procter, 'Parsons' early voluntarism'. Jeffrey Alexander calls the thesis that intentional action is not purely causally determined 'formal voluntarism', which he distinguishes from 'substantive voluntarism', his term for the content of Parsons's theory regarding the conditions under which the human potential for autonomy can be realized in action. Alexander sees this substantive voluntarism as embodied primarily in a theory of increasing differentiation.
4 Cf. for an example along these lines, H.G. Schütte, 'Handlungen, Rollen und Systeme'.
5 K.R. Popper, *Conjectures and Refutations*, London: Routledge, 1963; *Objective Knowledge. An Evolutionary Approach*, Oxford: Clarendon Press, 1972; I. Lakatos and A. Musgrave (eds), *Criticism and the*

Growth of Knowledge, Cambridge: Cambridge University Press, 1970; R. Münch, *Gesellschaftstheorie und Ideologiekritik*, pp. 178–212.

6 T. Parsons, *Structure*, 'The superego and the theory of social systems'; 'Social structure and the development of personality: Freud's contribution to the integration of psychology and sociology'; 'Durkheim's contribution to the theory of integration of social systems; 'Introduction to Max Weber's *The Sociology of Religion*', 'Durkheim on religion revisited: Another look at *The Elementary Forms of the Religious Life*', in *Action Theory and the Human Condition*, pp. 213–32.

7 In a review of the volume of critical essays on Parsons edited by Max Black – P. Selznick, 'Review of *The Social Theories of Talcott Parsons: A Critical Examination*, edited by M. Black', in *American Sociological Review* 26, 1961, p. 934 – Selznick writes: 'Does Parsons have a distinctive perspective, a "philosophy of sociology"? I think not. His writing has become so diffuse and eclectic in recent years that it is really difficult to identify him with a special point of view.' On the other hand, the continuity in Parsons's work is accentuated in E. Schwanenberg, *Soziales Handeln. Die Theorie und ihr Problem*; 'The two problems of order in Parsons' theory'; D.R. Gerstein, 'A note on the continuity of Parsonian action theory', in *Sociological Inquiry* 45, 1975, pp. 11–15; J.C. Alexander, 'Formal and substantive voluntarism in the work of Talcott Parsons'; *Theoretical Logic in Sociology*, Vol. IV: *The Modern Reconstruction of Classical Thought: Talcott Parsons*; H.P.M. Adriaansens, *Talcott Parsons and the Conceptual Dilemma*.

8 In the light of Popper's theory of the objective mind Parsons himself, in his late phase, did not create the Kantian core in his own theory, but rediscovered it as something which already existed. Cf. K.R. Popper, *Objective Knowledge*; T. Parsons, 'A paradigm of the human condition'. The same is true of Parsons's epistemology, for example, his concept of empirical fact. See. T. Parsons, 'Comment on R. Stephen Warner's "Toward a redefinition of action theory: Paying the cognitive element its due"', p. 1354: 'I had adapted this from L.J. Henderson, but it was basically Kantian.'

9 T. Parsons and E.A. Shils, 'Values, motives, and systems of action', in *Toward a General Theory of Action*, pp. 53–76.

10 T. Parsons, *The Social System*, p. 7.

11 T. Parsons and E.A. Shils, 'Values, motives, and systems of action', p. 109.

12 T. Parsons, *The Social System*, pp. 36–45, 201–48; T. Parsons and E.A. Shils, 'Values, motives and systems of action', pp. 146–58, 176–83, 202–4.

13 T. Parsons, 'On building social system theory', pp. 37–8.

14 S. Freud, *The Ego and the Id*; T. Parsons, *The Social Systems*, Chaps VI, VII; 'The superego and the theory of social systems'; 'Family structure and the socialization of the child'; 'The organization of personality as a system of action'; 'Social structure and the development of personality'; T. Parsons and J. Olds, 'The mechanisms of personality functioning with special reference to socialization', in T.

Parsons and R.F. Bales, *Family, Socialization and Interaction Process*, pp. 187-257.

15 T. Parsons, 'Family structure and the socialization of the child', pp. 77-94.

16 T. Parsons, 'The school class as a social system: Some of its functions in American society', in *Social Structure and Personality*, pp. 129-54; 'Social structure and the development of personality'; 'Toward a healthy maturity', in *Social Structure and Personality*, pp. 236-54; 'Youth in the context of American society', in *Social Structure and Personality*, pp. 155-82; T. Parsons and G.M. Platt, 'Higher education, changing socialization and contemporary student dissent', in M.W. Riley, M.E. Johnson and A. Foner (eds), *Aging and Society*, Vol. 3: *A Sociology of Age Stratification*, New York: Sage, 1972, pp. 236-91; *The American University*, pp. 163-224.

17 On this process of generalization, see T. Parsons and R.F. Bales, 'Conclusion: Levels of cultural generality and the process of differentiation'; T. Parsons and G.M. Platt, *The American University*, pp. 163-224.

18 In this fundamental postulate of the theory of socialization we may already see a convergence of the theoretical positions of Simmel, Durkheim, Mead and Piaget. Cf. G. Simmel, *Soziologie: Untersuchungen über die Formen der Vergesellschaftung*, Berlin: Duncker & Humblot (1908) 1968, part of which is translated in *The Sociology of Georg Simmel*, transl., ed. and intro. by K.H. Wolff, Glencoe, Ill.: Free Press, 1950; E. Durkheim, *Sociology and Philosophy*; G.H. Mead, *Mind, Self and Society from the Standpoint of a Social Behaviorist*, Chicago and London: University of Chicago Press (1934) 1972; J. Piaget, *The Moral Judgement of the Child*, New York: Free Press (1932) 1965. The positions of these classic authors are preserved in Parsons's theory of socialization. This makes it all the less comprehensible that there should be such a widespread opinion that Parsons's theory of socialization integrates individual and society by subjecting the individual completely to social norms. The misrepresentation of Parsons's concept of internalization begins when it is interpreted as the internalization of *social* norms and not – as it ought to be – that of *cultural* norms which are very different. The more the individual internalizes cultural norms the more he has general measures for criticizing social institutions at hand. The meaning of cultural norms always transcends their particular concretization in the institutions of a society. See, for example, D.H. Wrong, 'The oversocialized conception of man in modern sociology', in *American Sociological Review* 26, 1961, pp. 183-93; T.P. Wilson, 'Normative and interpretive paradigms in sociology', in J.D. Douglas (ed.), *Understanding Everyday Life: Toward the Reconstruction of Sociological Knowledge*, Chicago: Aldine, 1970, pp. 57-79; R. Reichwein, 'Sozialisation und Individuation in der Theorie von Talcott Parsons', in *Soziale Welt* 21, 1970, pp. 161-84; A.G. Brandenburg, *Systemzwang und Autonomie: Gesellschaft und Persönlichkeit in der Theorie von Talcott Parsons*, Düsseldorf: Bertelsmann Universitätsverlag, 1971; L. Krappmann,

Soziologische Dimensionen der Identität, Stuttgart: Klett, 1971; T.J. Morrione, 'Symbolic interactionism and social action theory', in *Sociology and Social Research* 59, 1975, pp. 201–18. For commentary on this interpretation, see T. Parsons, 'Individual autonomy and social pressure: an answer to Dennis H. Wrong', in *Psychoanalysis and Psychoanalytic Review* 49, 1962, pp. 70–80; 'Comment on J.H. Turner and L. Beeghley: "Current folklore in the criticism of Parsonian action theory"', in *Sociological Inquiry* 44, 1974, pp. 55–8; J.H. Turner and L. Beeghley, 'Current folklore in the criticism of Parsonian action theory'; R. Geissler, 'Die Sozialisationstheorie von Talcott Parsons: Anmerkungen zur Parsons-Rezeption in der deutschen Soziologie', in *Kölner Zeitschrift für Soziologie und Sozialpsychologie* 31, 1979, pp. 267–81.

19 T. Parsons and R.F. Bales, 'Conclusion: Levels of cultural generality and the process of differentiation', pp. 357–8.

20 T. Parsons, 'An approach to psychological theory in terms of the theory of action', in S. Koch (ed.), *Psychology: A Study of a Science*, Vol. 3, New York: McGraw-Hill, 1959, p. 708.

21 Parsons himself protested against this labelling of his work. Cf. T. Parsons, 'On building social system theory', pp. 48–50; 'The present status of "structural-functional" theory in sociology', in *Social Systems and the Evolution of Action Theory*, pp. 100–17; 'Review of Harold J. Bershady: *Ideology and Social Knowledge*', p. 127. In this connection, see Parsons's own attempt to distinguish himself from Merton in 'The present status of "structural-functional" theory in sociology', p. 108: 'I have differed from him mainly in my strong stress on the importance and centrality of the concept "system", on the inevitability of abstraction, and on the necessity for the self-conscious use of plural or multiple system references.' Cf. R.K. Merton, 'Manifest and latent functions', in *Social Theory and Social Structure*, New York: Free Press (1949) 1968, pp. 73–138. I disagree, therefore, with attempts made by Mullins, and also by Eisenstadt and Curelaru, to place Parsons without qualification in the camp of structural functionalism: N.C. Mullins, *Theories and Theory Groups in Contemporary American Sociology*, New York: Harper & Row, 1973; S.N. Eisenstadt and M. Curelaru, *The Form of Sociology: Paradigms and Crises*, New York: Wiley, 1976. Nor is there any reason to postulate a change from structural functionalism to functional structuralism, as Luhmann has done. Cf. N. Luhmann, 'Soziologie als Theorie sozialer Systeme', in *Soziologische Aufklärung*, Vol. 1, Opladen: Westdeutscher Verlag, 1970, pp. 113–46. Rocher also emphasizes the difference between Parsons's theory and structural functional theories, but he lets some of the criticisms of structural functionalist theories stand as valid criticisms of Parsons also: G. Rocher, *Talcott Parsons and American Sociology*.

22 T. Parsons, 'Some problems of General Theory in sociology', p. 253.

23 T. Parson, *The Social System,* Chaps III–V; 'Pattern variables revisited: A response to Robert Dubin', in *Sociological Theory and Modern Society*, pp. 192–219; T. Parsons and E.A. Shils, 'Values, motives, and systems of action', pp. 76–91; T. Parsons and R.F. Bales,

'The dimensions of action-space', in T. Parsons, R.F. Bales and E.A. Shils, *Working Papers in the Theory of Action*, pp. 63–109; T. Parsons, R.F. Bales and E.A. Shils, 'Phase movement in relation to motivation, symbol formation, and role structure', in *Working Papers in the Theory of Action*, pp. 163–269.

24 T. Parsons, 'The professions and social structure', in *Essays in Sociological Theory*, New York: Free Press, 1954, pp. 34–49; *The Social System*, Chap. X; 'Professions', in D.L. Sills (ed.), *International Encyclopedia of the Social Sciences*, Vol. 12, New York: Macmillan, 1968, pp. 536–47; 'Research with human subjects and the "Professional Complex"', in *Action Theory and the Human Condition*, pp. 35–65; 'The sick role and the role of the physician reconsidered', in *Action Theory and the Human Condition*, pp. 17–34; T. Parsons and G.M. Platt, *The American University*, Chap. 5.

25 T. Parsons, R.F. Bales and E.A. Shils, 'Phase movement in relation to motivation, symbol formation, and role structure', pp. 172–90.

26 T. Parsons, 'Pattern variables revisited'; R. Dubin, 'Parsons' actor: Continuities in social theory', in T. Parsons, *Sociological Theory and Modern Society,* pp. 521–36; J.J. Loubser, 'General introduction', in J.J. Loubser, R.C. Baum, A. Effrat and V.M. Lidz (eds), *Explorations in General Theory in Social Science*, pp. 1–23; H.P.M. Adriaansens, *Talcott Parsons and the Conceptual Dilemma*, pp. 58–115.

27 T. Parsons, R.F. Bales and E.A. Shils, 'Phase movement in relation to motivation, symbol formation, and role structure', pp. 172–90.

28 T. Parsons, 'Some problems of general theory in sociology', p. 245.

29 T. Parsons, R.F. Bales and E.A. Shils, 'Phase movement in relation to motivation, symbol formation, and role structure', pp. 172–9; T. Parsons, 'Some problems of general theory in sociology', 'A paradigm of the human condition'.

30 Unlike Parsons, I interpret administration as goal-specifying (G) and legislation through political exchange as adaptive (A) in regard to the articulation of interests.

31 Thomas Burger criticizes Parsons's analytical sociology as not empirically verifiable. He pleads for an empirical sociology in which the different factors which determine action will be incorporated directly into an empirical model. Burger fails to recognize that the various forces which control action must be analytically separated, in order to determine what their effect is in general, before they can be joined together in empirical applications. An adequate theory of action must include both an analytical model and a level of empirical interpretation. In a concrete empiricism such as Burger advocates, the union of theoretical order and empirical experience, in Kant's sense, would not be attainable. But to attain this union is precisely Parsons's theoretical programme. Cf. T. Burger, 'Talcott Parsons, the problem of order in society, and the program of an analytical sociology'; T. Parsons, 'Comment on Burger's critique'.

32 Parsons introduced this element of the theory after an intensive reading of recent developments in physiology and modern cybernetics: W.B. Cannon, *The Wisdom of the Body*, New York: Norton, 1932; N.

Wiener, *Cybernetics, or Control and Communication in the Animal and the Machine*, New York: Wiley (1948) 1961. Cf. T. Parsons, 'An approach to psychological theory in terms of the theory of action', pp. 681-8; 'An outline of the social system', in T. Parsons, E.A. Shils, K.D. Naegele and J.R. Pitts (eds), *Theories of Society*, New York: Free Press, 1961, Section 1; *Societies. Evolutionary and Comparative Perspectives*, Englewood Cliffs, N.J.: Prentice Hall, 1966, Chap. 2; 'Pattern variables revisited'; 'The point of view of the author', in M. Black (ed.), *The Social Theories of Talcott Parsons*, pp. 311-63; cf. N.J. Smelser, *Theory of Collective Behavior*, New York: Free Press, 1963, pp. 32-4; H.M. Johnson, 'The relevance of the theory of action to historians', in *Social Science Quarterly* 50, 1969, pp. 46-58; E. Schwanenberg, 'The two problems of order in Parsons' theory', pp. 577-9; *Soziales Handeln*, pp. 139-56; H. Reimann, *Kommunikations-Systeme. Umrisse einer Soziologie der Vermittlungs- und Mitteilungsprozesse*, Tübingen: Mohr Siebeck, 1974, pp. 32-73.

33 For an interesting conception of the four-function schema, cf. R.C. Baum, 'Communication and media', in J.J. Loubser, R.C. Baum, A. Effrat and V.M. Lidz (eds), *Explorations in General Theory in Social Science*, pp. 533-56; 'On societal media dynamics', in J.J. Loubser, R.C. Baum, A. Effrat and V.M. Lidz (eds), *Explorations in General Theory in Social Science*, pp. 579-608; 'Beyond the "Iron Cage"', in *Sociological Analysis* 38, 1977, pp. 309-30.

34 Here I refer to Luhmann's basic categories: experience and action, complexity and contingency. However, Luhmann backs away from constructing a generally applicable analytical schema. See N. Luhmann, 'Einführende Bemerkungen zu einer Theorie symbolisch generalisierter Kommunikationsmedien', in *Zeitschrift für Soziologie*, 3, 1974, pp. 236-55.

35 I have not used the order of the subsystems which is set out in *Economy and Society* (p. 68), but that which appeared in *Working Papers in the Theory of Action* (pp. 192, 195), as recommended by Mark Gould. Cf. M. Gould, 'Systems analysis, macrosociology, and the generalized media of social action', in J.J. Loubser, R.C. Baum, A. Effrat and V.M. Lidz (eds), *Explorations in General Theory in Social Science*, pp. 470-506. Only this ordering of the A-G-I-L schema brings out its full potential as a way of locating a multiplicity of subsystems between the poles of the ordering and dynamizing systems. It allows us to solve the theoretical problems raised by Luhmann. Cf. N. Luhmann, 'Interpenetration bei Parsons'.

36 Parsons never made a clear distinction between these types of relations. He tended to write as if *every* concrete action had to be thought of as a product of the interpenetration of subsystems. 'Interpenetration' here obviously has a very general meaning. But Parsons also uses the term 'interpenetration' in a much more specific sense. In this narrower sense, interpenetration signifies a specific type of relation between subsystems, one possible relation among others, though Parsons does not precisely define the other types of relationship. In this respect I have here taken a theoretical element already implicit in Parsons's action theory and

given it a more precise form.

37 T. Parsons, 'An approach to psychological theory in terms of the theory of action' p. 701; 'Some problems of general theory in sociology', pp. 249–60.

38 M. Weber, *Economy and Society*, Vol. 2, Part 2, Chap. VII (W/G 382–5); E. Durkheim, *The Division of Labor*; T. Parsons and N.J. Smelser, *Economy and Society*, pp. 101–84.

39 K. Marx, *Capital*, ed. by F. Engels, in *Great Books of the Western World, 50: Marx*, Chicago and London: Encyclopaedia Britannica, 1950, p. 61.

40 M. Weber, *From Max Weber: Essays in Sociology*, pp. 323–33 (RS I 536–46).

41 M. Weber, *The Religion of China*, pp. 107–70 (RS I 395–458).

42 T. Parsons, 'Christianity and modern industrial society', in *Sociological Theory and Modern Society*, pp. 385–421; 'Durkheim's contribution to the theory of integration of social systems'; 'Full citizenship for the negro American?', in *Sociological Theory and Modern Society*, pp. 422–65; *The System of Modern Societies*, Englewood Cliffs N.J.: Prentice Hall, 1971, Chap. 6; 'Comparative studies and evolutionary change', in *Social Systems and the Evolution of Action Theory*, pp. 279–320; 'Equality and inequality in modern society, or social stratification revisited', in *Social Systems and the Evolution of Action Theory*, pp. 321–80; 'Some theoretical considerations on the nature and trends of change of ethnicity', in *Social Systems and the Evolution of Action Theory*, pp. 381–404; S.M. Lipset, *The First New Nation*, New York: Basic Books, 1963; J.C. Alexander, 'Core solidarity, ethnic outgroup, and social differentiation: A multidimensional model of inclusion in modern societies', in J. Dofny and A. Akiwowo (eds), *National and Ethnic Movements*, London: Sage, 1980, pp. 5–28; 'The mass news media in systemic, historical, and comparative perspective', in E. Katz and T. Szecsko (eds), *Mass Media and Social Change*, London: Sage, 1981, pp. 17–51.

43 T. Parsons, 'Some problems of general theory in sociology', p. 254.

44 D. Lockwood, 'Social integration and system integration', in G.K. Zollschan and W. Hirsch (eds), *Explorations in Social Change*, London: Routledge, 1964, pp. 244–57.

45 Among those making this assumption is W. Schluchter, 'Gesellschaft und Kultur: Überlegungen zu einer Theorie institutioneller Differenzierung', in W. Schluchter (ed.), *Verhalten, Handeln und System*, pp. 115–16, 136–8.

46 That there are value conflicts in concrete cases, and that the capacity of the social-cultural system to guide and control the other systems is in reality frequently limited, are not facts which in themselves falsify the Parsonian theory of action. Nothing in the theory denies these facts. Therefore there is no need to replace the Parsonian theory with a 'realistic' theory of action, as has been proposed by Schluchter. Cf. W. Schluchter, 'Gesellschaft und Kultur', pp. 116–40. On fitting the relationship between normative and conditional factors into the cybernetic hierarchy of conditions and controls, cf. E. Schwanenberg,

Soziales Handeln, pp. 139–56; 'The two problems of order in Parsons' theory', pp. 577–9.

47 Dahrendorf's characterization of the 'theory of integration' as opposed to a 'theory of conflict' is a caricature of Parsons's theory of action. The central thesis of the theory of integration is that every society *rests* on a *de facto* consensus of its members. In this concrete formulation, such a proposition is to be found nowhere in Parsons; the reconstruction of the theory of action given here should show that such a proposition is incompatible with the theory. Cf. R. Dahrendorf, 'Out of utopia: Toward a reorientation of sociological analysis', 'Toward a theory of social conflict', in *Journal of Conflict Resolution* 2, 1958, pp. 170–83; C.W. Mills, *The Sociological Imagination*; R. Collins, 'A comparative approach to political sociology', in R. Bendix (ed.), *State and Society: A Reader in Comparative Political Sociology*, Berkeley: University of California Press, 1968, pp. 42–67; A.W. Gouldner, *The Coming Crisis of Western Sociology*. On the theory of social change in the context of voluntaristic action theory, see N.J. Smelser, *Theory of Collective Behavior;* A.L. Jacobson, 'A theoretical and empirical analysis of social change and conflict based on Talcott Parsons' ideas', in H. Turk and R.L. Simpson (eds), *Institutions and Social Exchange*, pp. 344–60; S.N. Eisenstadt, *Tradition, Change and Modernity,* New York: Wiley, 1973; J.C. Alexander, 'Revolution, reaction, and reform: The change theory of Parsons' middle period', in *Sociological Inquiry* 51, 1981, pp. 267–80. See also the contributions on social change in J.J. Loubser, R.C. Baum, A. Effrat and V.M. Lidz (eds), *Explorations in General Theory in Social Science*, Part V, pp. 662–797.

48 I have not followed Parsons in all aspects of the differentiation of the social system. Cf. T. Parsons and G.M. Platt, *The American University*, p. 428, fig. A. 2.

49 Here again I have not followed Parsons in all aspects of the differentiation of the action system. Cf. T. Parsons and G.M. Platt, *The American University*, fig. A. 6.

50 Here once again, the differentiation of the human condition system does not follow Parsons in all respects. Cf. T. Parsons, 'A paradigm of the human condition', p. 382, fig. 2.

51 T. Parsons and N.J. Smelser, *Economy and Society*; T. Parsons, 'On the concept of influence'; 'On the concept of political power'; and, in addition, 'On the concept of value-commitments'; H.M. Johnson, 'The generalized symbolic media in Parsons' theory', in *Sociology and Social Research* 57, 1973, pp. 208–21; R.C. Baum, 'Communication and media'; 'On societal media dynamics'; R. Münch, *Legitimität und politische Macht,* Opladen: Westdeutscher Verlag, 1976. For the media 'value-commitments' (L) and 'influence' (I), I would substitute 'argument' as the medium of social-cultural discursive action (L) and 'commitment' as the medium of communal action (I). We can imagine specifications of these media within the general framework of action. For example, we could propose 'interpretation' (L), 'consensus formation' (I), 'expertise' (G), and 'truth' (A) as submedia of 'argument'. Similarly, I understand 'value-commitments' as a normative-cultural

specification of 'commitments' which is found in the zone of interpenetration of communal action and cultural discursive action. 'Influence' is a conjunction of expertise and commitment to the societal community. For the concept of the 'fiduciary system', I would substitute that of the 'social-cultural system'. The concept of the fiduciary system already contains the professional aspect which is actually only the G component of the social-cultural system. The notion of the social-cultural system is more general in its meaning and refers to that aspect of social action which deals with symbolic understanding.

52 T. Parsons, 'Social structure and the symbolic media of interchange', in *Social Systems and the Evolution of Action Theory*, pp. 204–28; 'Some problems of general theory in sociology'; T. Parsons and G.M. Platt, *The American University*, pp. 73–7, 304–45.

53 T. Parsons, 'A paradigm of the human condition'.

54 M. Weber, *Economy and Society*, Vol. 2, Part 2, Chaps I–IV (W/G 181–233).

55 T. Parsons, 'Social structure and the symbolic media of interchange', pp. 204–14.

56 T. Parsons, 'On the concept of political power'.

57 T. Parsons and G.M. Platt, *The American University*, p. 434, fig. A. 4.

58 T. Parsons and N.J. Smelser, *Economy and Society*, Chaps I–III.

59 This core of the theory of media is not, for example, present in Blain's alternative formulation. Cf. R.R. Blain, 'An alternative to Parsons' four-function paradigm as a basis for developing general sociological theory', in *American Sociological Review* 36, 1971, pp. 678–92.

60 T. Parsons and N.J. Smelser, *Economy and Society*, p. 71.

61 Ibid., p. 54.

62 T. Parsons, 'On the concept of political power', p. 398; T. Parsons and N.J. Smelser, *Economy and Society*, pp. 51–81, 101–84.

63 T. Parsons and N.J. Smelser, *Economy and Society*, pp. 175–84.

64 T. Parsons, 'On the concept of political power', p. 399. Parsons himself calls for special caution in avoiding reification when the relevant formulations are interpreted and applied. This cannot be emphasized too strongly, either in the present context or in the later interpretations of the media paradigm as it applies to the general action system or to the system of the human condition. Parsons himself believed further revisions would still be necessary. At this point we should be concerned less with the individual formulations than with the interpretation of the paradigm's perspective, and with how it is integrated within the voluntaristic theory of action's more general framework. A further note of caution needed here is that the paradigm should not be sweepingly 'economized'. Cf. T. Parsons, 'A paradigm of the human condition', p. 393, footnote 89; T. Parsons and G.M. Platt, *The American University*, p. 431.

65 M. Weber, *Economy and Society*, Vol. 1, Part 1, Chap. II, 10–14; Vol. 2, Chap. II (W/G 45–62, 199–211). For a detailed study of the economic element in Parsons's work as a whole, see the doctoral thesis by K.-H. Saurwein *Das ökonomische Element in der soziologischen Theorie Talcott Parsons'*, University of Düsseldorf, 1984 (due to be published shortly).

66 T. Parsons, 'On the concept of political power', pp. 383–95; 'On the concept of value-commitments', pp. 467–9; T. Parsons and G.M. Platt, *The American University*, pp. 268–70, 304–10, 383–4.

67 T. Parsons, 'On the concept of political power', pp. 392–4; T. Parsons and G.M. Platt, *The American University*, pp. 310–45; R. Münch, *Legitimität und politische Macht*, pp. 135–74.

68 T. Parsons and G.M. Platt, *The American University*, pp. 430–4.

69 It is misleading to place the 'economic analogy' in the foreground of Parsons's theory of media without making these qualifications. Cf. T. Parsons, 'Some problems of general theory in sociology', pp. 238–44; E. Schwanenberg, 'The two problems of order in Parsons' theory', p. 579.

70 T. Parsons, 'Review of Harold J. Bershady: *Ideology and Social Knowledge*', p. 130.

71 Cf. Parsons's earlier formulation of the theory of interpenetration on the level of the general system of action before the formulation of the theory of media: T. Parsons, 'An approach to psychological theory in terms of the theory of action'.

72 T. Parsons and G.M. Platt, *The American University*, p. 446, fig. A. 12.

73 Ibid., pp. 33–102.

74 Stephen Warner advocates an expansion of the theory of action to include cognitive elements, without, however, taking up Parsons's work on the cognitive complex. The cognitive aspect of action is already integrated into Parsons's theoretical model. Warner is suggesting that the cognitive orientation toward norms and/or common cognitions could provide just as adequate a foundation for order as moral obligations and common norms. But purely cognitive orientations toward norms would provide only a contingent, factual order, such as can exist only in limiting cases. Common cognitions can exist only where the validity of common norms has already been accepted. Warner's attempt to interpret Calvinism as an example of a purely cognitive system which yet provides a foundation for order ignores these moral and societal fundamentals. Cf. R.S. Warner, 'Toward a redefinition of action theory: Paying the cognitive element its due'; T. Parsons, 'Comment on R. Stephen Warner's "Toward a redefinition of action theory: Paying the cognitive element its due"'; W. Pope and J. Cohen, 'Oh R. Stephen Warner's "Toward a redefinition of action theory: Paying the cognitive element its due"'.

75 T. Parsons and G.M. Platt, *The American University*, p. 57. The introduction of the behavioural system as a replacement for the behavioural organism in the general system of action goes back to Charles W. Lidz and Victor M. Lidz's integration into action theory of Piaget's cognitive psychology. The organism then occupies the place of the goal-specifying subsystem (G) of the human condition. Cf. C.W. Lidz and V.M. Lidz, 'Piaget's psychology of intelligence and the theory of action', in J.J. Loubser, R.C. Baum, A. Effrat and V.M. Lidz (eds), *Explorations in General Theory in Social Science*, pp. 195–239. Victor Lidz uses different terms for the action system's media which stem from his cooperative work with Parsons: Durkheim's 'collective representations' (L) and 'collective sentiments' (I), 'affect' (G) and 'intelligence'

(A). 'Affect' in this context, i.e. as a medium for the personality system, is an expression of spontaneous, emotional devotion to goals. On the other hand, 'affect' as a medium for the social system implies affective *attachment* to others. These, then, are two totally different interpretations of the term 'affect'. One can agree with Lidz to the extent that subjective, emotional devotion to goals undoubtedly does represent an essential element of goal-directed action. Though Durkheim's 'collective representations' are too firmly rooted in the social context to serve as an appropriate concept for the cultural medium, it is possible that the aspect of affective *attachment* which constitutes the social system's medium may be better brought out by the term 'collective sentiments' than the term 'affect'. Nevertheless, in the present work 'affect' should always be understood to mean affective attachment. Cf. V.M. Lidz, 'The law as index, phenomenon, and element – conceptual steps toward a general sociology of law', in *Sociological Inquiry* 49, 1979, pp. 5–25. A number of other particularly interesting contributions by Victor Lidz amongst his recent work follow the argument outlined above.

76 T. Parsons and G.M. Platt, *The American University*, pp. 435–40.

77 Ibid., p. 75.

78 Ibid., pp. 310–45.

79 Ibid., pp. 346–88; T. Parsons, 'The future of the university', in *Action Theory and the Human Condition*, pp. 96–114; 'Some considerations on the growth of the American system of higher education and research', in *Action Theory and the Human Condition*, pp. 115–32; 'Stability and change in the University', in *Action Theory and the Human Condition*, pp. 154–64; 'The university "bundle": A study of the balance between differentiation and integration', in *Action Theory and the Human Condition*, pp. 133–53; cf. N.J. Smelser, 'Epilogue: Social-structural dimensions of higher education', in T. Parsons and G.M. Platt, *The American University*, pp. 389–422.

80 T. Parsons, 'A paradigm of the human condition'.

81 Ibid., pp. 392–414.

82 R.N. Bellah, 'Civil religion in America', in *Beyond Belief: Essays on Religion in a Post-traditional World*, New York: Harper & Row, 1970, pp. 168–89; *The Broken Covenant: American Civil Religion in Time of Trial*, New York: Seabury Press, 1975.

83 T. Parsons, 'A paradigm of the human condition', pp. 355–401.

84 Ibid., pp. 368–70, 396–7.

85 Ibid., pp. 401–3.

86 Ibid., pp. 397–400.

87 Ibid., pp. 392–405.

88 Ibid., pp. 407–8.

89 Ibid., pp. 411–13.

90 E. Durkheim, *Sociology and Philosophy*; *The Elementary Forms of the Religious Life*.

91 M. Weber, *From Max Weber: Essays in Sociology*, pp. 323–59 (RS I 536–73); *Economy and Society*, Vol. 2, Part 2, Chap. VI, ix–xv (W/G 321–81).

92 T. Parsons, 'A paradigm of the human condition', pp. 409–10; L.J. Henderson, *The Fitness of the Environment: An Inquiry into the Biological Significance of the Properties of Matter*, New York: Macmillan, 1913.
93 T. Parsons, 'A paradigm of the human condition', pp. 410, 414–33; S. Freud, 'The ego and the id'.
94 T. Parsons, *Societies. Evolutionary and Comparative Perspectives;* 'Evolutionary universals in society', in *Sociological Theory and Modern Society*, pp. 490–520; *The System of Modern Societies*; 'Comparative studies and evolutionary change'.
95 T. Parsons, *Structure*, p. 3.
96 Ibid., pp. 583–5, 634–9, 641–2, 681, 764–5; 'Unity and diversity in the modern intellectual disciplines: The role of the social sciences', in *Sociological Theory and Modern Society*, pp. 166–91; 'Theory in the humanities and sociology', in *Daedalus* 99 (1), 1970, pp. 495–523; 'A paradigm of the human condition', pp. 382, 389–90, 393, 397, 403; 'On the relation of the theory of action to Max Weber's "Verstehende Soziologie"', in W. Schluchter (ed.), *Verhalten, Handeln und System*, pp. 150–63.
97 T. Parsons, *Structure*, pp. 67–8, 80–6, 110–14, 122–5, 219–28.
98 Cf. E. Mayr, *Populations, Species, and Evolution*, Cambridge, Mass.: Harvard University Press, 1970; B. Giesen, *Makrosoziologie: Eine evolutionstheoretische Einführung,* Hamburg: Hoffmann & Campe, 1980; K. Eder, *Die Entstehung staatlich organisierter Gesellschaften. Ein Beitrag zu einer Theorie sozialer Evolution*, Frankfurt: Suhrkamp, 1980.
99 Explanation of *action* within the framework of such a theory of evolution cannot, therefore, be purely teleonomic in character as Bershady assumes: H.J. Bershady, *Ideology and Social Knowledge*; 'Commentary on Talcott Parsons' review of Harold J. Bershady's *Ideology and Social Knowledge'*. On this question, see also T. Parsons, 'General introduction', in *Social Systems and the Evolution of Action Theory*, pp. 5–7; 'The present status of "structural-functional" theory in sociology', pp. 110–16; 'Review of Harold J. Bershady: *Ideology and Social Knowledge*', pp. 130–2. Cf. also the emphasis Parsons places on the assertion that, because categories from biological theory are integrated into action theory, this does not mean that action theory is to be subsumed under biological theory, in H.M. Johnson, 'Interview with Talcott Parsons', in *Revue Européenne des Sciences Sociales et Cahiers Vilfredo Pareto* 13 (34), 1975, p. 82. For a detailed study of the epistemological presuppositions, theoretical structure, explanatory programme and methodological corollaries of Parsons's work see the recent publication by B. Miebach, *Strukturalistische Handlungstheorie. Zum Verhältnis von soziologischer Theorie und empirischer Forschung in Werk Talcott Parsons'*, Opladen: Westdeutscher Verlag, 1984.
100 T. Parsons and G.M. Platt, *The American University*, pp. 169–81; T. Parsons, 'Comparative studies and evolutionary change'.
101 T. Parsons, 'An analytical approach to the theory of social

stratification', in *Essays in Sociological Theory*, pp. 69–88; 'A revised analytical approach to the theory of social stratification', in *Essays in Sociological Theory*, pp. 386–439; 'Equality and inequality in modern society, or social stratification revisited'.

102 For an argument along these lines, see B. Barber, 'Inequality and occupational prestige: Theory, research and social policy', in *Sociological Inquiry* 48, 1978, p. 76: 'The structure of values and the structure of occupational roles are in continual and complex interaction with one another, and neither is in any generalized way determinative of the other.' See also B. Barber, *Social Stratification*, New York: Harcourt, Brace, 1957.

103 K. Davis and W.E. Moore, 'Some principles of stratification', in *American Sociological Review* 10, 1945, pp. 242–9; K. Davis, 'Reply to Tumin', in *American Sociological Review* 18, 1953, pp. 394–7; 'The abominable heresy: a reply to Dr Buckley', in *American Sociological Review* 24, 1959, pp. 82–3; W.E. Moore, 'But some are more equal than others', in *American Sociological Review* 28, 1963, pp. 26–8; M.M. Tumin, 'Some principles of stratification: A critical analysis', in *American Sociological Review* 18, 1953, pp. 387–94; 'Reply to Kingsley Davis', in *American Sociological Review* 18, 1953, pp. 672–3; 'On inequality', in *American Sociological Review* 28, 1963, pp. 19–26; W. Buckley, 'Social stratification and the functional theory of social differentiation', in *American Sociological Review* 23, 1958, pp. 369–75; 'A rejoinder to functionalists Dr Davis and Dr Levy', in *American Sociological Review* 24, 1959, pp. 84–6; 'On equitable inequality', in *American Sociological Review* 28, 1963, pp. 799–801; M.J. Levy, Jr, 'Functionalism: A reply to Dr Buckley', in *American Sociological Review* 24, 1959, pp. 83–4; G.A. Huaco, 'A logical analysis of the Davis-Moore theory of stratification', in *American Sociological Review* 28, 1963, pp. 801–4; A.L. Stinchcombe, 'Some empirical consequences of the Davis-Moore theory of stratification', in *American Sociological Review* 28, 1963, pp. 805–8; G.A. Lenski, *Power and Privilege: A Theory of Social Stratification*, New York: McGraw-Hill, 1966.

104 G.A. Huaco, 'A logical analysis of the Davis-Moore theory of stratification', p. 804.

105 Cf. Bernard Barber's critique of Davis and Moore's stratification theory: B. Barber, 'Inequality and occupational prestige', pp. 80, 83–5.

106 G. Lenski, *Power and Privilege*.

107 E. Durkheim, *Suicide*, pp. 246–58 (272–88).

108 R.K. Merton, 'Social structure and anomie', in *Social Theory and Social Structure*, pp. 185–214; 'Continuities in the theory of social structure and anomie', in *Social Theory and Social Structure*, pp. 215–48.

109 E. Durkheim, *Suicide*, p. 251 (278–9). This represents a specification of the general problem of an order's legitimacy. Cf. T. Parsons, 'Social classes and class conflict in the light of recent sociological theory', in *Essays in Sociological Theory*, pp. 323–35.

110 Max Weber already draws a distinction along these lines, 'appreciation'

being linked to 'status' while 'life chances' are linked to 'class situation'. The latter is essentially equivalent to the distribution of economic, political and intellectual opportunities described earlier in this exposition. Another concept Weber deals with in this context, namely the party, is located on a different level. It signifies that an organizational conjunction to form a collective has already taken place, and that the collective has the purpose of aspiring to a share of power within a democratic order. See M. Weber *Economy and Society*, Vol. 1, Part 1, Chap. IV; Vol. 2, Part 2, Chap. IX, 6 (W/G 177-80, 531-40).

111 T. Parsons, 'Equality and inequality in modern society, or social stratification revisited', p. 341.

112 J. Rawls, *A Theory of Justice*, Cambridge, Mass.: Harvard University Press, 1971, p. 60.

113 R. Dubin, 'Parsons' actor: Continuities in social theory'.

114 T. Parsons, 'Pattern variables revisited', p. 219.

115 See for example T. Parsons, 'An approach to psychological theory in terms of the theory of action', p. 649; *Societies. Evolutionary and Comparative Perspectives*, p. 8.

116 This terminology is used, for example, by W. Schluchter in 'Gesellschaft und Kultur', pp. 111-14.

117 J. Habermas, 'Handlung und System. Bemerkungen zu Parsons' Medientheorie', in W. Schluchter (ed.), *Verhalten, Handeln und System*, pp. 68-105; 'Talcott Parsons – Probleme der Theorie-konstruktion', in J. Matthes (ed.), *Lebenswelt und soziale Probleme*, Frankfurt and New York: Campus, 1981, pp. 28-48; *Theorie des kommunikativen Handelns*, Vol. 2, pp. 297-443. For a further critical analysis of the break between action theory and systems theory in Parsons's work, see S.P. Savage, *The Theories of Talcott Parsons*, New York: St Martin, 1981.

118 T. Parsons, *Structure*, p. 670; see also pp. 74-7, 91-2, 309, 318, 389-99, 424-5, 440, 458, 499, 712.

119 J. Habermas, *Theorie des kommunikativen Handelns*, Vol. 2, pp. 304-22.

120 Ibid., pp. 322-84.

121 T. Parsons and E.A Shils, 'Values, motives, and systems of action', pp. 54-6.

122 On this conception of the action system and the action space, see in particular T. Parsons and R.F. Bales, 'The dimensions of action-space', pp. 85-99.

123 T. Parsons, 'Social systems', in *Social Systems and the Evolution of Action Theory*, pp. 179-80.

124 J. Habermas, *Theories des kommunikativen Handelns*, Vol. 2, pp. 338-51.

125 Ibid., pp. 343, 346.

126 Ibid., pp. 309.

127 Cf. for example, T. Parsons and E.A. Shils, 'Values, motives, and systems of action', pp. 202-4; T. Parsons, 'Introduction' to Culture and the Social System, in T. Parsons, E.A. Shils, K.D. Naegele and J.R. Pitts (eds), *Theories of Society*, pp. 976-9.

128 Among other sources, see T. Parsons, 'Introduction' to Culture and the Social System, pp. 971–6.
129 J. Habermas, *Theorie des kommunikatives Handelns,* Vol. 2, pp. 352–75.
130 Ibid., pp. 375–84.
131 Among other sources, see T. Parsons, 'Introduction' to Culture and the Social System; *Societies. Evolutionary and Comparative Perspectives*; *The System of Modern Societies*; 'Equality and inequality in modern society, or social statification revisited'; 'Comparative studies and evolutionary change'.
132 Cf. T. Parsons, 'On the concept of value-commitments'.
133 J. Habermas, *Theorie des kommunikativen Handelns,* Vol. 2, pp. 384–419.
134 T. Parsons, *Structure*, pp. 67, 79–81, 102–25.
135 Ibid., pp. 67, 81, 112–13.
136 Even in Parsons's empirically oriented works, no functionalistic explanatory strategy exists in the sense of the logic of functionalistic explanations which has been analysed by Hempel, among others. Cf. C.G. Hempel, 'The logic of functional analysis', in *Aspects of Scientific Explanation*, New York: Free Press, 1965, pp. 297–330. Nor do the studies on evolutionary theory work with a purely teleonomic principle of explanation. See, for example, T. Parsons, *Societies. Evolutionary and Comparative Perspectives*; *The System of Modern Societies*.
137 T. Parsons, 'On building social system theory', pp. 48–50; 'The present status of "structural-functional" theory in sociology'; 'Review of Harold J. Bershady: *Ideology and Social Knowledge'*, p. 127.
138 T. Parsons, 'On the concept of political power'; 'On the concept of influence'; 'On the concept of value-commitments'; 'Social structure and the symbolic media of interchange'; 'Levels of organization and the mediation of social interaction', in H. Turk and R.L. Simpson (eds), *Institutions and Social Exchange*, pp. 23–35; T. Parsons and G.M. Platt, *The American University*, pp. 304–45.
139 J. Habermas, *Theorie des kommunikativen Handelns,* Vol. 2, pp. 420–37.
140 Ibid., pp. 437–44.
141 Ibid., pp. 191–228, especially pp. 193, 214.
142 Ibid., pp. 118–41. I have borrowed the term 'bisected' from J. Habermas in his contribution 'Gegen einen positivistisch halbierten Rationalismus', in T.W. Adorno, H. Albert, R. Dahrendorf, J. Habermas, H. Pilot and K.R. Popper, *Der Positivismusstreit in der deutschen Soziologie*, Neuwied and Berlin: Luchterhand, 1969, pp. 155–91.
143 T. Parsons, *Structure*, pp. 757–75; 'Unity and diversity in the modern intellectual disciplines'; 'Theory in the humanities and sociology'; 'A paradigm of the human condition', pp. 392–405; 'On the relation of the theory of action to Max Weber's "Verstehende Soziologie"'; 'Rationalität und der Prozess der Rationalisierung im Denken Max Webers', in W.M. Sprondel and C. Seyfarth (eds), *Max Weber und die Rationalisierung sozialen Handelns*, Stuttgart: Enke, 1981, pp. 81–92.

144 T. Parsons, 'Theory in the humanities and sociology', pp. 507–10, 513–17.
145 Scott is therefore in error when he claims that, on an epistemelogical level, Parsons moves from the voluntarism of *The Structure of Social Action* to a cautious 'naturalism' in *The Social System* and later works. Cf. J.F. Scott, 'The changing foundations of the Parsonian action scheme', in *American Sociological Review* 28, 1963, pp. 716–35; 'Interpreting Parsons' work: A problem in method', in *Sociological Inquiry* 44, 1974, pp. 58–61. Cf. the critique by J.H. Turner and L. Beeghley, 'Current folklore in the criticism of Parsonian action theory'; 'Persistent issues in Parsonian action theory', in *Sociological Inquiry* 44, 1974, pp. 61–3; T. Parsons, 'Comment on J.H. Turner and L. Beeghley: "Current Folklore in the Criticism of Parsonian Action Theory"', D.R. Gerstein, 'A note on the continuity of Parsonian action theory', in *Sociological Inquiry* 49, 1979, pp. 27–39; I. Procter, 'Parsons' early voluntarism'. Right at the outset, in *The Structure of Social Action,* Parsons integrated the 'normative' and 'conditional' determinants of action into a voluntaristic frame of reference; this effort of integration was continually expanded upon right through to his *Action Theory and the Human Condition.* 'Idealism' and 'naturalism' are not alternatives we are forced to choose between; rather, we must integrate their true substance in a more comprehensive frame of reference, whilst rejecting that which is inherently false in them. Nor, as Bershady believes, does Parsons move away from the ideal of the Covering Law model of the natural sciences toward a second best scientific solution to the explanatory problem by way of a teleonomic model. Bershady's own proposal, namely a pragmatic interpretational model, is itself restricted to only one aspect of the comprehensive explanatory requirements posed by the theory of action. Cf. H.J. Bershady, *Ideology and Social Knowledge*; 'Commentary on Talcott Parsons' review of H.J. Bershady's *Ideology and Social Knowledge*'; T. Parsons, 'Review of Harold J. Bershady: *Ideology and Social Knowledge*'. On this theme, see also my own discussion with H. Fehr, 'Handlung, System und teleonomische Erklärungen', in *Soziale Welt* 31, 1980, pp. 490–8; R. Münch, '"Teleonomie" und voluntaristische Handlungstheorie', in *Soziale Welt* 31, 1980, pp. 499–511. The crucial weakness of most of the interpretations of Parsons's epistemology is that they only look at some of Parsons's explicitly made epistemological statements without any attempt to relate them to the epistemology which is present as a latent structure in Parsons's substantial work itself. In this respect Parsons's epistemological statements do not always represent the epistemology he really applies in his work. Many of these weaknesses have been overcome in B. Miebach, *Strukturalistische Handlungstheorie.*
146 On the various explanatory strategies, cf. the discussion in C.G. Hempel, *Aspects of Scientific Explanation*; E. Nagel, *The Structure of Science. Problems in the Logic of Scientific Explanation*, New York: Harcourt, Brace, 1961; W. Stegmüller, *Probleme und Resultate der Wissenschaftstheorie und Analytischen Philosophie*, Vol. 1: *Wissenschaft-*

liche Erklärung und Begründung, Berlin/Heidelberg/New York: Springer, 1969; B. Giesen and M. Schmid, *Basale Soziologie: Wissenschaftstheorie,* Opladen: Westdeutscher Verlag, 1977; H. Esser, K. Klenovits and H. Zehnpfennig, *Wissenschaftstheorie,* 2 vols, Stuttgart: Teubner, 1977; M. Schmid, *Handlungsrationalität. Kritik einer dogmatischen Handlungswissenschaft,* Munich: Fink, 1979.

147 Cf. M.U. Martel and A.C. Hayes, 'Some new directions for action theory', in *Sociological Inquiry* 49, 1979, p. 77: 'Action Theory is distinctive for its *double commitment* to the aims of nomonlogical ("lawful") social science, and to the interpretive (hermeneutic) understanding of human action "from the actor's point of view"'. See also M.U. Martel, 'Academentia praecox: The aims, merits and scope of Parsons' multisystemic language rebellion (1958–1968)', in H. Turk and R.L. Simpson (eds), *Institutions and Social Exchange,* pp. 175–211.

148 Cf. B. Giesen, *Makrosoziologie,* pp. 82–124.

149 K.R. Popper, *Conjectures and Refutations; Objective Knowledge,* Chap. 2; I. Lakatos, 'Falsification and the methodology of scientific research programmes', in I. Lakatos and A. Musgrave (eds), *Criticism and the Growth of Knowledge,* pp. 91–196; R. Münch, *Gesellschafts-theorie und Ideologiekritik,* pp. 178–205.

150 Parsons once again categorically emphasized these premises underlying scientific work in 'A paradigm of the human condition', pp. 352–60, by quoting extensively from Albert Einstein who also had a strong conviction on this matter. Cf. A. Einstein, 'Physik und Realität', in *Journal of the Franklin Institute,* 221(3), 1936, pp.314–15.

151 T. Parsons and W. White, 'The link between character and society', in T. Parsons, *Social Structure and Personality,* pp. 183–255; T. Parsons and G.M. Platt, *The American University,* pp. 40–89; T. Parsons, 'Comparative studies and evolutionary change'; 'Equality and inequality in modern society, or social stratification revisited'.

152 On this point, cf. H. Albert's clear distinction between value basis, object language and object domain in the sciences: 'Wertfreiheit als methodisches Prinzip. Zur Frage der Notwendigkeit einer normativen Sozialwissenschaft', in E. Topitsch (ed.), *Logik der Sozialwissen-schaften,* Cologne and Berlin: Kiepenheuer & Witsch, 1965, pp. 181–210.

153 M. Weber, *The Methodology of the Social Sciences,* transl. and ed. by E.A. Shils and H.A. Finch, New York: Free Press, 1949, pp. 76–112 (WL 175–214); cf. T. Parsons, *Structure,* pp. 593–601, 715; 'Evaluation and objectivity in social science: An interpretation of Max Weber's con-tributions', in *Sociological Theory and Modern Society,* pp. 85–7, 98–101; T. Parsons and G.M. Platt, *The American University,* pp. 86–9.

154 In his insightful interpretation of Parsons's work, François Bourricaud justifiably features the value concept of 'institutionalized individualism' as the normative basis for Parsons's theory of action: F. Bourricaud, *The Sociology of Talcott Parsons.* See also the following discussion of Bourricaud's work: H.M. Johnson, 'Review of *L'Individualisme institutionel: Essai sur la sociologie de Talcott Parsons,* by François Bourricaud', in *American Journal of Sociology* 84, 1979, pp. 1000–4;

J.C. Alexander, 'The French correction: Revisionism and followership in the interpretation of Parsons', in *Contemporary Sociology* 10 (4), 1981, pp. 500–5. Jeffrey Alexander, too, sees this as the heart of Parsons's substantive voluntarism, as distinct from his formal voluntarism which Alexander sees on the level of analytical theory: J.C. Alexander, 'Formal and substantive voluntarism in the work of Talcott Parsons'. See also Alexander's more recent comprehensive and profound work on action theory: J.C. Alexander, *Theoretical Logic in Sociology*, particularly Vol. IV: *The Modern Reconstruction of Classical Thought: Talcott Parsons.*

155 Cf. H.M. Johnson, 'The relevance of the theory of action to historians'. This was surely one of the most inappropriate and ill-informed criticisms of Parsons, branding him as ideologically conservative, which later became the conventional prejudice of many other sociologists. The view is contradicted, however, by writings such as Parsons's vehement criticism of establishment economism. But the ideology of the true community and value absolutism (the ethics of conviction) also stand counter to Parsons's idea of institutionalized individualism. For a final assessment, see T. Parsons, 'Law as an intellectual stepchild', in H.M. Johnson (ed.), *Social System and Legal Process*, San Francisco: Jossey Bass, 1977, pp. 11–58 (*Sociological Inquiry* 47, Nos 3/4); 'Religious and economic symbolism in the Western world', in H.M. Johnson (ed.), *Religious Change and Continuity*, San Francisco: Jossey Bass, 1979, pp. 1–48 (*Sociological Inquiry* 49, Nos. 2/3). See also the support he indicates for President Roosevelt's 'New Deal' in the 1930s: T. Parsons, 'On building social system theory', p. 63, note 20. On this issue, cf. J.C. Alexander, 'Sociology for liberals: The legacy of Talcott Parsons', in *The New Republic* 180 (22), 2 June, 1979, pp. 10–12. Jürgen Habermas, meanwhile, has clearly expressed the significance of Parsons's work for neo-Marxist positions: J. Habermas, *Theorie des kommunikativen Handelns*, Vol. 2, p. 297. Talcott Parsons was a representative of modernity, and was pledged to its fundamental values, with their roots in the Enlightenment: rationality and a universally oriented ethical activism, freedom and equality.

156 This difference is brought out at an early stage by A. de Tocqueville, *Democracy in America* (2 vols), transl. by H. Reeve, critical appraisal by J.S. Mills, New York: Schocken (1835/40) 1961.

157 T. Parsons, 'On the concept of influence'; 'Research with human subjects and the "Professional complex"'.

158 R. Dahrendorf, 'Out of utopia'; Toward a theory of social conflict'; C.W. Mills, *The Sociological Imagination*; R. Collins, 'A comparative approach to political sociology'; A.W. Gouldner, *The Coming Crisis of Western Sociology.*

159 J.S. Coleman, 'Collective decisions'; D.P. Ellis, 'The Hobbesian problem of order'; V. Vanberg, 'Kollektive Güter und kollektives Handeln'.

160 The criticism directed by Pope, Cohen, Hazelrigg and also Collins toward Parsons's thesis that Durkheim and Weber converge in a

voluntaristic theory of action manifestly overemphasizes the elements of sociologistic positivism in Durkheim and those of positivistic/individualistic power and conflict theory in Weber. This interpretation amounts to a one-sided reduction of the two classic authors. In terms of systematic theoretical development, it is a relapse into positivism. Yet a key point demonstrated by Parsons was that the above two variants of positivism could at best explain coincidental, *factual* orders, but not *normative* orders. Durkheim managed to progress beyond sociologistic positivism with his concept of moral obligation. Equally, Weber progressed beyond pure idealism and, in his studies on the origin of modern social order, did not in any way confine himself to the frame of reference of individualistic positivism — it is impossible to reconstruct Weber's studies using a frame of reference of this kind. Schluchter's more recent attempt to interpret the work of Weber is in essence a non-integrated combination of the pure developmental logic of rationalization and a positivistic, utilitarian theory of interests and power. It was Tenbruck who first brought developmental logic with its rationalization of world-views to the fore in his interpretation of Weber's comparative studies on the sociology of religion. In its own way, this idealistic interpretational approach is just as one-sided as it is to reduce Weber to the terms of the theory of interests and power. See R. Collins, 'A comparative approach to political sociology'; R. Bendix, 'Two sociological traditions'; W. Pope, 'Classic on classic: Parsons' interpretation of Durkheim'; 'Parsons on Durkheim revisited: Reply to Cohen and Parsons'; J. Cohen, 'Moral freedom through understanding in Durkheim: Comment on Pope'; J. Cohen, L.E. Hazelrigg and W. Pope, 'De-Parsonizing Weber: A critique of Parsons' interpretation of Weber's sociology'; W. Pope J. Cohen and L.E. Hazelrigg, 'On the divergence of Weber and Durkheim: A critique of Parsons' convergence thesis'; 'Reply to Parsons'; W. Schluchter, 'The paradox of rationalization'; *The Rise of Western Rationalism*; F.H. Tenbruck, 'Das Werk Max Webers'. Cf. the critical commentaries contained in T. Parsons, 'Review of Reinhard Bendix and Günther Roth: *Scholarship and Partisanship: Essays on Max Weber*'; 'Comment on "Parsons' interpretation of Durkheim" and on "Moral freedom through understanding in Durkheim": Comment on Pope and Cohen'; 'Reply to Cohen, Hazelrigg and Pope'; R. Münch, 'Max Webers Gesellschaftsgeschichte als Entwicklungslogik der gesellschaftlichen Rationalisierung?', in *Kölner Zeitschrift für Soziologie und Sozialpsychologie* 32, 1980, pp. 774–86. On the matter of convergence and divergence between Max Weber and Emile Durkheim see the comparative examination in the forthcoming R. Münch, *Understanding Modernity. Toward a New Perspective going beyond Durkheim and Weber*, London: Routledge & Kegan Paul, Chaps 1 and 2.

161 On different variants, and on Parsonianism's future development, see J.C. Alexander, 'Paradigm revision and "Parsonianism"', in *Canadian Journal of Sociology* 4, 1979, pp. 343–58; E.A. Tiryakian, 'Post-Parsonian sociology', in *Humboldt Journal of Social Relations* 7:1, 1979/80, pp. 17–32.

Chapter 3

* I was motivated to write the following chapter on the scope and the limits of influential theoretical approaches as a result of many controversial discussions with colleagues from the Deutsche Gesellschaft für Soziologie's sociological theory section who favour other approaches and who are not readily convinced of the explanatory power of the voluntaristic theory of action. This is an attempt to formally demonstrate the advance in knowledge voluntaristic action theory achieves over positivistic and idealistic action theories.

1 T. Parsons, *Structure*, pp. 3–125, 731–48; 'The present position and prospects of systematic theory in sociology', in *Essays in Sociological Theory*, pp. 212–37; 'Law as an intellectual stepchild'.
2 T. Parsons, *Structure*, pp. 43–86.
3 The idealistic dilemma presented here is an enlargement upon Parsons's systematic treatment of idealism.
4 On this point, cf. the similar distinctions drawn by J. Habermas, *The Theory of Communicative Action*, Vol. 1, pp. 273–337 (369–452).
5 Cf. R. Münch, *Theorie sozialer Systeme. Eine Einführung in Grundbegriffe, Grundannahmen und logische Struktur*, Opladen: Westdeutscher Verlag, 1976, pp. 38–62.
6 Cf. M. Weber, *Gesammelte Aufsätze zur Wissenschaftslehre*, Tübingen: Mohr Siebeck (1922) 1973, pp. 441–7.
7 Cf. T. Parsons and R.F. Bales, 'The dimensions of action-space', pp. 63–109; T. Parsons, R.F. Bales and E.A. Shils, 'Phase movement in relation to motivation, symbol formation, and role structure', pp. 163–90; T. Parsons, 'Pattern variables revisited'. For more on the dimensions of the action space, see Section 2.3 of this book.
8 T. Parsons and E.A. Shils, 'Values, motives, and systems of action', pp. 53–76.
9 At this point I have integrated the basic elements Parsons formulated for the action system in 1937 — namely, ends, situation (means, given conditions), selective standard — with the AGIL schema which was not constructed until the 1950s. Cf. T. Parsons, *Structure*, pp. 43–51; T. Parsons, R.F. Bales and E.A. Shils, *Working Papers in the Theory of Action*, pp. 172–90. In the process, it becomes clear that the symbolic frame of reference still needs to be introduced as a further basic element. In the 1937 version, it appears that the selective standard fulfils the function both of norms and of a frame of reference. The transfer of these elements of action to the AGIL schema should show yet again that the schema's introduction did not replace the 1937 fundamentals of action theory at all, but in fact provided a further differentiation of them. Hans P.M. Adriaansens has also transferred the action frame of reference to the four-function schema in an interesting way: see H.P.M. Adriaansens, *Talcott Parsons and the Conceptual Dilemma*, pp. 107–15. Adriaansens equates the AGIL schema's external-internal axis to that of given conditions and norms in the action frame of reference, and its instrumental-consummatory axis

231

with that of means and ends. Adriaansens stresses that, in combination
with the cybernetic hierarchy of conditions and controls and with
media theory, the four-function schema succeeds in overcoming the
inconsistencies of structural-functionalism by synthesizing positivism
and idealism, individualism and collectivism still more than in *The
Structure of Social Action* to form voluntarism.

10 The limits of these approaches are discussed elsewhere, using classical
political theories as an example: R. Münch, *Basale Soziologie:
Soziologie der Politik*, Opladen: Westdeutscher Verlag, 1982.

11 Habermas and Schluchter have both formulated particularly telling
examples of this type of unintegrated idealistic-positivistic rationalism.
See J. Habermas, *Theorie des kommunikativen Handelns*; W.
Schluchter, *The Rise of Western Rationalism*.

12 The following can be regarded as classic representations of power and
conflict theory: N. Machiavelli, *The Prince*, transl., intro. and
annotation by J.B. Atkinson, Indianapolis: Bobbs-Merrill (1532) 1976;
T. Hobbes, *Leviathan*. Examples of modern variants of power and
conflict theory are propounded by, for example, R. Dahrendorf,
Gesellschaft und Freiheit, Munich: Piper, 1961; A.W. Gouldner, *The
Coming Crisis of Western Sociology*; C.W. Mills, *The Sociological
Imagination*; R. Collins, *Conflict Sociology. Toward an Explanatory
Science*, New York: Academic Press, 1974. Marxism, too, contains
elements of power and conflict theory in a number of its variants. Cf.
for example, N. Poulantzas, *Political Power and Social Classes*,
London: Verso, 1978.

13 For classic representations of the utilitarian approach, cf. D. Hume,
*Enquiries Concerning the Human Understanding and Concerning the
Principles of Morals*; A. Smith, *The Theory of Moral Sentiments*, New
York: Bohn (1759) 1966; *The Wealth of Nations*, New York: Modern
Library (1776) 1937; J.S. Mill, *Three Essays (On Liberty,
Representative Government, The Subjection of Women)*, London:
Oxford University Press (1859, 1861, 1869) 1975. For modern
utilitarian approaches see, for example, G.S. Becker, *The Economic
Approach to Human Behavior*, Chicago: University of Chicago Press,
1976; J.M. Buchanan, *The Limits of Liberty – Between Anarchy and
Leviathan*; J.S. Coleman, *Collective Decisions*; A. Downs, *An
Economic Theory of Democracy*, New York: Harper & Row 1957; V.
Vanberg, *Kollektive Güter und kollektives Handeln*. On the above, see
L. Dumont's critical study, *From Mandeville to Marx: The Genesis and
Triumph of Economic Ideology*, Chicago: University of Chicago Press,
1977.

14 Idealistic culture theory is represented primarily by the philosophical
tradition of German idealism. Cf. G.W.F. Hegel, *Grundlinien der
Philosophie des Rechts*, in *Werke*, Vol. 7, ed. by E. Moldenhauer and
K.M. Michel, Frankfurt: Suhrkamp, 1970; W. Dilthey, 'The
construction of the historical world in the human studies', in *Selected
Writings*, ed. and transl. by H.P. Rickman, Cambridge: Cambridge
University Press, 1976, pp. 168–245; E. Husserl, *Logical Investigations*,
transl. of 2nd edn by J.N. Findlay, New York: Humanities Press (1900–

1) 1970; A. Schütz, *Collected Papers*, Vol. 1, The Hague: Nijhoff, 1962; J. Habermas, *Knowledge and Human Interests*, transl. by J. Shapiro, London: Heinemann, 1972; J. Habermas, *Theorie und Praxis*, Frankfurt: Suhrkamp, 1971 (abridged transl. by J. Viertel: J. Habermas, *Theory and Practice*, London: Heinemann, 1974); K.-O. Apel, *Transformation der Philosophie*, 2 vols, Frankfurt: Suhrkamp, 1976. Elements of idealism provide the foundations for the approaches of phenomenological sociology, ethnomethodology, objective hermeneutics and symbolic interactionism. Cf. for example, J.D. Douglas (ed.), *Understanding Everyday Life. Toward the Reconstruction of Sociological Knowledge*; Arbeitsgruppe Bielefelder Soziologen (eds), *Alltagswissen, Interaktion und gesellschaftliche Wirklichkeit*, 2 vols, Reinbek nr Hamburg: Rowohlt, 1972; P.L. Berger and T. Luckmann, *The Social Construction of Reality: A Treatise in the Sociology of Knowledge*, Garden City, N.Y.: Doubleday, 1966; A. Cicourel, *Cognitive Sociology*, New York: Free Press, 1974: E. Goffman, *Frame Analysis*, New York: Harper & Row, 1974; A. Schütz and T. Luckmann, *The Structures of the Life-World*, transl. by R.M. Zaner and H.T. Engelhardt jr, Evanston, Ill.: North Western University Press, 1973; R. Grathoff and W.M. Sprondel (eds), *Alfred Schütz und die Idee des Alltags in den Sozialwissenschaften*, Stuttgart: Enke, 1976. On the above, see the discussion between Parsons and Schütz: A. Schütz and T. Parsons, *The Theory of Social Action: The Correspondence of Alfred Schütz and Talcott Parsons*. The literature named here also, to a considerable extent, reaches into the field of the normative paradigm. It belongs in the class of idealistic culture theory to a greater extent, the more highly developed its tendency toward generalization. If that tendency is taken to an extreme, the works propound forms of idealistic developmental logic. This, for example, is the case with many interpretations of Max Weber's thesis of disenchantment which occur either in pure idealistic form or in combination, though without any integration, with components of positivistic power and conflict theory. See for example, P.L. Berger, *The Sacred Canopy. Elements of a Sociological Theory of Religion*, Garden City, N.Y.: Doubleday, 1967; F.H. Tenbruck, 'Das Werk Max Webers'; W. Schluchter, *The Rise of Western Rationalism*. Although in *Theorie des kommunikativen Handelns* (*The Theory of Communicative Action* (1984)), Habermas does take steps toward an integrated paradigm, his approach continues to carry the stamp of the unresolved conflict between idealistic and materialistic developmental logic. See also his earlier work: J. Habermas, *Zur Rekonstruktion des Historischen Materialismus*, Frankfurt: Suhrkamp, 1976 (4 essays, transl. by T. McCarthy, reproduced in: *Communication and the Evolution of Society*, London: Heinemann, 1979).

15 Normative theory is generally presented in combination with the theory of idealistic culture, with great emphasis placed on the normative control of action. The classic formulation can be found in J.-J. Rousseau, *The Social Contract*, transl. and intro. by M. Cranston, Harmondsworth: Penguin (1762) 1968. Within the tradition of German

idealism, normative theory is brought out especially strongly in A. Schäffle, *Bau und Leben des sozialen Körpers*, Tübingen: Mohr Siebeck, 1884; F. Tönnies, *Community and Association: Gemeinschaft und Gesellschaft*, transl. by C.P. Loomis, London: Routledge & Kegan Paul (1887) 1955. Among contemporary currents of thought, the main areas falling under the title of normative theory are 'life-world sociology' and especially ethnomethodology. These approaches both have normativism implicit within them. This applies all the more, the more they seek to grasp the particularity of distinct life-worlds. Hence, a great deal of the literature cited in note 14 is also attributable to normative theory's frame of reference. Examples of this in relatively recent literature are: J.D. Douglas (ed.), *Understanding Everyday Life*; Arbeitsgruppe Bielefelder Soziologen (eds), *Alltagswissen, Interaktion und gesellschaftliche Wirklichkeit*; A. Schütz and T. Luckmann, *The Structures of the Life-World*. On the above, cf. the critical discussion in J. Habermas, *Theorie des kommunikativen Handelns*, Vol. 2, pp. 182–228. Talcott Parsons criticized the approach of ethnomethodology as 'Gemeinschaft romanticism'. See E.A. Tiryakian, 'Letter from Talcott Parsons', in *Sociological Inquiry* 51, 1981, p. 36.

Concluding considerations

1 This is something which was already evident to Max Weber. Cf. M. Weber, *From Max Weber: Essays in Sociology*, pp. 141–2 (WL 596–7); *The Religion of China*, pp. 150–2 (RS I 439–40); *The Religion of India*, pp. 146–7 (RS II 146), 165–76 (RS II 165–76).

2 Cf. J. Ben-David, *The Scientist's Role in Society*, Englewood Cliffs, N.J.: Prentice Hall, 1971; J. Needham, *The Grand Titration. Science and Society in East and West*, London: Allen & Unwin, 1969; B. Nelson, *Der Ursprung der Moderne*, Frankfurt: Suhrkamp, 1977; E. Zilsel, *Die sozialen Ursprünge der neuzeitlichen Wissenschaft*, ed by W. Krohn, Frankfurt: Suhrkamp, 1976.

3 I. Kant, *Critique of Pure Reason*. Cf. R. Münch, *Gesellschaftstheorie und Ideologiekritik*, pp. 16–23.

4 I. Kant, *Critique of Practical Reason*. Cf. R. Münch, *Gesellschaftstheorie und Ideologiekritik*, pp. 23–30.

5 T. Parsons, 'Unity and diversity in the modern intellectual disciplines', p. 190; *Structure*, pp. 3–86, 727–75; 'Theory in the humanities and sociology'; 'Review of Harold J. Bershady: *Ideology and Social Knowledge*'. The fact that differing orientations of knowledge coincide is the basis for competition between different paradigms in sociology. On paradigm competition, cf. H. Strasser, *The Normative Structure of Sociology. Conservative and Emancipatory Themes in Social Thought*, London: Routledge, 1976; G. Ritzer, *Sociology. A Multiple Paradigm Science*, Boston: Allyn & Bacon, 1975; P. Sztompka, *Sociological Dilemmas: Toward a Dialectic Paradigm*, New York: Academic Press, 1979.

6 Cf. T. Parsons, 'Evaluation and objectivity in social science: An

interpretation of Max Weber's contributions'; 'Durkheim on religion
revisited: Another look at *The Elementary Forms of the Religious Life*';
'On the relation of the theory of action to Max Weber's "Verstehende
Soziologie"'.

7 For classic proponents of utilitarian social theory, see, for example,
D. Hume, *Enquiries Concerning the Human Understanding and
Concerning the Principles of Morals*; A. Smith, *The Theory of Moral
Sentiments*; for modern utilitarian approaches see, for example, G.S.
Becker, *The Economic Approach to Human Behavior*; J.M. Buchanan,
The Limits of Liberty – Between Anarchy and Leviathan. Cf. R.
Münch, *Basale Soziologie: Soziologie der Politik*, Section 2.3.

8 Normativism should be taken to primarily include approaches which
stress community formation in human action, generally as a normative
postulate. This group includes in particular: J.-J. Rousseau, *The Social
Contract*; F. Tönnies, *Community and Association: Gemeinschaft und
Gesellschaft*. Many works of ethnomethodology also incorporate an
implicit normativism. Cf. for example, J.D. Douglas (ed.), *Understanding Everyday Life*; A. Schütz and T. Luckmann, *The Structures of
the Life-World*. On the above, cf. R. Münch, *Basale Soziologie:
Soziologie der Politik*, Section 2.2.

9 The theory of reason has its most important roots in German idealism.
See, for example, G.W.F. Hegel, *Phenomenology of the Spirit*, transl.
by A.V. Miller, analysis by J.N. Findley, Oxford: Clarendon Press,
1977; W. Dilthey, 'The construction of the historical world in the
human studies'; E. Husserl, *Logical Investigations*; A. Schütz,
Collected Papers; J. Habermas, *Knowledge and Human Interests*.
Idealistic interpretations of Max Weber's sociology of religion should
also be viewed in this context. See, for example, F.H. Tenbruck, 'Das
Werk Max Webers'. Cf. R. Münch, *Basale Soziologie: Soziologie der
Politik*, Section 2.1.

10 For classic proponents of power and conflict theory, see: N.
Machiavelli, *The Prince*; T. Hobbes, *Leviathan*. For modern variants
see R. Dahrendorf, *Gesellschaft und Freiheit*; R. Collins, *Conflict
Sociology*. On the above, cf. R. Münch, *Basale Soziologie: Soziologie
der Politik*, Section 2.4.

11 The various theoretical approaches are located in the frame of reference
of voluntaristic action theory in chapter 3 of this book.

12 T. Parsons, *Structure*, pp. 43–51, 731–48; T. Parsons, R.F. Bales and
E.A. Shils, 'Phase movement in relation to motivation, symbol
formation, and role structure', pp. 172–90. Cf. chapter 3 of this book.

13 Cf. section 2.3 of this book.

14 Cf. T. Parsons, *Structure*, pp. 583–5, 588–9, 634–9, 681, 765; 'Unity and
diversity in the modern intellectual disciplines', pp. 182–91; 'A
paradigm of the human condition', pp. 382, 389–90, 393, 397, 403; 'On
the relation of the theory of action to Max Weber's "Verstehende
Soziologie"'.

15 Cf. T. Parsons, *Structure*, p. 732.

16 Cf. chapter 1 of this book.

17 These two additional poles of the action space result from the

introduction of the AGIL schema. Cf. sections 2.3 and 2.4 of this book.
18 T. Parsons, *Structure*, pp. 65–7, 91, 346–59.
19 Ibid., pp. 686–94.
20 Ibid., pp. 82, 473–87.
21 Ibid., pp. 81–2, 396, 439–40, 448–50, 572–3, 753–7, 762.

Bibliography

Adriaansens, H.P.M., *Talcott Parsons and the Conceptual Dilemma*, London: Routledge & Kegan Paul, 1980.

Albert, H., 'Wertfreiheit als methodisches Prinzip. Zur Frage der Notwendigkeit einer normativen Sozialwissenschaft', in E. Topitsch (ed.), *Logik der Sozialwissenschaften*. Cologne/Berlin: Kiepenheuer & Witsch, 1965, pp. 181–210.

Alexander, J.C., 'Formal and substantive voluntarism in the work of Talcott Parsons: A theoretical and idealogical reinterpretation', in *American Sociological Review* 43, 1978, pp. 177–98.

Alexander, J.C., 'Paradigm revision and "Parsonianism"', in *Canadian Journal of Sociology* 4, 1979, pp. 343–58.

Alexander, J.C., 'Sociology for liberals: The legacy of Talcott Parsons', in *The New Republic* 180 (22), 2 June 1979, pp. 10–12.

Alexander, J.C., 'Core solidarity, ethnic outgroup, and social differentiation: A multidimensional model of inclusion in modern societies', in J. Dofny and A. Akiwowo (eds), *National and Ethnic Movements*, London: Sage, 1980, pp. 5–28.

Alexander, J.C., 'The French correction: Revisionism and followership in the interpretation of Parsons', in *Contemporary Sociology* 10 (4), 1981, pp. 500–5.

Alexander, J.C., 'The mass news media in systemic, historical, and comparative perspective', in E. Katz and T. Szecsko (eds), *Mass Media and Social Change*, London: Sage, 1981, pp. 17–51.

Alexander, J.C., 'Revolution, reaction, and reform: The change theory of Parsons' middle period', in *Sociological Inquiry* 51, 1981, No. 3/4.

Alexander, J.C., *Theoretical Logic in Sociology*, 4 vols, Berkeley: University of California Press, 1982–4.

Almaraz, J., *La teoria sociologica de Talcott Parsons, La problemática de la constitución metodológica del objeto*, Madrid: Centro de Investigaciones Sociologicas, 1981.

Apel, K.O., *Transformation der Philosophie*, 2 vols, Frankfurt: Suhrkamp, 1976.

Arbeitsgruppe Bielefelder Soziologen (eds), *Alltagswissen, Interaktion und gesellschaftliche Wirklichkeit,* 2 vols, Reinbek nr Hamburg: Rowohlt, 1972.

Barber, B., *Social Stratification,* New York: Harcourt, Brace, 1957.

Barber, B., 'Inequality and occupational prestige: Theory, research, and social policy', in *Sociological Inquiry* 48, 1978, pp. 75-88.

Baum, R.C., 'Communication and media', in J.J. Loubser, R.C. Baum, A. Effrat and V.M. Lidz (eds), *Explorations in General Theory in Social Science,* New York: Free Press, 1976, pp. 533-56.

Baum, R.C., 'On societal media dynamics', in J.J. Loubser, R.C. Baum, A. Effrat and V.M. Lidz (eds), *Explorations in General Theory in Social Science,* New York: Free Press, 1976, pp. 579-608.

Baum, R.C., 'Beyond the "Iron Cage"', in *Sociological Analysis* 38, 1977, pp. 309-30.

Becker, G.S., *The Economic Approach to Human Behavior,* Chicago: University of Chicago Press, 1976.

Bellah, R.N., 'Civil religion in America', in *Beyond Belief: Essays on Religion in a Post-Traditional World,* New York: Harper & Row, 1970, pp. 168-89.

Bellah, R.N., *The Broken Covenant: American Civil Religion in Time of Trial,* New York: Seabury Press, 1975.

Ben-David, J., *The Scientist's Role in Society,* Englewood Cliffs, N.J.: Prentice Hall, 1971.

Bendix, R., 'Two sociological traditions', in R. Bendix and G. Roth, *Scholarship and Partisanship: Essays on Max Weber,* Berkeley: University of California Press, 1971, pp. 282-98.

Berger, P.L., *The Sacred Canopy. Elements of a Sociological Theory of Religion,* Garden City, N.Y.: Doubleday, 1967.

Berger, P.L. and T. Luckmann, *The Social Construction of Reality: A Treatise in the Sociology of Knowledge,* Garden City, N.Y.: Doubleday, 1966.

Berghe, P.L. van den. 'Dialectic and functionalism: Toward a theoretical synthesis', in *American Sociological Review* 28, 1963, pp. 695-705.

Bershady, H.J., *Ideology and Social Knowledge,* Oxford: Blackwell, 1973.

Bershady, H.J., 'Commentary on Talcott Parsons' review of H.J. Bershady's *Ideology and Social Knowledge',* in T. *Parsons, Social Systems and the Evolution of Action Theory,* New York: Free Press, 1977, pp. 134-41.

Black, M. (ed.), *The Social Theories of Talcott Parsons: A Critical Examination,* Englewood Cliffs, N.J.: Prentice Hall, 1961.

Blain, R.R., 'An alternative to Parsons' four-function paradigm as a basis for developing general sociological theory', in *American Sociological Review* 36, 1971, pp. 678-92.

Bourricaud, F., *The Sociology of Talcott Parsons (L'Individualisme instituionel),* transl. by A. Goldhammer, Chicago: University of Chicago Press, 1981 (*L'Individualisme institutionel. Essai sur la sociologie de Talcott Parsons,* Paris: Presses Universitaires de France, 1977).

Brandenburg, A.G., *Systemzwang und Autonomie: Gesellschaft und Persönlichkeit in der Theorie von Talcott Parsons,* Düsseldorf: Bertelsmann Universitätsverlag, 1971.

Buchanan, J.M., *The Limits of Liberty – Between Anarchy and Leviathan,*

Chicago: University of Chicago Press, 1975.

Buckley, W., 'Social stratification and the functional theory of social differentiation', in *American Sociological Review* 23, 1958, pp. 369–75.

Buckley, W., 'A rejoinder to functionalists Dr Davis and Dr Levy', in *American Sociological Review* 24, 1959, pp. 84–6.

Buckley, W., 'On equitable inequality', in *American Sociological Review* 28, 1963, pp. 799–801.

Burger, T., 'Talcott Parsons, the problem of order in society, and the program of an analytical sociology', in *American Journal of Sociology* 83, 1977, pp. 320–34.

Cannon, W.B., *The Wisdom of the Body*, New York: Norton, 1932.

Chazel, F., *La Théorie analytique de la société dans l'oeuvre de Talcott Parsons*, Paris: Mouton, 1974.

Cicourel, A., *Cognitive Sociology*, New York: Free Press, 1974.

Cohen, J., 'Moral freedom through understanding in Durkheim: comment on Pope', in *American Sociological Review* 40, 1975, pp. 104–6.

Cohen, J., Hazelrigg, L.E. and W. Pope, 'De-Parsonizing Weber: A critique of Parsons' interpretation of Weber's sociology', in *American Sociological Review*, 40, 1975, pp. 229–41.

Coleman, J.S., 'Collective decisions', in H. Turk and R.L. Simpson (eds), *Institutions and Social Exchange*, Indianapolis: Bobbs-Merrill, 1971, pp. 272–86.

Coleman, J.S., 'Inequality, sociology, and moral philosophy', in *American Journal of Sociology* 80, 1974, pp. 739–64.

Coleman, J.S., *Power and the Structure of Society*, New York: Norton, 1974.

Collins, R., 'A comparative approach to political sociology', in: R. Bendix (ed.), *State and Society: A Reader in Comparative Political Sociology*, Berkeley: University of California Press, 1968, pp. 42–67.

Collins, R., *Conflict Sociology. Toward an Explanatory Science*, New York: Academic Press, 1974.

Dahrendorf, R., 'Struktur und Funktion. Talcott Parsons und die Entwicklung der soziologischen Theorie', in *Kölner Zeitschrift für Soziologie und Sozialpsychologie* 7, 1955, pp. 491–519.

Dahrendorf, R., 'Out of utopia: Toward a reorientation of sociological analysis', in *American Journal of Sociology* 64, 1958, pp. 115–27.

Dahrendorf, R., 'Toward a theory of social conflict', in *Journal of Conflict Resolution* 2, 1958, pp. 170–83.

Dahrendorf, R., *Gesellschaft und Freiheit*, Munich: Piper, 1961.

Davis, K., 'Reply to Tumin', in *American Sociological Review* 18, 1953, pp. 394–7.

Davis, K., 'The abominable heresy: A reply to Dr Buckley', in *American Sociological Review* 24, 1959, pp. 82–3.

Davis, K. and W.E. Moore, 'Some principles of stratification', in *American Sociological Review* 10, 1945, pp. 242–9.

Dilthey, W., 'The construction of the historical world in the human studies', in *Selected Writings*, ed., transl. and intro. by H.P. Rickman, Cambridge: Cambridge University Press, 1976, pp. 168–245 (*Der Aufbau der geschichtlichen Welt in den Geisteswissenschaften*, ed. and intro. by M. Reidel, Frankfurt: Suhrkamp, 1970).

Douglas, J.D. (ed.), *Understanding Everyday Life. Toward the Reconstruction of Sociological Knowledge*, Chicago: Aldine, 1970.

Downs, A., *An Economic Theory of Democracy*, New York: Harper & Row, 1957.

Dubin, R., 'Parsons' actor: Continuities in social theory', in T. Parsons, *Sociological Theory and Modern Society*, New York: Free Press, 1967, pp. 521–36.

Dumont, L., *From Mandeville to Marx: The Genesis and Triumph of Economic Ideology*, Chicago: University of Chicago Press, 1977.

Durkheim, E., *Suicide*, transl. by J.A. Spaulding and G. Simpson, London: Routledge, 1952 (*Le Suicide*, Paris: Presses Universitaires de France (1897) 1973).

Durkheim, E., *Moral Education*, transl. by E.K. Wilson and H. Schnurer, New York: Free Press, 1961 (*L'Education morale*, Paris: Presses Universitaires de France (1925) 1974).

Durkheim, E., *The Division of Labor in Society*, transl. by G. Simpson, New York: Free Press, 1964 (*De la Division du travail social*, Paris: Presses Universitaires de France (1893) 1973) (*Über die Teilung der sozialen Arbeit*, Frankfurt: Suhrkamp, 1977).

Durkheim, E., *Sociology and Philosophy*, transl. by D.F. Pocock, London: Cohen & West, 1965 (*Sociologie et philosophie*, Paris: Presses Universitaires de France (1924) 1974).

Durkheim, E., 'The dualism of human nature and its social conditions', in *On Morality and Society*, ed. and intro. by R.N. Bellah, Chicago: University of Chicago Press, 1973, pp. 149–63 ('Le dualisme de la nature humaine et ses conditions sociales', in *La Science sociale et l'action*, ed. by J.C. Filloux, Paris: Presses Universitaires de France (1914) 1970, pp. 314–32).

Durkheim, E., *The Elementary Forms of the Religious Life*, transl. by J.W. Swain, London: Allen & Unwin, 1976 (*Les Formes élémentaires de la vie religieuse*, Paris: Presses Universitaires de France (1912) 1968).

Durkheim, E., *The Rules of Sociological Method*, transl. by W.D. Halls, London: Macmillan, 1982 (*Les Règles de la méthode sociologique*, Paris: Presses Universitaires de France (1895) 1973).

Eder, K., *Die Entstehung staatlich organisierter Gesellschaften. Ein Beitrag zu einer Theorie sozialer Evolution*, Frankfurt: Suhrkamp, 1980.

Einstein, A., 'Physik und Realität', in *Journal of the Franklin Institute*, 221 (3), 1936, March.

Eisenstadt, S.N., *Tradition, Change, and Modernity*, New York: Wiley, 1973.

Eisenstadt, S.N. and M. Curelaru, *The Form of Sociology: Paradigms and Crises*, New York: Wiley, 1976.

Ellis, D.P., 'The Hobbesian problem of order: A critical appraisal of the normative solution', in *American Sociological Review* 36, 1971, pp. 692–703.

Esser, H., Klenovits, K. and H. Zehnpfennig, *Wissenschaftstheorie*, 2 vols, Stuttgart: Teubner, 1977.

Faris, E., 'Review of T. Parsons: *The Social System*', in *American*

Sociological Review 18, 1953, pp. 103–6.

Fehr, H., 'Handlung, System und teleonomische Erklärungen', in *Soziale Welt* 31, 1980, pp. 490–8.

Freud, S., *The Ego and the Id*, authorised transl. by Joan Rivière, London: Institute of Psychoanalysis, 1927 ('Das Ich und das Es', in *Gesammelte Werke*, Vol. 13, 7th edn, Frankfurt: Fischer, 1972).

Geissler, R., 'Die Sozialisationstheorie von Talcott Parsons: Anmerkungen zur Parsons-Rezeption in der deutschen Soziologie', in *Kölner Zeitschrift für Soziologie und Sozialpsychologie* 31, 1979, pp. 267–81.

Genov, N., *Talcott Parsons and Theoretical Sociology*, Sofia: Bulgarian Academy of Sciences, 1982.

Gerstein, D.R., 'A note on the continuity of Parsonian action theory', in *Sociological Inquiry* 45, 1975, pp. 11–15.

Gerstein, D.R., 'Durkheim and *The Structure of Social Action*', in *Sociological Inquiry* 49, 1979, pp. 27–39.

Giesen, B., *Makrosoziologie: Eine evolutionstheoretische Einführung*, Hamburg: Hoffmann & Campe, 1980.

Giesen, B. and M. Schmid, *Basale Soziologie: Wissenschaftstheorie*, Opladen: Westdeutscher Verlag, 1977.

Goffman, E., *Frame Analysis*, New York: Harper & Row, 1974.

Gould, M., 'Systems analysis, macrosociology, and the generalized media of social action', in J.J. Loubser, R.C. Baum, A. Effrat and V.M. Lidz (eds), *Explorations in General Theory in Social Science*, New York: Free Press, 1976, pp. 470–506.

Gouldner, A.W., *The Coming Crisis of Western Sociology*, London: Heinemann, 1971.

Grathoff, R. and W.M. Sprondel (eds), *Alfred Schütz und die Idee des Alltags in den Sozialwissenschaften*, Stuttgart: Enke, 1976.

Hambermas, J., 'Gegen einen positivistisch halbierten Rationalismus', in T.W. Adorno, H. Albert, R. Dahrendorf, J. Habermas, H. Pilot and K.R. Popper, *Der Positivismusstreit in der deutschen Soziologie*, Neuwied/Berlin: Luchterhand, 1969, pp. 155–91.

Habermas, J., *Knowledge and Human Interest*, transl. by J. Shapiro, London: Heinemann, 1972 (*Erkenntnis und Interesse*, Frankfurt: Suhrkamp, 1968).

Habermas, J., *Theory and Practice*, transl. by J. Viertel, Boston: Beacon Press, 1973 (*Theorie und Praxis*, Frankfurt: Suhrkamp, 1971).

Habermas, J., *Zur Rekonstruktion des Historischen Materialismus*, Frankfurt: Suhrkamp, 1976.

Habermas, J., *Communication and the Evolution of Society*, transl. by T. McCarthy, London: Heinemann, 1979 (contains four essays transl. from *Zur Rekonstruktion des Historischen Materialismus* above).

Habermas, J., 'Handlung und System. Bemerkungen zu Parsons' Medientheorie', in W. Schluchter (ed.), *Verhalten, Handeln und System*, Frankfurt: Suhrkamp, 1980, pp. 68–105.

Habermas, J., 'Talcott Parsons – Probleme der Theoriekonstruktion' in J. Matthes (ed.), *Lebenswelt und soziale Probleme*, Frankfurt/New York: Campus, 1981, pp. 28–48.

Habermas, J., *Theorie des kommunikativen Handelns*, 2 vols, Frankfurt:

Suhrkamp, 1981 (Vol. 1 only is now available in translation: *Theory of Communicative Action,* transl. by T. McCarthy, Boston: Beacon Press, 1984).

Hegel, G.W.F., *Grundlinien der Philosophie des Rechts,* in *Werke,* Vol. 7, ed. by E. Moldenhauer and K.M. Michel, Frankfurt: Suhrkamp, 1970.

Hegel, G.W.F., *Phenomenology of the Spirit,* transl. by A.V. Miller, analysis by J.N. Findlay, Oxford: Clarendon, 1977 (*Phänomenologie des Geistes,* in *Werke,* Vol. 3, ed. by E. Moldenhauer and K.M. Michel, Frankfurt: Suhrkamp, 1976).

Hempel, C.G., *Aspects of Scientific Explanation,* New York: Free Press, 1965.

Hempel, C.G., 'The logic of functional analysis', in *Aspects of Scientific Explanation,* New York: Free Press, 1965, pp. 297–330.

Henderson, L.J., *The Fitness of the Environment: An Inquiry into the Biological Significance of the Properties of Matter,* New York: Macmillan, 1913.

Henderson, L.J., 'An approximate definition of fact', in *University of California Studies in Philosophy* 14, 1932, pp. 179–200.

Hobbes, T., *Leviathan,* in *Collected English Works of Thomas Hobbes,* ed. by W. Molesworth, Vol. 3, Aalen, W. Germany: Scientia (1651) 1966.

House, F.N., 'Review of T. Parsons: *The Structure of Social Action*', in *American Journal of Sociology* 45, 1939, pp. 129–30.

House, F.N., 'Review of T. Parsons: *The Structure of Social Action*', in *American Journal of Sociology* 55, 1950, pp. 504–5.

Huaco, G.A., 'A logical analysis of the Davis-Moore theory of stratification', in *American Sociological Review* 28, 1963, pp. 801–4.

Hume, D., *Enquiries Concerning the Human Understanding and Concerning the Principles of Morals,* ed. by L.A. Selby-Bigge, Oxford: Clarendon (1748/51) 1966.

Hume, D., 'An enquiry concering human understanding', 1st edn 1748, in *Enquiries Concerning the Human Understanding and Concerning the Principles of Morals,* ed. by L.A. Selby-Bigge, Oxford: Clarendon, (1748/51) 1966, pp. 5–165.

Hume, D., *A Treatise on Human Nature,* ed. by L.A. Selby-Bigge, Oxford: Clarendon (1739–40) 1973.

Husserl, E., *Logical Investigations,* transl. of 2nd edn by J.N. Findlay, New York: Humanities Press, 1970 (*Logische Untersuchungen,* Halle: M. Niemeyer (1900–1) 1928).

Inkeles, A. and B. Barber (eds), *Stability and Social Change,* Boston: Little, Brown, 1973.

Jacobson, A.L., 'A theoretical and empirical analysis of social change and conflict based on Talcott Parsons' ideas', in H. Turk and R.L. Simpson (eds), *Institutions and Social Exchange,* Indianapolis: Bobbs-Merrill, 1971, pp. 344–60.

Jensen, S., 'Interpenetration – Zum Verhältnis personaler und sozialer Systeme?', in *Zeitschrift für Soziologie* 7, 1978, pp. 116–29.

Jensen, S., *Talcott Parsons. Eine Einführung,* Stuttgart: Teubner, 1980.

Johnson, B., *Functionalism in Modern Sociology: Understanding Talcott Parsons,* Morristown, N.J.: General Learning Press, 1976.

Johnson, H.M., 'The relevance of the theory of action to historians', in *Social Science Quarterly* 50, 1969, pp. 46–58.

Johnson, H.M., 'The generalized symbolic media in Parsons' theory', in *Sociology and Social Research* 57, 1973, pp. 208–21.

Johnson, H.M., 'Interview with Talcott Parsons', in *Revue Européenne des Sciences Sociales et Cahiers Vilfredo Pareto* 13 (24), 1975, pp. 81–90.

Johnson, H.M., 'Review of *L'Individualisme institutionel: Essai sur la sociologie de Talcott Parsons*, by François Bourricaud', in *American Journal of Sociology* 84, 1979, pp. 1000–4.

Kant, I., *The Critique of Pure Reason*, transl. by J.M.D. Meiklejohn, in *Great Books of the Western World, 42: Kant*, Chicago/London, etc.: Encyclopaedia Britannica, 1952, pp. 1–250 (*Kritik der reinen Vernunft*, Hamburg: Meiner (1781) 1956).

Kant, I., *The Critique of Practical Reason*, transl. by J.M.D. Meiklejohn, in *Great Books of the Western World, 42: Kant*, Chicago/London, etc.: Encyclopaedia Britannica, 1952, pp. 291–361 (*Kritik der praktischen Vernunft*, Hamburg: Meiner (1797) 1967).

Kant, I., *The Critique of Judgement*, transl. by J.M.D. Meiklejohn, in *Great Books of the Western World, 42: Kant*, Chicago/London, etc.: Encyclopaedia Britannica, 1952, pp. 461–613 (*Kritik der Urteilskraft*, Hamburg: Meiner (1799) 1968).

Krappmann, L., *Soziologische Dimensionen der Identität*, Stuttgart: Klett, 1971.

Lakatos, I., 'Falsification and the methodology of scientific research programmes', in I. Lakatos and A. Musgrave (eds), *Criticism and the Growth of Knowledge*, Cambridge: Cambridge University Press, 1970, pp. 91–196.

Lakatos, I. and A. Musgrave (eds), *Criticism and the Growth of Knowledge*, Cambridge: Cambridge University Press, 1970.

Lenski, G.A., *Power and Privilege: A Theory of Social Stratification*, New York: McGraw-Hill, 1966.

Levy, M.J., Jr, 'Functionalism: A reply to Dr Buckley', in *American Sociological Review* 24, 1959, pp. 83–4.

Lidz, C.W. and V.M. Lidz, 'Piaget's psychology of intelligence and the theory of action', in J.J. Loubser, R.C. Baum, A. Effrat and V.M. Lidz (eds), *Explorations in General Theory in Social Science*, New York: Free Press, 1976, pp. 195–239.

Lidz, V.M., 'The law as index, phenomenon and element – conceptual steps toward a general sociology of law', in *Sociological Inquiry* 49, 1979, pp. 5–25.

Lipset, S.M., *The First New Nation*, New York: Basic Books, 1963.

Lockwood, D., 'Social integration and system integration', in G.K. Zollschan and W. Hirsch (eds), *Explorations in Social Change*, London: Routledge, 1964, pp. 244–57.

Loubser, J.J., 'General introduction', in J.J. Loubser, R.C. Baum, A. Effrat and V.M. Lidz (eds), *Explorations in General Theory in Social Science*, New York: Free Press, 1976, pp. 1–23.

Loubser, J.J., Baum, R.C., Effrat, A. and V.M. Lidz (eds), *Explorations in General Theory in Social Science. Essays in Honor of Talcott Parsons*,

New York: Free Press, 1976.

Luhmann, N., 'Soziologie als Theorie sozialer Systeme', in *Soziologische Aufklärung*, Vol. 1, Opladen: Westdeutscher Verlag, 1970, pp. 113–36.

Luhmann, N., 'Einführende Bemerkungen zu einer Theorie symbolisch generalisierter Kommunikationsmedien', in *Zeitschrift für Soziologie* 3, 1974, pp. 236–55.

Luhmann, N., 'Interpenetration – Zum Verhältnis personaler und sozialer Systeme', in *Zeitschrift für Soziologie* 6, 1977, pp. 62–76.

Luhmann, N., 'Interpenetration bei Parsons', in *Zeitschrift für Soziologie* 7, 1978, pp. 299–302.

Luhmann, N., 'Soziologie der Moral', in N. Luhmann and S. Pfürtner (eds), *Theorietechnik und Moral*, Frankfurt: Suhrkamp, 1978, pp. 8–116.

Luhmann, N., 'Talcott Parsons – Zur Zukunft eines Theorieprogramms', in *Zeitschrift für Soziologie* 9, 1980, pp. 5–17.

Luhmann, N., *The Differentiation of Society*, transl. by S. Holmes and C. Larmore, New York: Columbia University Press, 1982.

Luhmann, N., 'Durkheim on morality and the division of labor', in *The Differentiation of Society*, New York: Columbia University Press, 1982, pp. 3–19 ('Arbeitsteilung und Moral – Durkheims Theorie', introduction ('Einleitung') to: E. Durkheim, *Über die Teilung der sozialen Arbeit*, Frankfurt: Suhrkamp, 1977, pp. 17–35).

Machiavelli, N., *The Prince*, transl., intro. and annotation by J.B. Atkinson, Indianapolis: Bobbs-Merrill (1532) 1976.

Martel, M.U., 'Academentia praecox: The aims, merits, and scope of Parsons' multisystemic language rebellion (1958–1968)', in H. Turk and R.L. Simpson, *Institutions and Social Exchange*, Indianapolis: Bobbs-Merrill, 1971, pp. 175–211.

Marx, K., *Capital*, ed. by F. Engels, in *Great Books of the Western World, 50: Marx*, Chicago/London, etc.: Encyclopeadia Britannica, 1950 (*Das Kapital*, Vol. I, in: *Marx-Engels Werke (MEW)*, Vol. 23, Berlin: Dietz, 1970).

Mayr, E., *Populations, Species, and Evolution*, Cambridge, Mass.: Harvard University Press, 1970.

Mead, G.H., *Mind, Self and Society from the Standpoint of a Social Behaviorist*, Chicago/London: University of Chicago Press (1934) 1972.

Menzies, K., *Talcott Parsons and the Social Image of Man*, London: Routledge, 1977.

Merton, R.K., 'Continuities in the theory of social structure and anomie', in *Social Theory and Social Structure*, New York: Free Press (1949) 1968, pp. 215–48.

Merton, R.K., 'Manifest and latent functions', in *Social Theory and Social Structure*, New York: Free Press (1949) 1968, pp. 73–138.

Merton, R.K., 'Social structure and anomie', in *Social Theory and Social Structure*, New York: Free Press (1949) 1968, pp. 185–214

Mieback, B., *Strukturalistische Handlungstheorie. Zum Verhältnis soziologischer Theorie und empirischer Forschung im Werk Talcott Parsons'*, Opladen: Westdeutscher Verlag, 1984.

Mill, J.S., *Three Essays (On Liberty, Representative Government, The*

Subjection of Women), London: Oxford University Press (1859, 1861, 1869), 1975.

Mills, C.W., *The Sociological Imagination*, London: Oxford University Press, 1959.

Mitchell, W.C., *Sociological Analysis and Politics: The Theories of Talcott Parsons*, Englewood Cliffs, N.J.: Prentice Hall, 1967.

Moore, W.E., 'But some are more equal than others', in *American Sociological Review* 28, 1963, pp. 26–8.

Morrione, T.J., 'Symbolic interactionism and social action theory', in *Sociology and Social Research* 59, 1975, pp. 201–18.

Mullins, N.C., *Theories and Theory Groups in Contemporary American Sociology*, New York: Harper & Row, 1973.

Münch, R., *Gesellschaftstheorie und Ideologiekritik*, Hamburg: Hoffmann & Campe, 1973.

Münch, R., *Legitimität und politische Macht*, Opladen: Westdeutscher Verlag, 1976.

Münch, R., *Theorie sozialer Systeme. Eine Einführung in Grundbegriffe, Grundannahmen und logische Struktur*, Opladen: Westdeutscher Verlag, 1976.

Münch, R., 'Talcott Parsons und die Theorie des Handelns I: Die Konstitution des Kantianischen Kerns', in *Soziale Welt* 30, 1979, pp. 385–409 ('Talcott Parsons and the theory of action I. The structure of the Kantian core', in *American Journal of Sociology* 86, 1981, pp. 709–39 – the basis for Chapter 1 of this book).

Münch, R., 'Max Webers Gesellschaftsgeschichte als Entwicklungslogik der gesellschaftlichen Rationalisierung?', in *Kölner Zeitschrift für Soziologie und Sozialpsychologie* 32, 1980, pp. 774–86.

Münch, R., 'Talcott Parsons und die Theorie des Handelns II: Die Kontinuität der Entwicklung', in *Soziale Welt* 31, 1980, pp. 3–47 ('Talcott Parsons and the theory of action II. The continuity of the development', in *American Journal of Sociology* 87, 1982, pp. 771–826 – the basis for Chapter 2 of this book).

Münch, R., '"Teleonomie" und voluntaristische Handlungstheorie. Replik auf Helmut Fehr, "Handlung, System und teleonomische Erklärungen"', in *Soziale Welt* 31, 1980, pp. 499–511.

Münch, R., *Basale Soziologie: Soziologie der Politik*, Opladen: Westdeutscher Verlag, 1982.

Münch, R., *Die Struktur der Moderne. Grundmuster und differentielle Gestaltung des institutionellen Aufbaus der modernen Gesellschaften*, Frankfurt: Suhrkamp, 1984.

Münch, R., *Die Kultur der Moderne*, 2 vols, Frankfurt: Suhrkamp, 1986.

Nagel, E., *The Structure of Science. Problems in the Logic of Scientific Explanation*, New York: Harcourt, Brace, 1961.

Needham, J., *The Grand Titration. Science and Society in East and West*, London: Allen & Unwin, 1969.

Nelson B., *The Idea of Usury. From Tribal Brotherhood to Universal Otherhood*, Chicago: University of Chicago Press (1949) 1969.

Nelson, B., *Der Ursprung der Moderne*, Frankfurt: Suhrkamp, 1977. A collection published in German containing the following essays:

'Sciences and civilizations, "East" and "West"', in *Boston Studies*, Vol. XI, 1974, pp. 445–93; 'Civilizational complexes and intercivilizational encounters', in *Sociological Analysis*, Vol. 34, No. 2, 1973, pp. 79–105; 'The early modern revolution in science and philosophy', in *Boston Studies*, Vol. III, 1968, pp. 1–40; 'Eros, Logos, Nomos, Polis. Their changing balances and the vicissitudes of communities and civilizations', in A.W. Eister (ed.), *Changing Perspectives in the Scientific Study of Religion*, New York: Wiley, 1974, pp. 85–111; 'Probalists, anti-probalists, the quest for certitude in the 16th and 17th centuries', in *Actes du Xe congrès international d'histoire des sciences*, Paris: Herman, 1964; 'On the shoulders of the giants of the comparative historical sociology of science', in R. Whitley (ed.), *Social Processes of Scientific Development*, London: Routledge, 1974; 'The brother and the other: An epilogue', in *The Idea of Usury* (see above), pp. 135–8.

Parsons, T., 'Capitalism in recent German literature: Sombart and Weber, I', in *Journal of Political Economy* 36, 1928, pp. 641–61.

Parsons, T., 'Capitalism in recent German literature: Sombart and Weber, II', in *Journal of Political Economy* 37, 1929, pp. 31–51.

Parsons, T., 'Wants and activities in Marshall', in *Quarterly Journal of Economics* 46, 1931, pp. 101–40.

Parsons, T., 'Economics and sociology: Marshall in relation to the thought of his time', in *Quarterly Journal of Economics* 46, 1932, pp. 316–47.

Parsons, T., 'Pareto's central analytical scheme', in *Journal of Social Philosophy* 1, 1936, pp. 244–62.

Parsons, T., *The Social System*, Glencoe, Ill.: Free Press, 1951.

Parsons, T., 'An analytical approach to the theory of social stratification', in *Essays in Sociological Theory*, New York: Free Press, 1954, pp. 69–88.

Parsons, T., 'The present position and prospects of systematic theory in sociology', in *Essays in Sociological Theory*, New York: Free Press, 1954, pp. 212–37.

Parsons, T., 'The professions and social structure', in *Essays in Sociological Theory*, New York: Free Press, 1954, pp. 34–49.

Parsons, T., 'A revised analytical approach to the theory of social stratification', in *Essays in Sociological Theory*, New York: Free Press, 1954, pp. 386–439.

Parsons, T., 'Social classes and class conflict in the light of recent sociological theory', in *Essays in Sociological Theory*, New York: Free Press, 1954, pp. 323–35.

Parsons, T., 'Family structure and the socialization of the child', in T. Parsons and R.F. Bales, *Family, Socialization and Interaction Process*, London: Routledge, 1956, pp. 35–131.

Parsons, T., 'The organization of personality as a system of action', in T. Parsons and R.F. Bales, *Family, Socialization and Interaction Process*, London: Routledge, 1956, pp. 133–86.

Parsons, T., 'An approach to psychological theory in terms of the theory of action', in S. Koch (ed.), *Psychology: A Study of a Science*, Vol. 3, New York: McGraw-Hill, 1959, pp. 612–711.

Parsons, T., 'Introduction' to Culture and the Social System, in T. Parsons, E.A. Shils, K.D. Naegele and J.R. Pitts (eds), *Theories of Society*, New

York: Free Press, 1961, pp. 963–93.

Parsons, T., 'An outline of the social system', in: T. Parsons, E.A. Shils, K.D. Naegele and J.R. Pitts (eds), *Theories of Society*, New York: Free Press, 1961, pp. 30–79.

Parsons, T., 'The point of view of the author', in M. Black (ed.), *The Social Theories of Talcott Parsons*, Englewood Cliffs, N.J.: Prentice Hall, 1961, pp. 311–63.

Parsons, T., 'Individual autonomy and social pressure: An answer to Dennis H. Wrong', in *Psychoanalysis and Psychoanalytic Review* 49, 1962, pp. 70–80.

Parsons, T., 'The incest taboo in relation to social structure and the socialization of the child', in *Social Structure and Personality*, New York: Free Press, 1964, pp. 57–77.

Parsons, T., 'The school class as a social system: Some of its functions in American society', in *Social Structure and Personality*, New York: Free Press, 1964, pp. 129–54.

Parsons, T., 'Social structure and the development of personality: Freud's contribution to the integration of psychology and sociology', in *Social Structure and Personality* (see above), pp. 78–111.

Parsons, T., 'The superego and the theory of social system', in *Social Structure and Personality*, New York: Free Press, 1964, pp. 17–33.

Parsons, T., 'Toward a healthy maturity', in *Social Structure and Personality*, New York: Free Press, 1964, pp. 236–54.

Parsons, T., 'Youth in the context of American society', in: *Social Structure and Personality*, New York: Free Press, 1964, pp. 155–82.

Parsons, T., *Societies. Evolutionary and Comparative Perspectives*, Englewood Cliffs, N.J.: Prentice Hall, 1966.

Parsons, T., 'Christianity and modern industrial society', in *Sociological Theory and Modern Society* (see next below), pp. 385–421.

Parsons, T., 'Durkheim's contribution to the theory of integration of social systems', in *Sociological Theory and Modern Society*, New York: Free Press, 1967, pp. 3–34.

Parsons, T., 'Evaluation and objectivity in social science: An interpretation of Max Weber's contribution', in *Sociological Theory and Modern Society*, New York: Free Press, 1967, pp. 79–101.

Parsons, T., 'Evolutionary universals in society', in *Sociological Theory and Modern Society*, New York: Free Press, 1967, pp. 490–520.

Parsons, T., 'Full citizenship for the negro American?', in *Sociological Theory and Modern Society*, New York: Free Press, 1967, pp. 422–65.

Parsons, T., 'Introduction to Max Weber's *The Sociology of Religion*', in *Sociological Theory and Modern Society*, New York: Free Press, 1967, pp. 35–78.

Parsons, T., 'Pattern variables revisited: A response to Robert Dubin', in *Sociological Theory and Modern Society*, New York: Free Press, 1967, pp. 192–219.

Parsons, T., 'Unity and diversity in the modern intellectual disciplines: The role of the social sciences', in *Sociological Theory and Modern Society*, New York: Free Press, 1967, pp. 166–91.

Parsons, T., 'Pareto', in D.L. Sills (ed.), *International Encyclopedia of the*

Social Sciences, Vol. 11, New York: Macmillan (1933) 1968, pp. 576–8.

Parsons, T., 'Professions', in D.L. Sills (ed.), *International Encyclopedia of the Social Sciences*, Vol. 12, New York: Macmillan, 1968, pp. 536–47.

Parsons, T., *The Structure of Social Action*, New York: Free Press (1937) 1968.

Parsons, T., 'On the concept of influence', in *Politics and Social Structure*, New York: Free Press, 1969, pp. 405–38.

Parsons, T., 'On the concept of political power', in *Politics and Social Structure*, New York: Free Press, pp. 352–404.

Parsons, T., 'On the concept of value-commitments', in *Politics and Social Structure*, New York: Free Press, 1969, pp. 439–72.

Parsons, T., 'Theory in the humanities and sociology', in *Daedalus* 99 (1), 1970, pp. 495–523.

Parsons, T., 'Review of Reinhard Bendix and Günther Roth: *Scholarship and Partisanship: Essays on Max Weber*', in *Contemporary Sociology* 1, 1972, pp. 200–3.

Parsons, T., 'Levels of organization and the mediation of social interaction', in H. Turk and R.L. Simpson (eds), *Institutions and Social Exchange*, Indianapolis: Bobbs-Merrill, 1971, pp. 23–35.

Parsons, T., *The System of Modern Societies*, Englewood Cliffs, N.J.: Prentice Hall, 1971.

Parsons, T., 'Comment on J.H. Turner and L. Beeghley: "Current folklore in the criticism of Parsonian action theory"', in *Sociological Inquiry* 44, 1974, pp. 55–8.

Parsons, T., 'Comment on "Parsons' interpretation of Durkheim" and on "Moral freedom through understanding in Durkheim": Comment on Pope and Cohen', in *American Sociological Review* 40, 1975, pp. 106–11.

Parsons, T., 'Reply to Cohen, Hazelrigg and Pope', in *American Sociological Review* 41, 1976, pp. 361–5.

Parsons, T., 'On building social system theory: A personal history', in *Social Systems and the Evolution of Action Theory*, New York: Free Press, 1977, pp. 22–76.

Parsons, T., 'Comment on Burger's critique', in *American Journal of Sociology* 83, 1977, pp. 335–9.

Parsons, T., 'Comparative studies and evolutionary change', in *Social Systems and the Evolution of Action Theory*, New York: Free Press, 1977, pp. 279–320.

Parsons, T., 'Equality and inequality in modern society, or social stratification revisited', in *Social Systems and the Evolution of Action Theory*, New York: Free Press, 1977, pp. 321–80.

Parsons, T., 'General introduction', in *Social Systems and the Evolution of Action Theory*, New York: Free Press, 1977, pp. 5–7.

Parsons, T., 'Law as an intellectual stepchild', in H.M. Johnson (ed.), *Social System and Legal Process*, San Francisco: Jossey Bass, 1977, pp. 11–58 (*Sociological Inquiry* 47, Nos 3/4).

Parsons, T., 'The present status of "structural-functional" theory in sociology', in *Social Systems and the Evolution of Action Theory*, New York: Free Press, 1977, pp. 100–17.

Parsons, T., 'Review of Harold J. Bershady: *Ideology and Social Knowledge*', in *Social Systems and the Evolution of Action Theory*, New York: Free Press, 1977, pp. 122–34.

Parsons, T., 'Social structure and the symbolic media of interchange', in *Social Systems and the Evolution of Action Theory*, New York: Free Press, 1977, pp. 204–28.

Parsons, T., 'Social systems', in *Social Systems and the Evolution of Action Theory*, New York: Free Press, pp. 177–203.

Parsons, T., 'Some problems of general theory in sociology', in *Social Systems and the Evolution of Action Theory* pp. 229–69.

Parsons, T., 'Some theoretical considerations on the nature and trends of change of ethnicity', in *Social Systems and the Evolution of Action Theory*, New York: Free Press, 1977, pp. 381–404.

Parsons, T., *Action Theory and the Human Condition*, New York: Free Press, 1978.

Parsons, T., 'Comment on R. Stephen Warner's "Toward a redefinition of action theory: Paying the cognitive element its due"', in *American Journal of Sociology* 83, 1978, pp. 1350–8.

Parsons, T., 'Death in the Western world', in *Action Theory and the Human Condition*, New York: Free Press, 1978, pp. 331–51.

Parsons, T., 'Durkheim on religion revisited: Another look at *The Elementary Forms of the Religious Life*', in *Action Theory and the Human Condition*, New York: Free Press, 1978, pp. 213–32.

Parsons, T., 'The future of the university', in *Action Theory and the Human Condition*, New York: Free Press, 1978, pp. 96–114.

Parsons, T., 'A paradigm of the human condition', in *Action Theory and the Human Condition*, New York: Free Press, 1978, pp. 352–433.

Parsons, T., 'Research with human subjects and the "professional complex"', in *Action Theory and the Human Condition*, New York: Free Press, 1978, pp. 35–65.

Parsons, T., 'The sick role and the role of the physician reconsidered', in *Action Theory and the Human Condition*, New York: Free Press, 1978, pp. 17–34.

Parsons, T., 'Some considerations on the growth of the American system of higher education and research', in *Action Theory and the Human Condition*, New York: Free Press, 1978, pp. 115–32.

Parsons, T., 'Stability and change in the American university', in *Action Theory and the Human Condition*, New York: Free Press, 1978, pp. 154–64.

Parsons, T., 'The university "bundle": A study of the balance between differentiation and integration', in *Action Theory and the Human Condition*, New York: Free Press, 1978, pp. 133–53.

Parsons, T., 'Religious and economic symbolism in the Western world', in H.M. Johnson (ed.), *Religious Change and Continuity*, San Francisco: Jossey Bass, 1979, pp. 1–48 (*Sociological Inquiry* 49, Nos 2/3).

Parsons, T., 'On the relation of the theory of action to Max Weber's "Verstehende Soziologie"', in W. Schluchter (ed.), *Verhalten, Handeln und System*, Frankfurt: Suhrkamp, 1980, pp. 150–63.

Parsons, T., 'Rationalität und der Prozess der Rationalisierung im Denken

Max Webers', in W.M. Sprondel and C. Seyfarth (eds), *Max Weber und die Rationalisierung sozialen Handelns*, Stuttgart: Enke, 1981, pp. 81–92.

Parsons, T. and R.F. Bales, 'The dimensions of action-space', in T. Parsons, R.F. Bales and E.A. Shils, *Working Papers in the Theory of Action*, Glencoe, Ill.: Free Press, 1953, pp. 63–109.

Parsons, T. and R.F. Bales, 'Conclusion: Levels of cultural generality and the process of differentiation', in T. Parsons and R.F. Bales, *Family, Socialization and Interaction Process*, London: Routledge, 1956, pp. 353–94.

Parsons, T. and R.F. Bales, *Family, Socialization and Interaction Process*, London: Routledge, 1956.

Parsons, T., Bales, R.F. and E.A. Shils, 'Phase movement in relation to motivation, symbol formation, and role structure', in *Working Papers in the Theory of Action*, Glencoe, Ill.: Free Press, 1953, pp. 163–269.

Parsons, T., Bales, R.F. and E.A. Shils, *Working Papers in the Theory of Action*, Glencoe, Ill.: Free Press, 1953.

Parsons, T., and J. Olds, 'The mechanisms of personality functioning with special reference to socialization', in T. Parsons and R.F. Bales, *Family, Socialization and Interaction Process*, London: Routledge, 1956, pp. 187–257.

Parsons, T. and G.M. Platt, 'Higher education, changing socialization and contemporary student dissent', in M.W. Riley, M.E. Johnson and A. Foner (eds), *Aging and Society*, Vol. 3: *A Sociology of Age Stratification*, New York: Sage, 1972, pp. 236–91.

Parsons, T. and G.M. Platt, *The American University*, Cambridge, Mass.: Harvard University Press, 1973.

Parsons, T. and E.A. Shils (eds), *Toward a General Theory of Action*, Cambridge, Mass.: Harvard University Press, 1951.

Parsons, T. and E.A. Shils, 'Values, motives, and systems of action', in *Toward a General Theory of Action*, Cambridge, Mass.: Harvard University Press, 1951, pp. 45–275.

Parsons, T. and N.J. Smelser, *Economy and Society*, New York: Free Press, 1956.

Parsons, T. and W. White, 'The link between character and society', in T. Parsons, *Social Structure and Personality*, New York: Free Press, 1964, pp. 183–235.

Piaget, J., *The Moral Judgement of the Child*, New York: Free Press, 1965 (*Le Jugement moral chez l'enfant*, Paris: Alcan, 1932).

Pope, W., 'Classic on classic. Parsons' interpretation of Durkheim', in *American Sociological Review* 38, 1973, pp. 399–415.

Pope, W., 'Durkheim as a functionalist', in *Sociological Quarterly* 16, 1975, pp. 361–79.

Pope, W., 'Parsons on Durkheim, revisited: Reply to Cohen and Parsons', in *American Sociological Review* 40, 1975, pp. 111–15.

Pope, W., Cohen, J. and L.E. Hazelrigg, 'On the divergence of Weber and Durkheim: A critique of Parsons' convergence thesis', in *American Sociological Review* 40, 1975, pp. 417–27.

Pope, W., Cohen, J. and L.E. Hazelrigg, 'Reply to Parsons', in *American*

Sociological Review 42, 1977, pp. 809–11.

Pope, W., and J. Cohen, 'On R. Stephen Warner's "Toward a redefinition of action theory: Paying the cognitive element its due"', in *American Journal of Sociology* 83, 1978, pp. 1359–67.

Popper, K.R., *Conjectures and Refutations*, London: Routledge, 1963.

Popper, K.R., *Objective Knowledge. An Evolutionary Approach*, Oxford: Clarendon, 1972.

Poulantzas, N., *Political Power and Social Classes*, transl. from French by T. O'Hagan *et al.*, London: Verso, 1978.

Procter, I., 'Parsons' early voluntarism', in *Sociological Inquiry* 48, 1978, pp. 37–48.

Rawls, J., *A Theory of Justice*, Cambridge, Mass.: Harvard University Press, 1971.

Reichwein, R., 'Sozialisation und Individuation in der Theorie von Talcott Parsons', in *Soziale Welt* 21, 1970, pp. 161–84.

Reinmann, H., *Kommunikations-Systeme. Umrisse einer Soziologie der Vermittlungs- und Mitteilungsprozesse*, Tübingen: Mohr Siebeck, 1974.

Ritzer, G., *Sociology. A Multiple Paradigm Science*, Boston: Allyn & Bacon, 1975.

Rocher, G., *Talcott Parsons and American Sociology*, London: Nelson, 1974.

Rousseau, J.-J., *The Social Contract*, transl., intro. by M. Cranston, Harmondsworth: Penguin, 1968 (*Du Contrat social, ou principes du droit politique*, Paris: Garnier (1762) 1926).

Saurwein, K.-H., *Das ökonomische Element in der soziologischen Theorie Talcott Parsons*, doctoral thesis, University of Düsseldorf, 1984 (to be published shortly).

Savage, S.P., *The Theories of Talcott Parsons*, New York: St Martins, 1981.

Schäffle, A., *Bau und Leben des sozialen Körpers*, Tübingen: Mohr Siebeck, 1884.

Schluchter, W., 'Max Webers Gesellschaftsgeschichte. Versuch einer Explikation', in *Kölner Zeitschrift für Soziologie und Sozial-psychologie*, 30, 1978, pp. 438–67.

Schluchter, W., 'The paradox of rationalization: On the relation of ethics and world', in G. Roth and W. Schluchter, *Max Weber's Vision of History*, Berkeley: University of California Press, 1979, pp. 11–64 ('Die Paradoxie der Rationalisierung. Zum Verhältnis von "Ethik" und "Welt" bei Max Weber', in *Zeitschrift für Soziologie* 5, 1976, pp. 256–84).

Schluchter, W., 'Gesellschaft und Kultur: Überlegungen zu einer Theorie institutioneller Differenzierung', in W. Schluchter (ed.), *Verhalten, Handeln und System. Talcott Parsons' Beitrag zur Entwicklung der Sozialwissenschaften*, Frankfurt: Suhrkamp, 1980, pp. 106–49.

Schluchter, W., *The Rise of Western Rationalism: Max Weber's Developmental History*, transl., intro. by G. Roth, Berkeley: University of California Press, 1981 (*Die Entwicklung des okzidentalen Rationalismus. Eine Analyse von Max Webers Gesellschaftsgeschichte*, Tübingen: Mohr Siebeck, 1979).

Schluchter, W. (ed.), *Verhalten, Handeln und System. Talcott Parsons'*

Beitrag zu einer Entwicklung der Sozialwissenschaften, Frankfurt: Suhrkamp, 1980.

Schmid, M., *Handlungsrationalität, Kritik einer dogmatischen Handlungswissenschaft*, Munich: Fink, 1979.

Schütte, H.G., 'Handlungen, Rollen und Systeme. Überlegungen zur Soziologie M. Webers und T. Parsons'', in H. Lenk (ed.), *Handlungstheorie interdisziplinär IV*, Munich: Fink, 1977, pp. 17–57.

Schütz, A., *Collected Papers*, Vol. 1, The Hague: Nijhoff, 1962.

Schütz, A. and T. Luckmann, *The Structures of the Life-World*, transl. by R.M. Zaner and H.T. Engelhardt jr, Evanston, Ill.: Northwestern University Press, 1973.

Schütz, A. and T. Parsons, *The Theory of Social Action: The Correspondence of Alfred Schütz and Talcott Parsons*, ed. by R. Grathoff, Bloomington: Indiana University Press, 1978.

Schwanenberg, E., *Soziales Handeln – Die Theorie und ihr Problem*, Berne: Huber, 1970.

Schwanenberg, E., 'The two problems of order in Parsons' theory: An analysis from within', in *Social Forces* 49, 1971, pp. 569–81.

Scott, J.F., 'The changing foundations of the Parsonian action scheme', in *American Sociological Review* 28, 1963, pp. 716–35.

Scott, J.F., 'Interpreting Parsons' Work: a problem in method', in *Sociological Inquiry* 44, 1974, pp. 58–61.

Selznick, P., 'Review of *The Social Theories of Talcott Parsons: A Critical Examination*, edited by M. Black', in *American Sociological Review* 26, 1961, pp. 932–5.

Simmel, G., *Soziologie: Untersuchungen über die Formen der Vergesellschaftung*, Berlin: Duncker & Humblot (1908) 1968.

Smelser, N.J., *Theory of Collective Behavior*, New York: Free Press, 1963.

Smelser, N.J., 'Epilogue: Social-structural dimensions of higher education', in T. Parsons and G.M. Platt, *The American University*, Cambridge, Mass.: Harvard University Press, 1973, pp. 389–422.

Smith, A., *The Wealth of Nations*, New York: Modern Library (1776) 1937.

Smith, A., *The Theory of Moral Sentiments*, New York: Bohn (1759) 1966.

Stegmüller, W., *Probleme und Resultate der Wissenschaftstheorie und analytischen Philosophie*, Vol. 1: *Wissenschaftliche Erklärung und Begründung*, Berlin/Heidelberg/New York: Springer, 1969.

Stinchcombe, A.L., 'Some empirical consequences of the Davis-Moore theory of stratification', in *American Sociological Review* 28, 1963, pp. 805–8.

Strasser, H., *The Normative Structure of Sociology. Conservative and Emancipatory Themes in Social Thought*, London: Routledge & Kegan Paul, 1976.

Sztompka, P., *Sociological Dilemmas. Toward a Dialectic Paradigm*, New York: Academic Press, 1979.

Tenbruck, F.H., 'Das Werk Max Webers', in *Kölner Zeitschrift für Soziologie und Sozialpsychologie* 27, 1975, pp. 663–702.

Tiryakian, E.A., 'Post-Parsonian sociology', in *Humboldt Journal of Social Relations* 7:1, 1979/80, pp. 17–32.

Tiryakian, E.A., 'Letter from Talcott Parsons', in *Sociological Inquiry* 51,

1981, pp. 35–6.

Tocqueville, A. de, *Democracy in America*, 2 vols, transl. by H. Reeve, critical appraisal by J.S. Mill, New York: Schocken (1835/40) 1961.

Tocqueville, A. de, *OEuvres complètes*, Paris: Gallimard, 1977.

Tönnies, F., *Community and Association: Gemeinschaft und Gesellschaft*, transl. by C.P. Loomis, London: Routledge, 1955 (*Gemeinschaft und Gesellschaft*, Darmstadt: Wissenschaftliche Buchgesellschaft (1887) 1963).

Tumin, M.M., 'Reply to Kingsley Davis', in *American Sociological Review* 18, 1953, pp. 672–3.

Tumin, M.M., 'Some principles of stratification: A critical analysis', in *American Sociological Review* 18, 1953, pp. 387–94.

Tumin, M.M., 'On inequality', in *American Sociological Review* 28, 1963, pp. 19–26.

Turner, J.H., *The Structure of Sociological Theory*, Homewood, Ill: Dorsey (1974) 1978.

Turner, J.H. and L. Beeghley, 'Current folklore in the criticism of Parsonian action theory', in *Sociological Inquiry* 44, 1974, pp. 47–55.

Turner, J.H. and L. Beeghley, 'Persistent issues in Parsonian action theory', in *Sociological Inquiry* 44, 1974, pp. 61–3.

Turner, J.H. and L. Beeghley, *The Emergence of Sociological Theory*, Homewood, Ill: Dorsey, 1981.

Vanberg, V., *Die zwei Soziologien. Individualismus und Kollektivismus in der Sozialtheorie*, Tübingen: Mohr Siebeck, 1975.

Vanberg, V., 'Kollektive Güter und kollektives Handeln. Zur Bedeutung neuerer ökonomischer Theorieentwicklungen für die Soziologie', in *Kölner Zeitschrift für Soziologie und Sozialpsychologie* 30, 1978, pp. 652–79.

Van den Berghe, P.L. – *see* Berghe, P.L. van den

Warner, R.S., 'Toward a redefinition of action theory: Paying the cognitive element its due', in *American Journal of Sociology* 83, 1978, pp. 1317–49.

Weber, M., *The Methodology of the Social Sciences*, transl. and ed. by E.A. Shils and H.A. Finch, New York: Free Press, 1949.

Weber, M., *Ancient Judaism*, transl. and ed. by H.H. Gerth and D. Martindale, New York: Free Press, 1952 (*Gesammelte Aufsätze zur Religionssoziologie,* Vol. III, Tübingen: Mohr Siebeck (1920) 1971) (RS III).

Weber, M., *The Religion of China. Confucianism and Taoism*, transl. and ed. by H.H. Gerth, New York: Free Press, 1964 (*Gesammelte Aufsätze zur Religionssoziologie*, Vol. I, Tübingen: Mohr Siebeck (1920) 1972, pp. 276–536) (RS I).

Weber, M., *The Religion of India. The Sociology of Hinduism and Buddhism*, transl. and ed. by H.H. Gerth and D. Martindale, New York: Free Press, 1967 (*Gesammelte Aufsätze zur Religionssoziologie*, Vol. II, Tübingen: Mohr Siebeck (1920) 1972) (RS II).

Weber, M., *Economy and Society. An Outline of Interpretive Sociology*, 3 vols, ed. by G. Roth and C. Wittich, New York: Bedminster Press, 1968 (*Wirtschaft und Gesellschaft*, Tübingen: Mohr Siebeck (1922) 1976) (W/G).

Weber, M., *Gesammelte Aufsätze zur Wissenschaftslehre*, Tübingen: Mohr Siebeck (1922) 1973 (WL).

Weber, M., *The Protestant Ethic and the Spirit of Capitalism*, transl. by T. Parsons, New York: Charles Scribner's Sons, 1976 (*Gesammelte Aufsätze zur Religionssoziologie*, Vol. I, Tübingen: Mohr Siebeck (1920) 1972, pp. 17–209) (RS I).

Weber, M., *From Max Weber: Essays in Sociology*, transl., ed., intro. by H.H. Gerth and C.W. Mills, Oxford/New York: Oxford University Press, 1979.

Whitehead, A.N., *Science and the Modern World*, New York: Macmillan (1925) 1967.

Wiener, N., *Cybernetics, or Control and Communication in the Animal and the Machine*, New York: Wiley (1948) 1961.

Wilson, T.P., 'Normative and interpretive paradigms in sociology', in J.D. Douglas (ed.), *Understanding Everyday Life: Toward the Reconstruction of Sociological Knowledge*, Chicago: Aldine, 1970, pp. 57–79.

Wrong, D.H., 'The oversocialized conception of man in modern sociology', in *American Sociological Review* 26, 1961, pp. 183–93.

Zilsel, E., *Die sozialen Ursprünge der neuzeitlichen Wissenschaft*, ed. by W. Krohn, Frankfurt: Suhrkamp, 1976.

Index of Names

INDEX OF NAMES

Subject Index

SUBJECT INDEX